In-Memory Data Management Research

Series Editor

Prof. Dr. Dr. h.c. Hasso Plattner
Hasso Plattner Institute
Potsdam, Germany

For further volumes:
http://www.springer.com/series/11642

Jürgen Müller

A Real-Time In-Memory Discovery Service

Leveraging Hierarchical Packaging Information in a Unique Identifier Network to Retrieve Track and Trace Information

Springer

Jürgen Müller
Hasso Plattner Institute
Potsdam
Germany

ISBN 978-3-642-37127-1   ISBN 978-3-642-37128-8 (eBook)
DOI 10.1007/978-3-642-37128-8
Springer Heidelberg New York Dordrecht London

Library of Congress Control Number: 2013934388

© Springer-Verlag Berlin Heidelberg 2013
This work is subject to copyright. All rights are reserved by the Publisher, whether the whole or part of the material is concerned, specifically the rights of translation, reprinting, reuse of illustrations, recitation, broadcasting, reproduction on microfilms or in any other physical way, and transmission or information storage and retrieval, electronic adaptation, computer software, or by similar or dissimilar methodology now known or hereafter developed. Exempted from this legal reservation are brief excerpts in connection with reviews or scholarly analysis or material supplied specifically for the purpose of being entered and executed on a computer system, for exclusive use by the purchaser of the work. Duplication of this publication or parts thereof is permitted only under the provisions of the Copyright Law of the Publisher's location, in its current version, and permission for use must always be obtained from Springer. Permissions for use may be obtained through RightsLink at the Copyright Clearance Center. Violations are liable to prosecution under the respective Copyright Law.
The use of general descriptive names, registered names, trademarks, service marks, etc. in this publication does not imply, even in the absence of a specific statement, that such names are exempt from the relevant protective laws and regulations and therefore free for general use.
While the advice and information in this book are believed to be true and accurate at the date of publication, neither the authors nor the editors nor the publisher can accept any legal responsibility for any errors or omissions that may be made. The publisher makes no warranty, express or implied, with respect to the material contained herein.

Printed on acid-free paper

Springer is part of Springer Science+Business Media (www.springer.com)

Dedication

Writing this dissertation was a complex and cumbersome process.

I want to thank my *colleagues* from our research group for five very interesting years. Impressions of our (scientific) adventures will not be forgotten.

Andrea Bärtig, Dr. Joos H. Böse, Anja Grigoleit, Martin Heinig, Martin Lorenz, Dr. Sarah Kappes, Thomas Kowark, Jens Krüger, Alexander Neumann, Jan Schaffner, Matthieu P. Schapranow, Dr. Matthias Uflacker, thank you for proof-reading and helpful advice.

Dr. William R. Killingsworth, thank you for your scientific support throughout my Ph.D. project.

Furthermore, I want to offer my deepest admiration and gratitude for *Prof. Dr. Hasso Plattner*. Thanks for what you made possible with "your five guys in Potsdam". All the best to you and the ones you are associated with.

Finally, I am thankful for the vast support I got from my friends, my beloved girlfriend *Anja*, her family, and my much-loved family, especially *Emilia, Heinz, Albert, Gabi, Alex, Lisa, Norman, Raffi, Jana, Regina*, and *Heinrich*

塞翁失马
sài wēng shī mǎ
The old man from the border loses a horse
(Chinese Ideom)

Contents

1	**Introduction and Motivation**		1
	1.1 Definition of Key Terms		3
		1.1.1 Basic Terms	3
		1.1.2 Discovery Service	8
		1.1.3 Unique Identifier Network	10
	1.2 Use Case: Securing the European Pharmaceutical Supply Chain		10
	1.3 Contributions		15
	1.4 Design Science Research Approach		15
		1.4.1 Environment	16
		1.4.2 Knowledge Base	17
	1.5 Assumptions for This Thesis		17
	1.6 Outline		18
2	**Underlying Technologies and Related Work**		21
	2.1 Underlying Technologies		21
		2.1.1 Automatic Identification and Data Capture Technologies	21
		2.1.2 Unique Identifier Network Technology and Standards	24
	2.2 Approaches to Retrieve Track and Trace Information Without Discovery Services		31
		2.2.1 A Central Data Store for Each Item	31
		2.2.2 Daisy Chain Approach	32
		2.2.3 E-Pedigree	33
		2.2.4 Entry-Exit Testing	35
		2.2.5 A Federated Read Event Repository Database System	35
		2.2.6 Summary	38
	2.3 Related Work on Discovery Services		39
		2.3.1 Literature Review	39
		2.3.2 Requirements Elicitation	43

	2.3.3	Existing Discovery Service Approaches..............	49
	2.3.4	Qualitative Evaluation...........................	55

3 An In-Memory Hierarchical-Packaging-Aware Discovery Service: Overview and Communication Protocol 63
   3.1 Overview of the Hierarchical-Packaging-Aware Discovery Service...................................... 63
   3.2 A Novel Discovery Service Communication Protocol 63
       3.2.1 Processing Lifecycle Queries 64
       3.2.2 Processing Last-Seen Queries..................... 66

4 A Recursive Search Algorithm to Find all Potentially Relevant Read Events 71
   4.1 Data Structure for the Discovery Service 71
   4.2 Description of the Search Algorithm 74
   4.3 Mode of Operation Exemplified with a Simple Supply Chain... 75
   4.4 Handling Returnable Transport Items..................... 78
   4.5 Handling Situations with an Incomplete Read Event Sequence... 81
       4.5.1 Missing Packing Read Events..................... 82
       4.5.2 Missing Unpacking Read Events................... 86
       4.5.3 A Missing Pair of Corresponding Read Events........ 89
       4.5.4 Various Missing Corresponding Read Events 91
   4.6 Critical Discussion of the Search Algorithm 92
       4.6.1 No Notification Messages at All................... 93
       4.6.2 No Packaging Read Events 94
       4.6.3 No Hierarchical-Packaging Relationship 94
       4.6.4 Hierarchical-Packaging Relationships 95
   4.7 Limitations... 95

5 A Filter Algorithm to Extract the Relevant Read Events 97
   5.1 Data Structure for the Algorithm........................ 97
   5.2 Description of the Filter Algorithm 98
   5.3 Mode of Operation Exemplified with a Simple Supply Chain... 100
   5.4 Handling Interim Re-use of a Box....................... 104
   5.5 Handling Situations with an Incomplete Read Event Sequence... 107
       5.5.1 Missing Packing Read Events..................... 108
       5.5.2 Missing Unpacking Read Events................... 115
       5.5.3 A Missing Pair of Corresponding Read Events........ 116
       5.5.4 Various Missing Corresponding Read Events 117
   5.6 Critical Discussion of the Filter Algorithm 118
       5.6.1 Leveraging a Stack to Represent the Packaging Hierarchy.. 118
       5.6.2 Discussion of Filter Decisions 121

		5.6.3	The Stack for the Reverse Filter Algorithm	121
		5.6.4	Discussion of Filter Decisions for the Reverse Filter Algorithm	124
	5.7	Summary		124

6 System Design and Implementation Considerations 127
   6.1 High-Level Design. 127
   6.2 Bulk Loading Read Events into the Discovery Service. 129
   6.3 In-Memory Data Management. 130
       6.3.1 Expected Data Volume 130
       6.3.2 Target Hardware. 133
       6.3.3 Expected Query Performance 134
       6.3.4 Leveraging Partitioning 134
       6.3.5 Expected Bulk Loading Performance. 137
   6.4 Static Structure of the System. 137
   6.5 Dynamic Behavior of the System 138
       6.5.1 Processing Notification Messages 138
       6.5.2 Processing Lifecycle Queries 140
       6.5.3 Processing Last-Seen Queries 140
       6.5.4 Storing and Processing Standing Queries 140
   6.6 Summary 142

7 Evaluation 143
   7.1 Data Volume at the Discovery Service. 143
       7.1.1 Experiment Setup and Procedure 144
       7.1.2 Results. 145
       7.1.3 Discussion and Conclusion. 147
   7.2 Notification Message Processing 147
       7.2.1 Experiment Setup and Procedure 148
       7.2.2 Results. 149
       7.2.3 Discussion and Conclusion. 150
   7.3 Query Performance 150
       7.3.1 Experiment Setup and Procedure 151
       7.3.2 Results. 152
       7.3.3 Discussion and Conclusion. 152
   7.4 Scalability 152
   7.5 Summary 155

8 Conclusion and Future Work 157
   8.1 Summary 157
   8.2 Future Work 157

References 159

Figures

Fig. 1.1	Use cases for discovery services....................	8
Fig. 1.2	Schematic visualization of unique identifier Network Sets....	10
Fig. 1.3	Overview of the European pharmaceutical supply chain	12
Fig. 1.4	Lifecycle of a package of pharmaceuticals including read events and discovery service query in the European pharmaceutical supply chain	13
Fig. 1.5	Design science research cycles.......................	16
Fig. 2.1	Overview of barcodes and encoding schemes.............	22
Fig. 2.2	Schematic illustration of an RFID tag.................	23
Fig. 2.3	A typical RFID deployment...........................	24
Fig. 2.4	The EPC network interface standards	27
Fig. 2.5	Example of a singly-linked list in the daisy chain approach...	32
Fig. 2.6	Example for a doubly-linked list in the daisy chain approach.....................................	33
Fig. 2.7	Simplified example E-pedigree document	34
Fig. 2.8	Simplified concept for a federated discovery service database (database table "ObjectEvents" only)	37
Fig. 2.9	Very simple supply chain used to exemplify principles of operation for different discovery service approaches......	50
Fig. 2.10	Process of gathering lifecycle information following the directory look-up approach.......................	51
Fig. 2.11	Process of gathering lifecycle information following the query relay approach...........................	52
Fig. 2.12	Process of gathering lifecycle information following the fat discovery service approach	54
Fig. 3.1	Overview of the hierarchical-packaging-aware discovery service	64
Fig. 3.2	Process of gathering lifecycle information following the hierarchical-packaging-aware discovery service approach	65

Fig. 3.3	Process of gathering last-seen information about the item of interest following the hierarchical-packaging-aware discovery service approach	67
Fig. 3.4	Example values for the number of messages necessary to retrieve last-seen information about an item of interest	68
Fig. 4.1	Normalized database schema for the discovery service	72
Fig. 4.2	Denormalized database schema for the discovery service with two tables	73
Fig. 4.3	Denormalized database schema for the discovery service with one table	74
Fig. 4.4	Leveraging lower and upper boundaries to limit the search space	77
Fig. 4.5	Re-use of a box	79
Fig. 4.6	Read events to be identified in a common supply chain with a missing packing AggregationEvent and desired behavior of the search algorithm with regard to search spaces	82
Fig. 4.7	Actual identified events in a common supply chain with a missing packing AggregationEvent and respective search spaces	84
Fig. 4.8	Database schema for the discovery service with action field	84
Fig. 4.9	Events to be identified in a common supply chain with a missing unpacking AggregationEvent and desired behavior of the search algorithm with regard to search spaces	85
Fig. 4.10	Rules to determine lower boundary and upper boundary	87
Fig. 4.11	Events in a supply chain with a missing pair of AggregationEvents	89
Fig. 4.12	A situation with a missing AggregationEvent pair but the trace can be completely reconstructed	90
Fig. 4.13	A situation with a missing AggregationEvent Pair but the Trace can be Partly Reconstructed	90
Fig. 4.14	Events in a common supply chain with two missing AggregationEvents affecting distinct pairs	91
Fig. 4.15	Interim re-use of a box	96
Fig. 5.1	Class diagram for events	98
Fig. 5.2	A simple supply chain	101
Fig. 5.3	State of the filter algorithm after read event ①	102
Fig. 5.4	State of the filter algorithm after read event ②	102
Fig. 5.5	State of the filter algorithm after read event ④	102

Fig. 5.6	State of the filter algorithm after read event ⑥	103
Fig. 5.7	State of the filter algorithm after read event ⑭	103
Fig. 5.8	Interim re-use of a box	104
Fig. 5.9	State of the filter algorithm after read event ⑥	105
Fig. 5.10	State of the filter algorithm after read event ⑧	106
Fig. 5.11	State of the filter algorithm after read event ⑫	106
Fig. 5.12	State of the filter algorithm after read event ⑮	106
Fig. 5.13	Final state of the filter algorithm	107
Fig. 5.14	Events to be identified in a common supply chain with a missing packing AggregationEvent	108
Fig. 5.15	Final state of the filter algorithm	109
Fig. 5.16	Events to be identified in a common supply chain with a missing packing AggregationEvent	112
Fig. 5.17	Initial state of the reverse filter algorithm	112
Fig. 5.18	State of the reverse filter algorithm after read event ⑧	113
Fig. 5.19	State of the reverse filter algorithm after read event ③	113
Fig. 5.20	Interim re-use of a box	114
Fig. 5.21	State of the reverse filter algorithm after read event ⑯	114
Fig. 5.22	State of the reverse filter algorithm after read event ⑬	115
Fig. 5.23	A supply chain with a missing unpacking AggregationEvent	116
Fig. 5.24	State of the adjusted filter algorithm after read event ⑫	116
Fig. 5.25	A situation with a missing AggregationEvent pair but the trace can be partly reconstructed	117
Fig. 5.26	Events in a common supply chain with two missing AggregationEvents affecting distinct pairs	118
Fig. 5.27	Decision tree with regard to stack modifications	119
Fig. 5.28	Dynamic representation of the packaging hierarchy by the stack	121
Fig. 5.29	Decision tree with regard to read event evaluations	122
Fig. 5.30	Decision tree for the reverse filter algorithm with regard to stack modifications	122
Fig. 5.31	Dynamic representation of the packaging hierarchy by the stack	123
Fig. 5.32	Decision tree with regard to read event evaluations for the reverse filter algorithm	124
Fig. 6.1	Simplified architecture of the hierarchical-packaging-aware discovery service prototype	128
Fig. 6.2	Simplified bulk loading process	129
Fig. 6.3	Dictionary compression at the discovery service	131
Fig. 6.4	Simplified class diagram of the discovery service	138
Fig. 6.5	Retrieving and processing notification messages (simplified)	139
Fig. 6.6	Processing lifecycle queries (simplified)	139

Fig. 6.7	Processing last-seen queries (simplified)	141
Fig. 6.8	Storing standing queries (simplified)	141
Fig. 6.9	Processing standing queries (simplified)	142
Fig. 7.1	Determining main memory consumption	144
Fig. 7.2	Data volume at the discovery service (summary and extrapolated values)	147
Fig. 7.3	Assessing notification message processing performance	148
Fig. 7.4	Notification message processing performance	149
Fig. 7.5	Query performance measurement	151
Fig. 7.6	Query performance measurement results	152
Fig. 7.7	Simplified deployment of a discovery service with one database server and one application server	153
Fig. 7.8	Simplified deployment of a discovery service with multiple database servers and multiple application servers	154
Fig. 7.9	Data replication in a long chain to leverage servers for fail-over and load variations	154

Tables

Table 1.1	Overview of test data scenarios	14
Table 2.1	EPC information services event types and attributes [45, 184]	30
Table 2.2	Evaluation of discovery service alternatives	39
Table 2.3	Overview of related papers identified by going backward	42
Table 2.4	Overview of papers in the literature review	43
Table 2.5	Concept matrix of relevant literature (ordered by year ascending)	44
Table 2.6	Fulfillment of selected requirements by different discovery service approaches	61
Table 3.1	Overview of the number of messages necessary to retrieve lifecycle information about an item of interest	67
Table 3.2	Example values for the number of messages necessary to retrieve last-seen information about of item of interest	68
Table 4.1	Example data that could be stored at the discovery service for the simple supply chain shown in Fig. 4.4	77
Table 4.2	Example data that could be stored at the discovery service for the supply chain shown in Fig. 4.5	79
Table 4.3	Example data that could be stored at the discovery service for the simple supply chain shown in Fig. 4.6	83
Table 4.4	Example data that could be stored at the discovery service for the simple supply chain shown in Fig. 4.9	87
Table 4.5	Example data that could be stored at the discovery service for the supply chain shown in Fig. 4.14	91
Table 5.1	Example data that could be stored at the discovery service for the simple supply chain shown in Fig. 5.2	101
Table 5.2	Example data that could be stored at the discovery service for the supply chain shown in Fig. 5.8	105

Table 5.3	Example data that could be stored at the discovery service for the simple supply chain shown in Fig. 5.14	108
Table 6.1	Data volume by column in the discovery service database (ca. 73.5 bn event records per year)	133
Table 7.1	Data volume by column in the discovery service database, scenario 1:2000, 1 year (32,566,968 event records)	145
Table 7.2	Data volume by column in the discovery service database, scenario 1:1000, 1 year (68,108,434 event records)	145
Table 7.3	Data volume by column in the discovery service database, scenario 1:100, 1 year (679,475,785 event records)	146
Table 7.4	Data volume by column in the discovery service database, scenario 1:10, 1 year (ca. 7.2 bn event records)	146
Table 7.5	Data volume by column in the discovery service database, scenario 1:1, 1 year (ca. 73.5 bn event records)	146

Listings

Listing 4.1	Search algorithm to retrieve read events for an item of interest...........................	76
Listing 4.2	Algorithm to retrieve the complete list of read events for an item of interest leveraging the action attribute for missing packing read events....................	86
Listing 4.3	Algorithm to retrieve the complete list of read events for an item of interest leveraging the action attribute for missing AggregationEvents	88
Listing 5.1	Algorithm to filter exactly the related read events out of the initial event list........................	99
Listing 5.2	Adjusted algorithm to retrieve exactly the related read events	110
Listing 5.3	Reverse algorithm to filter exactly the related read events out of the initial event list....................	111

Symbols

Symbols with Regard to the Unique Identifier Network

a	Action; part of a read event $re \in RE$
AE	Set of all AggregationEvents
$AE^{ADD}_{i\_distinct}$	AggregationEvents related to item i with the action 'ADD' and distinct parent_epcs
$\lvert AE^{ADD}_{i\_distinct} \rvert$	Cardinality of $AE^{ADD}_{i\_distinct}$, i.e., number of AggregationEvents related to item i with the action 'ADD' and distinct parent_epcs
ae_{start}	An AggregationEvent indicating that a hierarchical packaging relationship created
ae_{end}	An AggregationEvent indicating that a hierarchical packaging relationship was broken up
B	Set of all boxes in a unique identifier network
b	A box $b \in B$
C	Set of all clients that may issue requests to a discovery service
c	A client $c \in C$
C^L_i	A legitimate client with respect to an item of interest i
C^U_i	An unauthorized client with respect to an item of interest i
CO	Set of all containers in a unique identifier network
co	A container $co \in CO$
ER	Set of all EventRecords
$\lvert ER \rvert$	Cardinality of ER, i.e., number of event records
er	An event record $er \in ER$, the representation of a read event in a database
HPR	Set of all hierarchical packaging relationships in a unique identifier network
hpr	A hierarchical packaging relationship $hpr \in HPR$
I	Set of all uniquely identified items in a unique identifier network
i	A uniquely identified item of interest $i \in I$
ID_I	Set of identifiers dedicated to uniquely identifying items

id_I	A unique identifier of a uniquely identified item $id_I \in ID_I$
ID_R	Set of identifiers dedicated to uniquely identifying readers
id_R	A unique identifier of a uniquely identified reader $id_R \in ID_R$
ID_{RER}	Set of identifiers dedicated to uniquely identifying read event repositories
id_{RER}	A unique identifier of a uniquely identified read event repository $id_{RER} \in ID_{RER}$
ID_{TC}	Set of identifiers dedicated to uniquely identifying transport containers
id_{TC}	A unique identifier of a uniquely identified transport container $id_{TC} \in ID_{TC}$
M	Additional attributes of a read event sent to the discovery service
N_{AE}	Set of notification messages for AggregationEvents sent to the discovery service
n_{AE}	A notification message for an AggregationEvent $n_{ae} \in N_{AE}$
N_{OE}	Set of notification messages for ObjectEvents sent to the discovery service
n_{OE}	A notification message for an ObjectEvent $n_{oe} \in N_{OE}$
N_{RE}	Set of notification messages sent to the discovery service
$|N_{RE}|$	Cardinality of N_{RE}, i.e., total number of notification messages
n_{RE}	A notification message $n_{re} \in N_{RE}$
OE	Set of all ObjectEvents
oe	An ObjectEvent $oe \in OE$
P	Set of all participants in the unique identifier network
p	A participant $p \in P$
R	Set of all reader devices in the unique identifier network
r	A reader device $r \in R$
RE	Set of all read events in the unique identifier network
re	A read event $re \in RE$
RE_p	Set of all read events that took place at participant p. $RE_p \subseteq RE$
RER	Set of all read event repositories in the unique identifier network
rer	A read event repository $rer \in RER$
SC	Set of all supply chains in the unique identifier network
sc_i	Supply chain for the uniquely identified item i
t	Time when a read event happened part of a read event $re \in RE$
TC	Set of all transport containers in the unique identifier network
tc	A transport container $tc \in TC$
TTI_i	Track and trace information for the item of interest i

Symbols with Regard to In-Memory Data Management

Ω Number of partitions that are affected by a query
Φ Number of available cores
Π Number of partitions
π A partition $\pi \in \Pi$
S Number of database servers
Θ Variable defining how many days data should be stored in main-memory

About the Book

The given work with the title "A Real-Time In-Memory Discovery Service" discusses how to efficiently retrieve track and trace information for an item of interest that took a certain path through a complex network of manufacturers, wholesalers, retailers and consumers.

An example that is used throughout this work is the European pharmaceutical supply chain, which faces the challenge that more and more counterfeit medicinal products are being introduced. Between October and December 2008, more than 34 million fake drug pills were detected at customs control at the boarders of the European Union. These fake drugs can put lives in danger as they were supposed to fight cancer, take effect as painkiller or antibiotics, among others. The European Commission is aware of this problem and wants to leverage supply chain validity in order to determine whether a certain package of pharmaceuticals is genuine or not. While using this example, the work is applicable to many other scenarios as well.

This will be possible in the future because all products are equipped with a unique identifier. At strategic points in the supply chain, readers are installed. If a uniquely identified item is in the perimeter of the reader, a read event is created. Read events are stored in read event repositories, which are operated by the company where the read event took place. As items can be packed into uniquely identified boxes and containers, hierarchical packaging relationships are created and have to be considered. The supply chain for an item of interest comprises all companies the item passed in it's lifecycle.

As read events are company-sensitive data, they are not shared with the public. Thus, a special information system is necessary to identify all relevant read events for a certain item of interest—this is the discovery service. Put in relation to read event repositories, the discovery service is a superordinate entity that supports and coordinates inter-organizational collaboration and information retrieval in a so called unique identifier network.

In the course of this work, a discovery service is designed that explicitly includes hierarchical packaging relationships. That way, it differentiates from all existing discovery service approaches. This innovation allows for a new communication concept between requestor, discovery service, and relevant read event repositories, such that a minimal number of messages has to be exchanged. Furthermore, requestors get the response in real-time and the discovery service usage is more simplistic. Thus, also thin devices such as point-of-sale terminals and mobile devices can easily submit queries to the discovery service. Only required data is transferred from read event repositories to the discovery service. The companies that own the read event repositories remain full data ownership about their read event repositories. The resulting complexity at the discovery service is dealt with by two algorithms. The first algorithm is an efficient and heuristic search algorithm. The second algorithm iscalled filter algorithm as it processes all read events returned by the search algorithm and evaluates whether they are valid for a given item of interest or not.

In addition to the communication protocol, the search algorithm, and the filter algorithm, the data management, which is developed in the dissertation is optimized for column-oriented in-memory databases with dictionary encoding. This opens the opportunity to handle the data volume that occurs in so called "Unique Identifier Networks". In the example of the European pharmaceutical supply chain, approximately 15 billion packages of prescription-only pharmaceuticals are sold per year. These packages are subject to unique identification, which results in about 35 billion read events that have to be processed by the discovery service.

In the present work, the discovery service was prototypically implemented using JAVA as the programming language and SAP HANA as the database of choice. The evaluation shows that the data volume of a large unique identifier network could be reduced to a manageable size. For the complete European pharmaceutical supply chain, only 600 GB of main memory is necessary a size, which is commercially available for enterprise servers. The compression factor is approximately 17. Furthermore, it is shown that

- the data can be loaded into the discovery service fast enough, i.e., the required 8,000 read events per second can be processed.
- the throughput of the discovery service is high enough, i.e., about 20 servers are sufficient to cope with 2,000 discovery service queries in the European pharmaceutical supply chain.
- the developed discovery service is scalable.

Selected further areas of application are the effective support of recalls, company spanning supply chain optimization, and pattern recognition in supply chains. As the presented discovery service approach explicitly integrates changes in packaging hierarchies, this approach can easily be mapped to bill of material problems, e.g., to identify all parts of an airplane and their history at an arbitrary point in time.

The author already published 20 scientific articles with regard to the present topic.

Chapter 1
Introduction and Motivation

Since the invention of the container in 1956, global logistics experienced an enormous boost. With this highly efficient transportation concept, the Tayloristic method division of labor has spread across continents leveraging competitive advantages such as low labor costs in different regions of the world.

This, together with the Toyota Production System became widely adopted in the concepts of lean production [122]. In combination with principles such as Just-in-Time (JIT) deliveries, this led to the situation we see today with China as the production house of the world and companies having their warehouses on the streets [122, 199]. With the advent of Material Resource Planning (MRP) and, later on, Enterprise Resource Planning (ERP), companies were able to coordinate their planning and operations in an integrated manner [142, p. 56]. Many companies are focussing on their core competencies and outsourcing the rest of their operations and production.

The concepts of division of labor, lean production, and JIT have generated the need for coordination not only within one enterprise but across company borders [172]. From the 1990s, the term and discipline Supply Chain Management (SCM) was formed. It comprises "... the management of a network of interconnected businesses involved in the ultimate provision of product and service packages required by end customers" [77]. SCM heavily uses Information Technology (IT), for example, to exchange information about expected deliveries. Products need to be identified in many process steps such as incoming goods, warehousing, shipment, or point-of-sale. The need for automatic identification in order to increase process efficiency became obvious. A major breakthrough was the Universal Product Code (UPC) that was introduced in 1974 [68]. The first application included printing the UCP as a barcode on products to identify product manufacturer and product type automatically during checkout in supermarkets. After a long period of slow diffusion, this technology proved its value by increased process efficiencies and customer responsiveness due to more accurate and real-time information [68]. Nowadays, nearly all products have a barcode attached. The areas of application are not only bound to logistics but span from document management to membership cards to patient tracking.

In recent years, more and more companies investigate in the direction of unique serialization. Whereas the UPC barcode is able to identify a product's manufacturer and the product type, unique identification is the next level. The UPC is a unique serial number for each and every item. The identification of items is usually conducted using data matrix codes (also called 2D barcodes) or Radio Frequency Identification (RFID) technology [98, 179]. For example, products "designed by Apple in California" are produced in China and directly shipped to customers all over the world. Customers can track the delivery process from the production plant to the point of destination. This is possible because each product is uniquely identified and it's status is recorded at several points in the Apple supply chain.

Unique identification gives companies the opportunity to furthermore optimize their processes, e.g. Just-in-Sequence (JIS) production in the automotive industry would not be possible without the unique identification of cars and components. In addition, it is technically feasible to uniquely identify items over their complete lifecycle from production to the point-of-sale and beyond.

Even using traditional barcode technology, huge amounts of data are generated, e.g. point-of-sale data. With the advent of unique serialization, the data volume increases exponentially. This also drives the demand for an appropriate information system for storing and using the data for analytics, among others. The number of items to be tracked per year easily reaches billions. Two examples illustrate this circumstance:

1. 30 billion packages of pharmaceuticals are produced, distributed, and consumed in the European pharmaceutical supply chain per year [67].
2. Tobacco companies evaluate unique serialization for packages of cigarettes as a measure to prevent smuggling [10]. About 150 million packages of cigarettes are produced per day in Europe [190]. This results in more than 55 billion packages per year in Europe.

Products that are subject to unique serialization are equipped with a data matrix code or an RFID tag. Subsequently, the data matrix code or RFID tag is recognized at strategic points in the supply chain. This results in events containing the information "which item?"; "when was it seen?"; "where was the item seen?"; "why was it scanned?"; "what business step was the item involved in?". This information is stored in a read event repository operated by the company that owns the reader that recorded the read event. Especially in the context of reduced safety stocks in enterprises and JIT/JIS deliveries, it is important to know a product's location in order to avoid out-of-stock situations or production stops due to missing material. Despite the huge value for enterprises, it is not the aim of this thesis to discuss the impacts of track and trace information. The interested reader is referred to the respective references for details about the related desire to reduce inventory levels [172], fight counterfeiting and gray markets [88, 89], improve product recall precision [66], or prevent out-of-stock situations [172], among others.

This thesis contributes a missing puzzle piece, the "discovery service", that makes it possible to efficiently and effectively identify and aggregate information with regard to an item of interest. It discusses how track and trace information can be provided using a discovery service if the read events are distributed amongst several read event repositories. This concept is well-established within a single company. But as SCM inherently affects multiple companies, a mechanism is necessary to share relevant read events across company borders. As this read event data can be used to reconstruct a company's supply chain, this information is considered to be highly confidential and must only be shared with authorized partners.

This is where the present thesis comes into play. No applicable concept exists today to extract the relevant read events for an item of interest out of billions of read events, which are stored in several supply chain partners' read event repositories. This missing piece is an information system referred to as "discovery service". If such a discovery service existed, inter-company cooperation and coordination could enter a new era. Following a study conducted by MIT, such a discovery service could not be realized by the fact that previous database technology was not capable of handling the huge amounts of data [198].

Leveraging latest developments in hardware and software, this thesis strives to craft a discovery service using in-memory database technology. Concepts for the in-memory database SAP HANA were developed at our research chair [153] and this database already showed it's capabilities in several proof-of-concepts, e.g. by accelerating a dunning process by factor 1,200 [153, p. 181] or processing 64 million point-of-sale entries on-the-fly [153, p. 184].

1.1 Definition of Key Terms

Items are equipped with a unique identifier, which makes them a uniquely identified item. Clients can state interest in a uniquely identified item, which is then called item of interest. Readers are able to read unique identifiers in order to create read events. Readers are owned by unique identifier network participants that store read events in read event repositories. Notification messages are sent to the discovery service. Uniquely identified items can be put into transport containers such as boxes and containers, which results in hierarchical packaging relationships. The goal of the discovery service is to identify and collect track and trace information about the supply chain for an item of interest.

To create a common understanding, this section defines key terms used in the title and the remainder of this thesis. Basic terms are defined first before discussing the central term in this dissertation, the "discovery service".

1.1.1 Basic Terms

Item

In this thesis, an item is understood as any kind of physical entity. An item can be equipped with a unique identifier.

Unique Identifier

A unique identifier $id \in ID$ helps distinguish physical items by assigning an unambiguous signifier, a Uniform Resource Identifier (URI) [14]), to it. More specifically, it is a unique Uniform Resource Name (URN) [175]. The unique identifier meant in this thesis is not to be mistaken for an identifier only distinguish manufacturer and product type like a classical barcode. The assumption is that each unique identifier is computer-readable. ID_I is the set of identifiers dedicated to uniquely identify items.

Uniquely Identified Item

Let I be the set of all uniquely identified items. Unique identification of items can be seen as a function assigning a unique identifier $id_I \in ID_I$ to each item $i \in I$. $f : I \rightarrow ID_I$. The function f is injective: for $i_1, i_2 \in I$ the following applies: $i_1 \neq i_2 \Rightarrow f(i_1) \neq f(i_2)$. There might be identifiers $id_I \in ID_I$ that are not used.

Client

Let C be the set of clients that may issue requests about the track and trace information with regard to a uniquely identified item with the unique identifier id. This interest in id might be legitimate or unauthorized. A legitimate client with respect to id, $c_{id}^L \in C$ is understood as a person or organization that has justifiable interest in a uniquely identified item. This interest is legitimate if one of the following conditions are met.

1. c_{id}^L is or was in physical possession of the unique item identified by id,
2. c_{id}^L is involved in processing the unique item identified by id in it's lifecycle, or
3. c_{id}^L is an organization with the respective legitimation, e.g. governmental organizations, customs, disease prevention, or border control with the authorization to gather information about id.

If a client $c \in C$ does not fulfill the criteria above but nevertheless proclaims its interest in an item identified by id, he is defined as an unauthorized client with regard to id, c_{id}^U.

Item of Interest

In this thesis, the term item of interest will be used frequently. An item $i \in I$ is an item of interest if a client $c \in C$ articulates its interest in information about i.

Reader

A reader $r \in R$ is a physical device capable of retrieving the identifier id_I of an item if the item is in the reader's perimeter. The identification of the unique identifier can be seen as a function $g : I \rightarrow ID_I$. Readers are identified by unique identifiers

1.1 Definition of Key Terms

$id_R \in ID_R$ with ID_R being the set of unique identifiers dedicated to identifying readers.

Read Event

Each time id_I is read from i, a read event re is recorded and added to the set of all read events RE. Two kinds of read events exist: ObjectEvents $oe \in OE$ and AggregationEvents $ae \in AE$. $RE = OE \cup AE$. Each time a read event indicates that the packaging hierarchy of an item changed, it is called AggregationEvent. This happens if, for example, an item is packed into a box or a box is packed into a container or unpacked again. If the packaging hierarchy of an item is not changed, the read event is called ObjectEvent.

Each $oe \in OE$ is defined as a 5-tuple $\langle t, ID_I, a, id_R, M \rangle$ with t being the time when the read event happened. ID_I defines one or multiple unique identifier id_I assigned to the items $i \in I$ that were identified by the reader $r \in R$. Usually, exactly one uniquely identified item is involved in an ObjectEvent. The tuple a defines an action that took place. This action determines the context in which a read event took place, e.g. if id_i was just added to i, or an item is packed or unpacked from/ to a transport container. id_R is the unique identifier of the reader r. M is a set of optional additional attributes, which will be described later in this thesis.

In contrast, an AggregationEvent $ae \in AE$ is a 6-tuple $\langle t, ID, id_{TC}, a, id_R, M \rangle$ with ID as the unique identifier(s) of the item(s) added to or removed from a transport container. Usually, one uniquely identified item or transport container identified by id_I or id_{TC} is involved in an AggregationEvent. In the context of this thesis, all transport containers $tc \in TC$ are uniquely identified with $id_{TC} \in ID_{TC}$. The tuple id is either the unique identifier $id_i \in ID_I$ of a uniquely identified item or the unique identifier $id'_{TC} \in ID_{TC}$ of a uniquely identified transport container under the condition that $id_{TC} \neq id'_{TC}$.

Participant

A participant $p \in P$ is a company, organization, or corporation that processes uniquely identified items or transport containers. Each reader $r \in R$ belongs to a participant $p \in P$. The unique identifier of a reader is used to deduct the respective participant the reader belongs to. Thus, $h : ID_R \rightarrow P$. This function is surjective, meaning that $\forall id_R \in ID_R : \exists p \in P : f(id_R) = p$.

In the course of this thesis, a company, organization, or corporation is only a participant $p \in P$ if at least one read event exists that occurred at one of the readers of p, meaning that $\exists re \in RE : f(id_R) = p$. A participant $p \in P$ may also be a client $c \in C$.

Read Event Repository

In this thesis, it is assumed that each $p \in P$ operates exactly one read event repository $rer \in RER$. Thus, the function $i : P \rightarrow RER$ is bijective.

In addition, a read event repository $rer \in RER$ belongs to exactly one participant $p \in P$. The function $f : rer \to p$ is bijective. Let $rer_P \in RER$ be the read event repository of the participant $p \in P$. A $rer_P \in RER$ is an information system that stores the read events RE_P that took place at a participant $p \in P$, meaning that $RE_P \subseteq RE := \{re \mid f(id_R) = p\}$. These read events are referred to as read events of participant P.

Read event repositories are also identified by unique identifiers. Let ID_{RER} be the set of unique identifiers dedicated to identifying read event repositories. A Uniform Resource Locator (URL) [15] $id_{RER} \in ID_{RER}$ can be used to retrieve the respective read event repository: $j : ID_{RER} \to RER$.

Notification Message

For each read event $re \in RE$, a notification message $n_{RE} \in N_{RE}$ is sent to the discovery service. The set of all notification messages is $N_{RE} = N_{OE} \cup N_{AE}$.

A notification message $n_{OE} \in N_{OE}$ of an ObjectEvent $oe \in OE$ is a 4-tuple $\langle t, ID_I, a, id_{RER} \rangle$ with t as the point in time when the object event took place. ID_I represents the unique identifier(s) of the uniquely identified items that were involved in the read event. a defines the read event action. id_{RER} is the URL of the read event repository where the read event is stored. In comparison with the ObjectEvent as a 5-tuple $\langle t, ID_I, a, id_R, M \rangle$, id_R and M are not transmitted to the discovery service.

A notification message $n_{AE} \in N_{AE}$ of an AggregationEvent $ae \in AE$ is a 5-tuple $\langle t, ID_I, id_{TC}, a, id_{RER} \rangle$ with a indicating whether a packaging process or an unpacking process took place and id_{TC} being the identifier of the transport container. In comparison with the AggregationEvent as a 6-tuple $\langle t, ID, id_{TC}, a, id_R, M \rangle$, id_R and M are not transmitted to the discovery service.

Transport Container, Box, Container

Items are usually not transported as bulk goods from the manufacturer to the retailer. Instead, transport containers $tc \in TC$ are used. Transport containers are also identified by unique identifiers. Unique identification of transport containers can then be seen as a function assigning a unique identifier $id_{TC} \in ID_{TC}$ to each transport container $tc \in TC$. $k : TC \to ID_{TC}$. The function k is injective: for $tc_1, tc_2 \in TC$ the following applies: $tc_1 \neq tc_2 \Rightarrow f(tc_1) \neq f(tc_2)$. Thus, there might be identifiers $id_{TC} \in ID_{TC}$ that are not used.

Let B be the set of all boxes and CO the set of all containers ($B \cup CO = TC$). Transport containers are defined to be either boxes or containers ($B \cap CO = \emptyset$). A box b can be used to store one or multiple items. A box b_1 can be used to shelter another box b_2. A container $co \in CO$ can be used to store any number of items, boxes and containers.

Hierarchical Packaging Relationship

If an item $i \in I$ is packed into a box $b \in B$, this is referred to as a hierarchical packaging relationship hpr between i and b. The same term is used if

1.1 Definition of Key Terms

- A box $b_1 \in B$ is packed into an other box $b_2 \in B$ (subject to $b_1 \neq b_2$),
- A box $b \in B$ is packed into a container $co \in CO$, or
- A container $co_1 \in CO$ is packed into an other container $co_2 \in CO$ (subject to $co_1 \neq co_2$).

Each time a hierarchical packaging relationship $hpr \in HPR$ is created or broken up, an AggregationEvent $ae \in AE$ is created. A hierarchical packaging relationship $hpr \in HPR$ is defined by a 2-tuple $\langle ae_{start}, ae_{end}\rangle$. ae_{start} represents the AggregationEvents that was recorded at the point in time the hierarchical packaging relationship was created. ae_{end} describes the AggregationEvent that was recorded at the point in time the hierarchical packaging relationship was broken up. ae_{end} is not defined as long as the hierarchical packaging relationship is not broken up: $ae_{end} = ae \in AE \cup \emptyset$. If the hierarchical packaging relationship is not broken up, the second tuple of hpr is $\emptyset$.

As we will see in the course of this dissertation, all previous attempts to design discovery services neglected the fact that hierarchical packaging relationships exist at all. This is one reason why other discovery service design ideas are inefficient. In the discovery service design proposed in the present thesis, I incorporate the fact that hierarchical packaging relationships not only exist but are omnipresent in today's supply chains.

Supply Chain

In the remainder of this thesis, a supply chain is understood as a set of participants. A supply chain is always seen in the context of an item of interest. For a given i, the respective supply chain consists of all participants that have read events stored in their read event repositories, meaning that

$$sc_i \subseteq P := \{p \mid \exists re \in RE : f(id_I) = i, f(id_R) = p\}.$$

The set of all supply chains SC is composed of the supply chains for all uniquely identified items $i \in I$.

Track and Trace Information / Relevant Read Events

The goal of the discovery service is to retrieve track and trace information. In this thesis, track and trace information TTI_i for an arbitrary item i is defined as the subset of all relevant read events $re \in RE$. Let TTI_i be the set of all relevant read events for the item identified by i. First, for a given i, this is $TTI_i^{OE} \subseteq OE := \{oe \mid f(id_I) = i\}$. In addition, this is $TTI_i^{AE} \subseteq AE := \{ae \mid f(id_I) = i\}$. The relevant read events are subject to hierarchical packaging relationships. Thus, additional read events might be relevant for the given i. In fact, all read events TTI_i^{HPR} that happened to a transport container $tc \in TC$ while the item was present onto that tc are also relevant. The exact determination of TTI_i^{HPR} events will be described throughout this dissertation. Thus, $TTI_i = TTI_i^{OE} \cup TTI_i^{AE} \cup TTI_i^{HPR}$.

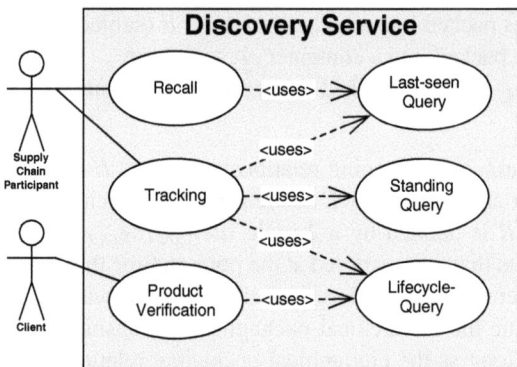

Fig. 1.1 Use cases for discovery services

1.1.2 Discovery Service

The term discovery service is ambiguously used in different research communities, applications, and environments.

In the understanding of this thesis, a discovery service D is an information system to find and retrieve track and trace information TTI_i for a given unique identifier id_i. Put in relation to read event repositories RER, the discovery service is a superordinate entity that supports and coordinates inter-participant collaboration and information retrieval in a unique identifier network.

To this end, the discovery service retrieves the notification messages N_{RE} from the participants where the respective read event took place. The actual read event data is not replicated to the discovery service but only a subset of the data is shared with the discovery service.

The use cases and stakeholders for a discovery service are depicted in Fig. 1.1. A use case that is supported using discovery services is product recall. This means that the discovery service is used to identify the last position of a set of items, e.g. ones that were produced in a certain time period. This is implemented using a last-seen query [45]. To optimize supply chain management, participants can track certain identifiers in the unique identifier network. Three options with regard to product tracking exist. A participant can invoke a last-seen query. He also can register for certain identifiers and is notified once a new event for this identifier appears. This is implemented using a so called standing query [45]. Standing queries have the same characteristic as normal queries but are performed regularly. In addition, the complete lifecycle of an item of interest can be queried invoking a so called lifecycle query. A legitimate client $c_i^L \in C$ conducting a product verification also uses the lifecycle query that identifies all relevant read events TTI_i for the item of interest i. In other research communities and industry applications, a discovery service is understood as something different. I will briefly describe the other meanings and distinguish the discovery service for a unique identifier network afterwards.

1.1 Definition of Key Terms

- *Web Services Dynamic Discovery (WS-Discovery)*: WS-Discovery is a standard describing how to discover Web services in a local network using multicasting [138, 147]. Two modes exist: In ad-hoc mode, clients send messages via multicast to the local network in order to discover a target service of interest [138]. Respective target services respond directly to the client indicating they can fulfill the service request. In managed mode, service providers send service descriptions to a discovery service. When queried by a client, the discovery service looks up whether a respective service has advertised itself and replies on behalf of the target services [138].
- *Universal Description, Discovery and Integration (UDDI)*: UDDI defines services, which support describing and discovering Web service providers and their Web service offerings as well as a concept to access these Web services [137]. It is based on industry standards such as Hypertext Transfer Protocol (HTTP) [63], Extensible Markup Language (XML) [20], XML Schema [61], and Simple Object Access Protocol (SOAP) [121]. The scope includes public Web services as well as services that are only accessible from within a company. The browser-accessible UDDI Business Registry, which became public shortly after the UDDI specification was standardized, contains three types of information [37]:
  - white pages for basic information about the service such as the Web address,
  - yellow pages providing a categorization of the Web service, and
  - green pages including technical details.
- *Association Rule Mining*: Association rule mining, also referenced to as association rule learning, belongs to the research areas of data mining and knowledge discovery [62]. It describes the methods to discover relations between variables [8]. These relations are condensed to a small set of rules [112]. It is used, for example, to analyze point-of-sale data or Web usage patterns [32]. The most famous story about association rule learning might be the pretended observation that diapers are regularly bought together with beer. But even if this story might not be true [155], association rule mining is used in many applications today, for example, to advertise what "other customers also bought". A discovery service or discovery algorithm, in this sense, is responsible for identifying rules by mining a given database.
- *Workflow and Process Mining*: Other areas of data mining are concerned with workflow and process mining. Workflows and process models can be discovered from event logs using data mining techniques [7]. The term process mining is connected to "distilling a structured process description from a set of real executions" [193]. One of the main challenges is the rediscovery problem stating the question whether an original workflow WF_1, which produced a workflow log WL_1 and a workflow WF_2, that is derived from WL_1, are equivalent [192].
- *Information or Resource Discovery*: In many publications, a discovery service is referred to as a tool to find information or resources. This relates to search engines [19] as well as resources in a network, ad-hoc, or grid environments [79, 83]. Each of these discovery services is used in its respective domain and fulfills a certain task.

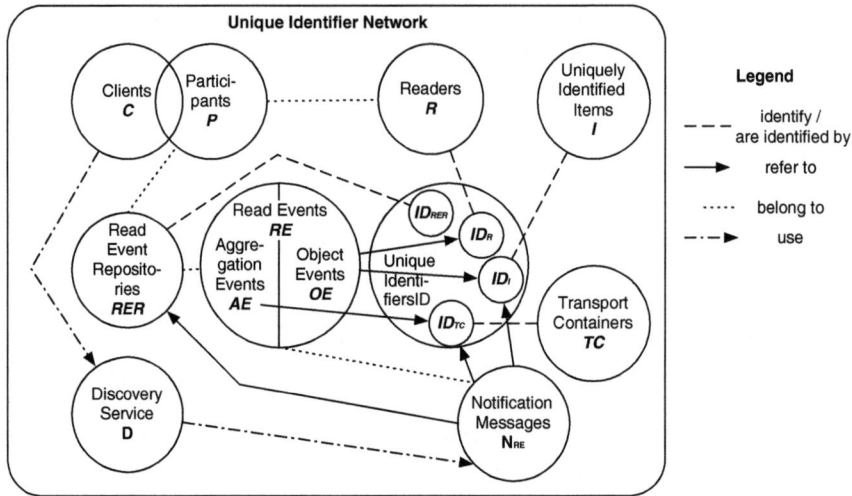

Fig. 1.2 Schematic visualization of unique identifier Network Sets

1.1.3 Unique Identifier Network

This thesis is conducted in the context of a unique identifier network. A unique identifier network UIN is understood as the set of clients, participants, readers, uniquely identified items, read event repositories, read events, transport containers, notification messages, and the discovery service: $UIN = I \cup ID_I \cup C \cup R \cup ID_R \cup RE \cup P \cup RER \cup ID_{RER} \cup N_{RE} \cup TC \cup ID_{TC} \cup D$ (see Fig. 1.2).

1.2 Use Case: Securing the European Pharmaceutical Supply Chain

This chapter introduces the use case of the pharmaceutical industry, which was addressed in the introduction. Here, discovery services are highly relevant securing the legal supply chain from counterfeits. Many other use cases exist, but this one is sufficient to explain the general concept and requirements with regard to requirements on a discovery service.

As production in low-wage regions and global trade increases, opportunities for producing and selling counterfeit products also arise. The Organization for Economic Co-operation and Development (OECD) estimates that the trade volume of pirated and counterfeit goods in 2009 reached up to USD 250 billion excluding domestically produced and consumed products and pirated digital products [140, 141]. This is an equivalent of about 2% of the world trade volume [140, 141]. This poses a financial risk to companies because fake or smuggled goods reduce their sales volume and reputation.

More and more counterfeit medicinal products appear in the legal European pharmaceutical supply chain [168, 53]. It is of utmost concern that counterfeiters have not

1.2 Use Case: Securing the European Pharmaceutical Supply Chain

hesitated to introduce fake prescription-only medicines. The pharmaceutical industry moved to public focus by the operation MEDI-FAKE conducted by custom authorities in all EU member states. More than 34 million fake drug tablets were detected at customs control at the boarders of the European Union between October and December 2008 [88]. These fake drugs can put lives in danger as they were supposed to fight cancer, take effect as painkiller or antibiotics, among others. Instead, they contain active pharmaceutical ingredients, wrong ingredients, wrong doses, or other harmful substances. Pharmaceutical companies reacted and attached verification characteristics to their products but counterfeiters copy them to perfection. The IP Crime Report 2009–2010 reports that 280,000 tablets of counterfeit pharmaceuticals were seized in two operations conducted in the UK [89]. Currently, imported medicinal products are only checked once, when they pass the borders of the European Community. No additional verification is possible after that [67].

The European Commission is aware of this problem and proposed an amendment of a directive related to medicinal products for human use [30] as well as a tender for a track and trace service for medicines [31, 55]. This amendment stipulates that identification, traceability, and authenticity of prescription medicinal products is to be ascertained. These initiatives resulted in the directive 2011/62/EU [54], which enforces unique identification of prescription-only pharmaceuticals and verification at the point of sale or the point of dispensing, respectively. These requirements are abstract and no guideline for an implementation is given.

However, it is foreseeable that the pharmaceutical supply chain has to change as follows to fulfill the minimum standards demanded by the 2011 directive [54]:

1. Unique identifiers are attached to each prescription-only drug ($id_I \in ID_I$) as well as packages, boxes, and containers ($id_{TC} \in ID_{TC}$) that are used to transport pharmaceuticals.
2. At strategic points in the supply chain, the participants $p \in P$ document the unique identifier id_I and additional data in a read event re.
3. Traceability and authenticity verification of medicinal products is enabled by a system retrieving and analyzing track and trace information TTI_i that is related to a particular item of interest $i \in I$, e.g. when a product is sold or dispensed.

Thus, following point (1), the prescription-only package of pharmaceuticals can be seen as a uniquely identified item $i \in I$ in the context of the pharmaceutical supply chain. The transport containers directly correspond to the transport containers TC defined for the unique identifier network UIN. With regard to point (2), each participant $p \in P$ has to deploy a reader $r \in R$ at each strategic point in the part of the supply chain covered by p. Each time a uniquely identified item $i \in I$ passes a strategic point in the supply chain, a read event $re \in RE$ is generated and stored in the read event repository rer_P. Point (3) implies that track and trace information TTI_i, i.e. all relevant read events for a given item of interest i can be retrieved by some information system. This information system is the discovery service.

Following the 2011 directive [54], legitimate clients c_{id}^L should be able to use the unique identifier id_I to query an information system in order to verify the authenticity of a particular medicinal product. A client in this use case could be a supply chain

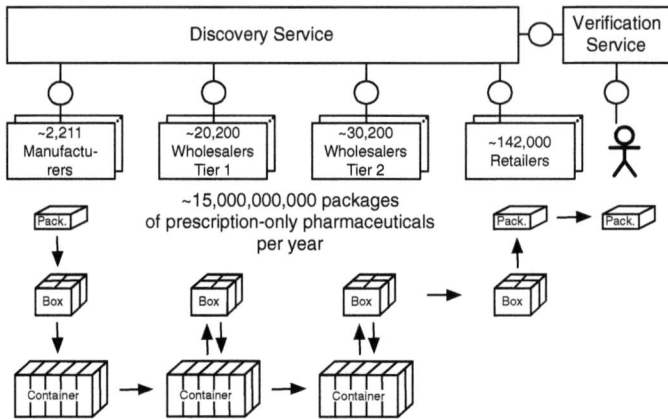

Fig. 1.3 Overview of the European pharmaceutical supply chain

participant, a consumer, or customs, for example. Leveraging the discovery service, a verification service can gather all read events for the item i and determine if this package of pharmaceuticals was produced by a certified manufacturer and handled by trustworthy distributors and retailers only. The new legal requirements raise the need for new information systems enabling supply chain partners to share data in a secure, cost-efficient, and effective way [105]. Estimated total costs to fulfilling these requirements including respective hardware, process adaptations, and information systems are 6–11 billion € [67].

The route of one specific package of pharmaceuticals through the pharmaceutical supply chain is usually composed of a manufacturer, a wholesaler (wholesaler tier 1) who buys the medicinal products and resells them to another wholesaler (wholesaler tier 2), and a retailer which in general is a pharmacy or hospital [67] as depicted in Fig. 1.3.

These entities can be seen as the most important participants in P in this use case. The European pharmaceutical supply chain incorporates about 2,211 manufacturers [97], 50,400 wholesalers [33, 42], and 142,000 retailers [56, 148, 197].

Each year, about 30 billion packages of pharmaceuticals are produced or imported into the European market [67]. Approximately 15 billion packages of pharmaceuticals are only available for prescription. The rest are over-the-counter products [67]. The highest priority with regard to anti-counterfeiting are prescription-only pharmaceuticals as they are more expensive and counterfeits of these medicines are most crucial to human well-being.

Before shipping, manufacturers usually aggregate packages of pharmaceuticals to a box and also aggregate multiple boxes to a container. The wholesalers disaggregate containers, re-aggregate them and forwards goods in containers (wholesaler 1 to wholesaler 2) or boxes (wholesaler 2 to retailer). Retailers only receive boxes and customers only receive packages of pharmaceuticals. The aforementioned strategic points in the supply chain are (see Fig. 1.4):

1.2 Use Case: Securing the European Pharmaceutical Supply Chain

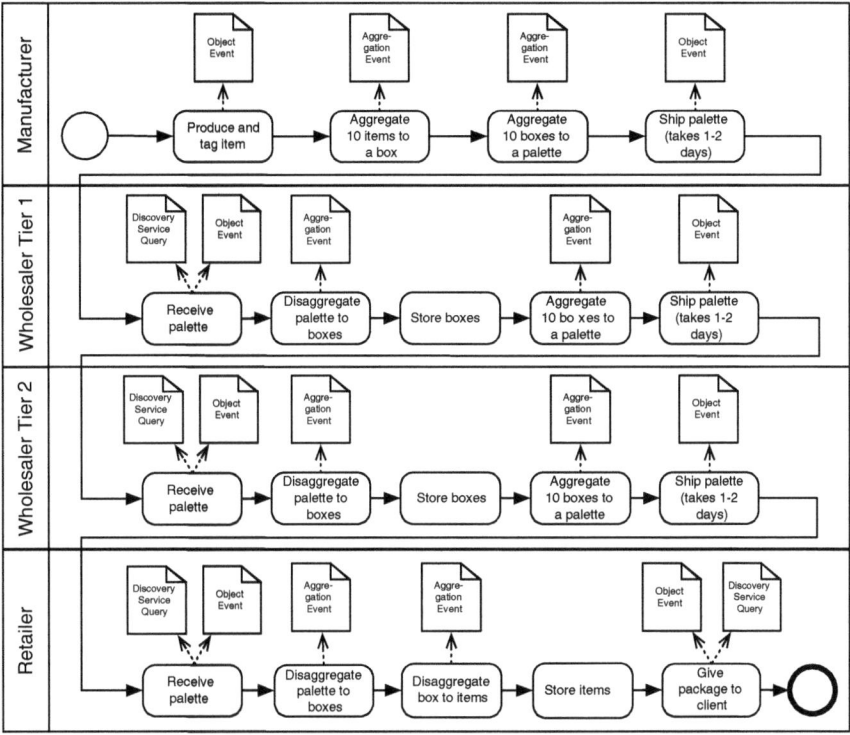

Fig. 1.4 Lifecycle of a package of pharmaceuticals including read events and discovery service query in the European pharmaceutical supply chain

- The initial tagging of the package of pharmaceuticals after its production,
- Each change of hierarchical packaging relationships,
- Each goods issue to a supply chain partner,
- Each goods receiving from a supply chain partner, and
- Selling or dispensing of the pharmaceutical product.

Before the product is sold or dispensed, the verification service is invoked, which results in a lifecycle-query to the discovery service. Optionally, a verification request is additionally conducted at every goods receipt.

A success factor in software engineering projects is working with real data. As no real data exists for discovery services, I gathered and analyzed the structure of the pharmaceutical supply chain as well as quantity structures. Evaluations using realistic test data is missing in the discovery service research community. Instead, only small sets of test data is used to validate discovery services, i.e. dozens or hundreds of events. Thus, I created a simulator to generate realistic test data [128]. The simulation model works according to the process described in Fig. 1.4. For each read event re, the simulator generates a data set, which is written to a file and can be used to evaluate discovery services or read event repositories [128]. These data

Table 1.1 Overview of test data scenarios

Scaling factor	1:2000			1:1000			1:100		
Simulated time	1 Month	1 Year	5.5 Years	1 Month	1 Year	5.5 Years	1 Month	1 Year	5.5 Years
# Manufacturer	1			2			20		
# Wholesaler	25			50			504		
# Retailer	71			142			1,420		
# Read events	709 k	16.3 m	96.7 m	1.4 m	32.5 m	194.1 m	14.2 m	325 m	1.9 bn
# Queries	18.5 k	6.7 m	43.1 m	37 k	13.3 m	86.3 m	369 k	133 m	864 m
# File size	13 MB	4.8 GB	30 GB	37 MB	10 GB	60 GB	914 MB	90 GB	597 GB

k = thousand; m = million; bn = billion

sets can be used to replay the read events RE when evaluating a system under test. For different purposes, different sizes of test data are needed. Consequently, I defined several scenarios. A selection of them is publicly available at http://epic.hpi.uni-potsdam.de/Home/RfidTestData. The smallest scenario scales the real European pharmaceutical supply chain down by factor 2,000. Thus, one manufacturer, 25 wholesalers, and 71 retailers are included in the model. This model is run for different periods of time, the shortest being one simulated month. This results in approximately 710,000 read events and 18,000 discovery service queries (assuming a query for each goods receipt). The file size is about 12 Mega Byte (MB). The largest scenario available scales the supply chain down by factor 100 resulting in 22 manufacturers, 504 wholesalers, and 1,420 retailers. This model of the 1:100 supply chain is run for 5.5 simulated years and results in 1.9 billion read events as well as 0.9 billion lifecycle queries. The resulting file has a size of about 600 Giga Byte (GB) (Table 1.1).

I use these numbers to approximate the number of events in the real European pharmaceutical supply chain. For a factor 1:1, the 15 billion prescription-only packages of pharmaceuticals result in about 35 billion read events ($1.9[\frac{bn}{year}] \times \frac{100}{5.5[years]} \cong 35[bn]$) and 16 billion discovery service queries ($0.9[\frac{bn}{year}] \times \frac{100}{5.5[years]} \cong 16[bn]$) per year. This test data set should be sufficient for most researchers. Thus, no 1:1 model is generated. Instead, the test data of the 1:100 model can be replicated if necessary. This test data is not only used in the context of this thesis but it is also adopted by researchers of SAP Research Dresden and Technical University of Munich.

I assume that the European pharmaceutical supply chain is active for 50 weeks a year with 6 days each week and 14 h per day. This results in 8.3 million read events per hour, thus, about 2,300 read events per second. Respectively, about 1,000 discovery service queries per second have to be handled by a discovery service on average. Including buffers and peak situations, I assume that a discovery service should be able to cope with 8,000 read events per second and 2,000 queries per second. The buffer for read events is higher because of bulk shipments in the supply chain in contrast to relatively homogeneous sales and dispensing activities. As the simulator is not at the core of this dissertation, the interested reader is referred to the respective contributions, where I describe the simulator and the resulting test data in detail [128, 130].

1.3 Contributions

This section provides an overview of contributions within this thesis.

In the field of unique identification of physical objects, many standards already exist. The respective standardization organization is EPCglobal. The standards describe how unique identifiers are stored on a tag [52], how the data is read by a reader [48], in which format it is passed to a middleware [47, 129, 132], and how it can be stored in and queried from a read event repository $rer \in RER$ [45, 124], among others. A detailed description of the standards takes place in Sect. 2.1.2.

The missing piece is the discovery service [50]. A standard for discovery services is still to be developed [44]. This dissertation tackles the problem of how a discovery service for a unique identifier network UIN should be designed and can be implemented.

The ultimate goal is to complete the existing infrastructure of unique identification to enable tracking and tracing of goods in supply chains with an arbitrary number of involved companies, which is not possible up to now. To this end, a first-of-its-kind discovery service is designed, prototypically implemented, and evaluated. This thesis is only about the discovery service and does not cope with other hardware or software systems.

The contributions of the thesis are as follows:

1. *Communication Protocol*: A communication protocol between clients C, discovery service D, and the participant's read event repositories RER is defined, such that short response times, low complexity at the client, and confidentiality of participants can be achieved.
2. *Identification of Relevant Read Events*: Two algorithms to identify relevant read events TTI_i when queried with the unique identifier i are specified.
3. *Data Management*: A data structure and partitioning schema is developed that supports bulk loading, data compression, and the provision of appropriate query performance for the developed discovery service D.

The discovery service that is crafted within this dissertation is called Hierarchical-Packaging-aware Discovery Service (HPDS) because hierarchical packaging relationships $hpr \in HPR$ are explicitly included in the design of the discovery service.

1.4 Design Science Research Approach

This thesis follows the design science research approach depicted in Fig. 1.5. It distinguishes three parts:

- *Relevance Cycle*: The researcher is in mutual exchange with the research environment. In particular, requirements are gathered and field testing is conducted. Thus, the result of the research is presumed to be relevant.

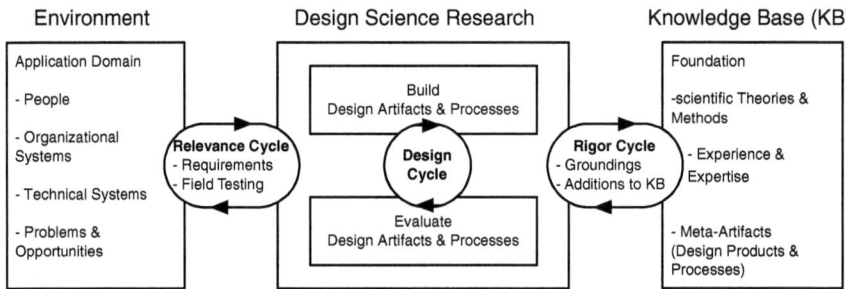

Fig. 1.5 Design science research cycles (adopted from [80])

- *Rigor Cycle*: The researcher leverages existing knowledge from the knowledge base to understand the background, related work, and current state of the research subject. Furthermore, results of the research are added to the knowledge base, for example, as conference papers. That way, the research conducted is presumed to be rigorous.
- *Design Cycle*: With the grounding of the knowledge base and the exchange with the environment, the researcher conducts his research by building design artifacts as well as processes and evaluates them.

In the following, I briefly describe the environment I worked in and how I interacted with the knowledge base. The design science part is described in the remainder of this thesis.

1.4.1 Environment

Throughout my work at the Hasso Plattner Institute and in my dissertation project, I was honored to work with many people from research as well as industry such as pharmaceutical companies and consultancies, fashion companies, tobacco companies, enterprise software vendors, RFID implementers, RFID device management providers, RFID hardware vendors, and the European Commission. In addition, I was part of the Massachusetts Institute of Technology (MIT) Forum for Supply Chain Innovation in the European section and at MIT, where I met additional knowledgeable people from academia, industry and government organizations.

Furthermore, I gained hands-on experience with different RFID systems given the fact that we operate an RFID laboratory at our research group and I coached students of nine RFID-related seminars in the Bachelor's and Master's curriculum.

This gave me valuable insights into the system landscape, existing problems, requirements, opportunities, and, finally, the open research questions I address with this thesis.

1.4 Design Science Research Approach   17

Throughout the past few years, I presented my research at multiple conferences and was given valuable feedback from the research community as well as practitioners, which helped maturing my ideas and concepts.

Notably, SAP is interested in the results of my research and initiated a project to convert my concepts and prototypical implementations into a real product. In addition, the European Commissioner for health and consumer policy, John Dalli, invited me to present my research so that he would be able to include the research results in the final EU directive with regard to a track and trace service for medicines in the European pharmaceutical supply chain.

With my research, I feel that I was able to give valuable information back to the people and companies I worked with. Most notably among these is that, with the support of SAP, my main research contributions are filed as patents in Europe and the USA. Furthermore, after a case study conducted together with the German fashion company Gerry Weber, RFID was introduced on item-level in their complete supply chain. In addition, the massive amount of realistic test data for the European pharmaceutical supply chain that I produced are already in use at SAP Research Dresden and Technical University of Munich.

1.4.2 Knowledge Base

I founded my research on intensive literature review and had the pleasure to learn from the experience and expertise of the people I worked with or got to know at conferences and expert meetings.

My additions to the existing research knowledge base comprise 34 publications, 20 of them directly related to the content of this dissertation. In projects conducted with project partners, we were able to deliver valuable information and prototypes for the respective stakeholders.

1.5 Assumptions for This Thesis

The goal of this thesis is to describe a discovery service concept that is feasible, viable, and desirable with regard to using it in real industry scenarios in the next years. As it is one of the first comprehensive discovery service concepts and the fact that one dissertation cannot cover all aspects of such a system, I make several assumptions.

The first assumption I make is that from a network perspective, a central discovery service can be realized. Furthermore, all aspects of fail-over and recovery are left out of the discussion.

Security is a huge issue if companies share data with each other. For the present thesis, I exclude all security topics that are not directly related to discovery services. I do not cover further security topics such as the interface between RFID tag and reader devices because other comprehensive contributions concerned with security are available [58, 59, 60, 164, 166, 201].

Discovery services will be needed in many use cases. Given the sheer amount of data and the fact that supply chains in many industries are disconnected, it is reasonable to deploy multiple discovery services. These discovery services could, for example, partition the read events RE by industry and geographical region. In reality, this separation is not complete. For example, Wal-Mart sells pharmaceuticals as well as fashion articles, which also might be uniquely identified. At the point-of-sale, both product types have to be validated as being non-counterfeit. Thus, Wal-Mart would have to identify the respective discovery service for both products. Nevertheless, I solve the discovery service problem assuming that only one single discovery service exists. The interested reader is referred to [114] where I present a preliminary approach of a distributed discovery service design.

Finally, I assume that a verification service exists. In a practical deployment, it is not enough to have all relevant read events, thus the track and trace information TTI_i, at hand. To decide whether an item $i \in I$ is counterfeit or not, a decision function is needed. This decision function will be implemented in a verification service that receives all read events related to an item of interest as the input. Then, it applies heuristics to decide whether the product is genuine or counterfeit [106]. As it will be described in the course of this thesis, the discovery service will not always be able to retrieve a complete list of read events. The verification service has to decide wether important read events are missing or if the item of interest can be flagged as genuine. In addition, the verification service would analyze track and trace information with regard to patterns of missing or unrealistic data because this could be a way for counterfeiters to outmaneuver the verification system. Possible solutions could be rule-based anti-counterfeiting or statistical track and trace data analysis, among others [9].

1.6 Outline

The thesis is structured as follows: Chap. 2 lays the foundation of this work by presenting important underlying technologies and discussing related work. In Chaps. 3, 4, 5, the main contributions of this thesis are described: Chap. 3 presents an innovative communication protocol that is the foundation for the hierarchical-packaging-aware discovery service. It allows for a design where participants have full control over their read events RE_p. At the same time, the client faces low complexity and queries issued to the discovery service can be processed quickly. To identify potentially relevant read events, a search algorithm is developed in Chap. 4. This algorithm exploits a data structure designed to support the hierarchical-packaging-aware discovery service in the context of a column-oriented in-memory database. Several extensions to this search algorithm are made in order to make it robust even in situations where read events are missing. Situations might occur where the search algorithm is efficient but identifies read events that are not relevant for a certain item of interest $i \in I$.

1.6 Outline

Thus, a filter algorithm is introduced in Chap. 5 to reduce the result set to exactly the relevant read events TTI_i. Again, extensions to the algorithm are made such that it returns the best results possible in situations with incomplete track and trace information. After these contributions, implementation considerations are presented in Chap. 6. This includes the system design as well as in-memory data management at the hierarchical-packaging-aware discovery service. Chapter 7 is dedicated to evaluating the hierarchical-packaging-aware discovery service. A conclusion and an outlook are given in Chap. 8.

Chapter 2
Underlying Technologies and Related Work

2.1 Underlying Technologies

This section gives an introduction into Automatic Identification and Data Capture (AIDC) technologies. Barcode and RFID technology is presented in Sect. 2.1.1. Section 2.1.2 focusses on the components of a unique identifier network UIN and a concrete example, the EPC Network that will be used in the remainder of the thesis to apply the developed concepts. In addition, Sect. 2.2 discusses approaches enabling unique identification and track and trace without using a discovery service.

2.1.1 Automatic Identification and Data Capture Technologies

Unique identification is conducted with AIDC technologies [174]. These include optical character recognition, smart cards, biometrical systems like finger print or voice recognition, classical barcode, data matrix code, and RFID.

For the given background of this thesis, which is a unique identifier network UIN, the data matrix system and RFID technology are most relevant. The advantages and disadvantages of these technologies are well-known and not of importance for this thesis. Thus, I refer the interested reader to Finkenzeller's RFID Handbook [65]. For this thesis, the only relevant aspects are:

- A unique identifier $id \in ID$ can be stored on a data matrix code or RFID tag,
- The data matrix code or RFID tag can be attached to an item, which thereby becomes an uniquely identified item $i \in I$ and
- The unique identifier can be read by any reader $r \in R$ once the item i is in the readers' perimeter.

Barcode

Barcodes are optical machine-readable representations of data. The most often used barcodes are the 1-dimensional barcode and the matrix code, which is also called 2-dimensional barcode or data matrix code.

In the 1-dimensional barcode, the data to be encoded is represented by parallel lines with varying width and spacing. Different barcode standards exist. The first one was the Universal Product Code (UPC) that was introduced in North America in 1973 [81]. It encodes 12 decimal digits. The European Article Number (EAN) was introduced in 1975. It encodes 13 decimal digits and, together with other naming schemata, was renamed to 'Global Trade Item Number' (GTIN) in 2009 [73, 180].

The matrix code is comprised of black and white squares and can store arbitrary information up to 2 kB [87, 149]. It was invented in the 1990s [13, 98]. With this increased capacity, it can store not only the GTIN describing the manufacturer and the product type but the Serialized Global Trade Item Number (SGTIN), which adds a unique serial number for each product to the GTIN [52]. In the context of this thesis, a SGTIN is used as unique identifier $id_I \in ID_I$ for each uniquely identified item $i \in I$.

An overview of barcodes is presented in Fig. 2.1. The leading numbers at the barcodes and the data matrix code are header information. The last digit at the UPC is a checksum. The last digit at the GTIN-13 is a quiet zone necessary for barcode readers to work properly.

All barcodes comprise a 'Manager Code', which identifies the manufacturer of the product, e.g. Coca Cola. The 'Product Type Code' denotes the type of product, e.g. a 1.5 l bottle of original Coca Cola. The matrix code also stores a 'Serial Number', which makes it possible to distinguish two products of the same product type.

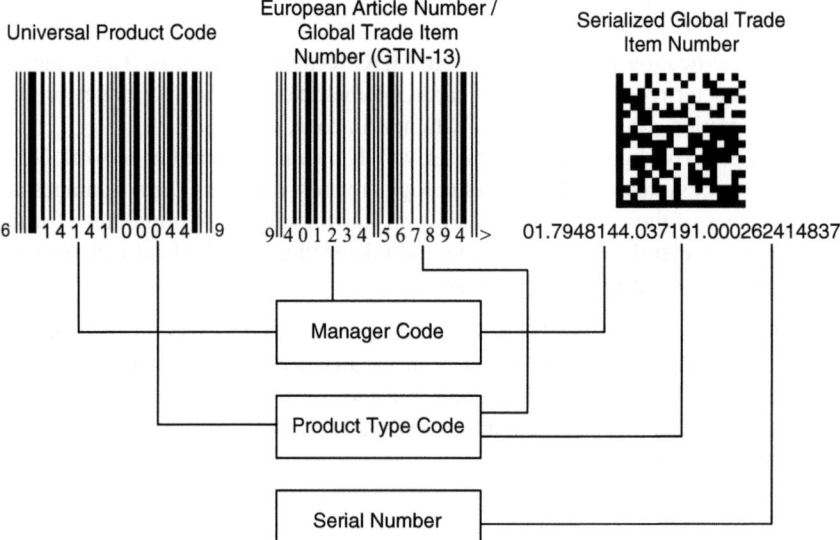

Fig. 2.1 Overview of barcodes and encoding schemes (adopted from [21] and [74])

2.1 Underlying Technologies 23

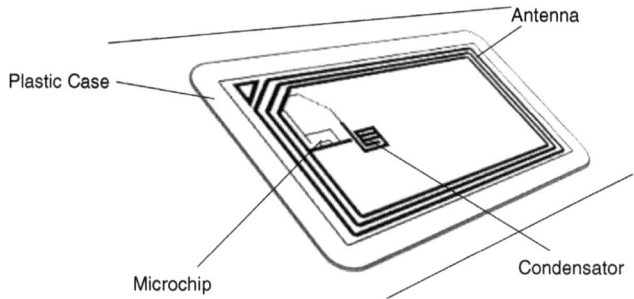

Fig. 2.2 Schematic illustration of an RFID tag (adopted from [93, p. 75])

Radio-Frequency Identification

RFID was first used in World War II for friend-or-foe identification and later on used for unique serialization without the need for line of sight. The main concept behind RFID is that tags store data that can be read by RFID readers by means of reflected power [179].

The SGTIN can also be stored on an RFID tag. Different kinds of RFID tags exist. The commonality is that (Fig. 2.2):

- An RFID tag can store data in a microchip,
- It has an antenna to retrieve and emit radio waves,
- A condenser is used to buffer the energy retrieved from radio waves, and
- The RFID tag has some kind of plastic or paper case where the antenna, microchip, and condenser are embedded.

Most commonly used are passive RFID tags without any onboard power source. The power needed to retrieve the data that is stored in the microcontroller on the tag and transmit it is retrieved from the RFID reader that emits power in the form of radio waves [107, pp. 9]. For details on RFID tags, I refer the interested reader to [69, pp. 55].

The data stored on the RFID tag can be read using an RFID reader. The reader is comprised of an antenna, a controller, and a network interface. A controller instructs the antenna to emit radio waves according to a tag protocol [69, pp. 77]. The tag receives the request to send its data, energizes itself, emits the response using its own antenna and the reader's antenna receives the respective response. Using the network interface, the reader forwards the received data to an RFID middleware, which then processes the data.

RFID printers are used to encode tags and attach them to the items that shall be uniquely identified.

2.1.2 Unique Identifier Network Technology and Standards

The term unique identifier network was already defined, but the underlying technology was excluded. It will be covered in this section.

In general, the goal of unique identification is to lower costs by, for example, more precise and efficient recalls or increasing sales volume because of fewer out-of-stock situations. To achieve these goals, simply equipping items with unique identifiers is not enough: a complete infrastructure with readers, device management, middleware, ERP integration and read event repositories needs to be deployed and processes have to be adopted in order to realize the potential improvements.

Hardware and Software Components in a Unique Identifier Network

To illustrate the components in a unique identifier network as well as their interplay, Fig. 2.3 presents a typical RFID deployment. RFID readers and writers interact with RFID tags. Additional sensors help monitoring what happens in the real world, i.e. light sensors are used to determine the direction an RFID reader is passed. Raw read events are sent to a device management, which is often included in an RFID middleware. From there, related systems such as ERP systems are informed about what was detected by these automatic identification technologies. In addition, read events are persistently stored in a read event repository. Clients can access read events by using the object name service or an application, which leverages a discovery service. The variety of RFID deployments is unlimited. Nevertheless, they consist of typical building blocks. These can be divided into hardware and software. In the next subsections, the particular components are depicted.

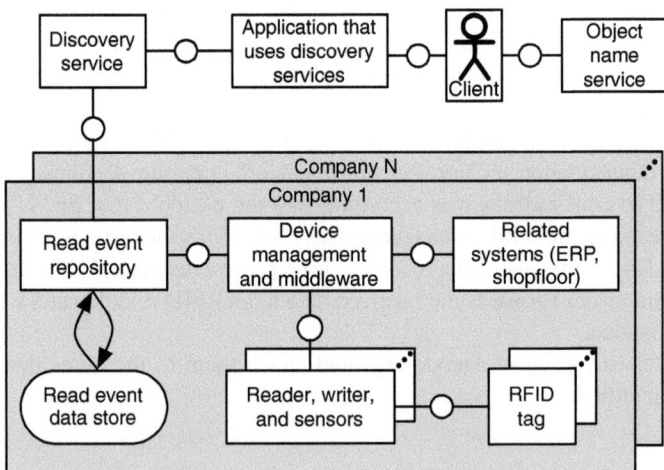

Fig. 2.3 A typical RFID deployment

Hardware Components

Each unique identification application uses RFID tags or data matrices to store the unique identifiers that are attached to items, boxes, or containers. Tags can also store more information than just the identifier. This is described in the so called data-on-tag approach [41].

At the beginning of the tag lifetime, the data has to be written onto the tag. This is done using RFID writer devices such as RFID printers.

Many RFID deployments use additional hardware such as infrared sensors, weighting machines, or temperature sensors. Infrared sensors are applied to switch RFID readers on and off and to determine the direction of moving items, e.g., through an RFID-equipped gate.

Software Components

In most RFID deployments a device management software is used to configure, manage, and control the attached RFID readers and the additional hardware [129]. This software also filters the read events [90] and represents the border between the RFID-related, hardware-oriented layer and business layers that consume well-formatted and context-enriched data. The device management software can be configured to directly communicate with related systems or read event repositories, but in most situations it makes sense to deploy an RFID middleware [18].

RFID middleware processes the incoming read events. This includes initiating certain business processes such as goods receipt or goods issue in related systems, e.g., an Enterprise Resource Planning or Inventory Management System. Furthermore, read events $re \in RE$ are propagated to a read event repository $rer \in RER$. Read event repositories are in charge of the reliable storage of read events because ERP systems are not designed to handle unique identifier information [18]. Furthermore, access rights can be defined at the read event repository to prevent unauthorized access.

As read events RE are stored locally at each participant P, the discovery service D is necessary to collect read events RE_p that are distributed at multiple participants. Related to this, an application that accesses the discovery service, e.g., a verification service, completes the unique identifier network components.

Electronic Product Code Network Standards

The organization Global Standards 1 (GS1) is an association with the goal to develop and implement global standards related to supply chain management. It was founded in 1977 and is a not-for-profit organization. Currently, GS1 is active in four areas: barcodes, electronic messaging standards for enterprises, global data synchronization, and track and trace in supply chains. In the latter, it collaborates with EPCglobal. EPCglobal is a joint venture of formerly EAN International (now GS1) and formerly

Uniform Code Council (now GS1 US). EPCglobal has the goal to standardize unique identification technology and, thus, foster its adoption.

The so called Electronic Product Code (EPC) Network consists of several standards approved by EPCglobal [50]. Several companies joined the standardization process and coordinated their efforts with regard to serialization concepts. Therefore, the EPC Network is the most mature collection of standardization documents at the moment [133].

To increase the practical applicability and increase the relevance of my work, I use the EPC Network as a foundation for my research and integrate my research into the existing standards. Nevertheless, the described concepts are applicable for all unique identifier networks.

Eleven standards were issued by EPCglobal so far. They can be categorized into data standards and interface descriptions. The relevant standards for this dissertation are marked with an (X) and described in more detail in the following. The data standards in the EPC Network are:

- Tag data standard (X),
- Tag data translation standard,
- Certificate profile standard, and
- Pedigree standard (X).

The interface standards in the EPC Network are:

- Tag protocol standard (X),
- Low level reader protocol standard,
- Reader protocol standard,
- Reader management standard,
- Application level event standard,
- EPC information services standard (X), and
- Object name service standard (X).

The mapping of these standards to the components of a unique identifier network is illustrated in Fig. 2.4. The data standards are relevant for multiple components and therefore not integrated in the figure.

Tag Data Standard

The tag data standard [52] defines the Electronic Product Code. The EPC is used as unique identifier $id \in ID$ for physical items within the EPC network. To this end, "epc" was added as a URN namespace [117]. Furthermore, the tag data standard defines different EPC data formats for distinct items to be tagged. Selected data formats in the EPC network are:

- A Serial Shipping Container Code (SSCC) to uniquely identify transport containers [52, pp. 31, pp. 98]. The SSCC is encoded in 96 bit that contain header information (14 bit, "urn:epc:id:sscc:"), a company code of the owner (between 20 and 40 bit,

2.1 Underlying Technologies

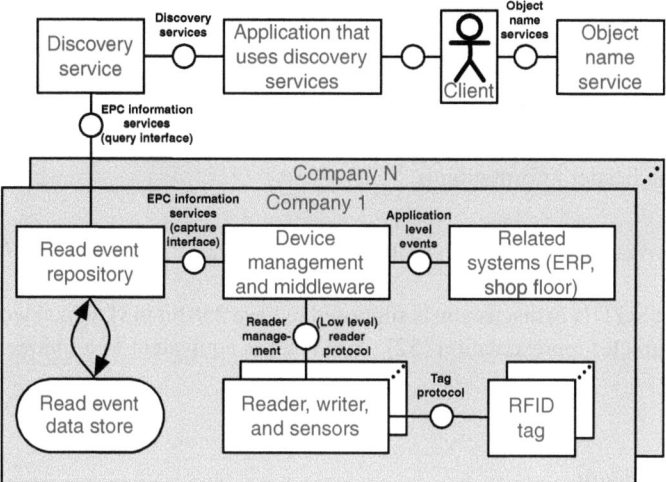

Fig. 2.4 The EPC network interface standards

e.g. "0063870"), a serial number (between 38 and 18 bit, e.g. "1234535654"), and a reserved block (24 bit). An example of a SSCC in a string representation including header information is

urn:epc:id:sscc:0063870.1234535654.

In this dissertation, a SSCC is used as unique identifier $id_{TC} \in ID_{TC}$ for each transport container $tc \in TC$.

- The Serialized Global Location Number (SGLN) uniquely identifies business locations [52, pp. 31, pp. 99]. The SGLN can be encoded in 96 bit or 195 bit. I use the 96 bit version in the remainder of this thesis. Thus, it consists of header information (14 bit, "urn:epc:id:sgln:"), a company code (between 20 and 40 bit, e.g. "7948144"), a location reference (between 21 and 1 bit, e.g. "015163"), and an extension (41 bit, e.g. "1234567881430"). An example in a string representation including header information is

urn:epc:id:sgln:7948144.015163.1234567881430.

In this thesis, a SGLN is used as unique identifier $id_R \in ID_R$ for each reader $r \in R$.

- The Serialized Global Trade Item Number (SGTIN) to uniquely identify physical objects such as items [52, pp. 30, pp. 95]. Two variations of the SGTIN exist: one with 198 bit and one with 96 bit. The 96 bit version is more commonly used and therefore, I use this one in the remainder of this thesis. The SGTIN consists of four parts: header information (14 bit, "urn:epc:id:sgtin:"), a manager code (between 20 and 40 bit, e.g. "7948144") that identifies the company responsible for the initial assignment of the EPC to a physical item, a product type code (between 24 and 4 bit, e.g. "037191") that describes the product type, and a serial number (38 bit, e.g. "123262414837") that is used to uniquely identify all product instances of that particular product type. An example of a SGTIN in a string representation including header information is

$$\text{urn:epc:id:sgtin:7948144.037191.123262414837.}$$

The largest SGTIN in discussion is supposed to have 256 bit [43], which would result in a 61 character representation [52]. A SGTIN is equivalent to a unique identifier $id_I \in ID_I$.

Pedigree Standard

The pedigree standard [46] describes an architecture for maintaining and exchanging electronic pedigree documents used in the pharmaceutical supply chain. A pedigree is a certified record containing information about the complete lifecycle of a prescription drug.

Tag Protocol Standard

The tag protocols defines the air interface between RFID tags and readers. Protocols for Ultra High Frequency (UHF) communication, Class-1 Generation-2 [48] as well as High Frequency (HF) communication [51] are in place.

EPC Information Services Standard

EPC Information Services (EPCIS) [45] are the interfaces to a read event repository $rer \in RER$. They define a capture interface and a query interface. In the context of the EPC network, read event repositories are implemented as EPCIS servers. Using the capture interface, an RFID middleware or other software can send read events re that shall be stored to the read event repository. Using the query interface, clients $c \in C$ can submit queries against a read event repository $rer \in RER$. Basically, read event repositories answer the questions:
- When did a read event happen?
- What actually happened?
- Where did the read event take place?
- Why did the read event appear?

The interface definitions are also used for data transfer between different IT systems [45].

EPCIS servers can serve two different types of queries: one-off queries and standing queries. One-off queries are performed by a client once and no further communication between client and EPCIS server is planned. Standing queries are subscriptions, which can be time-controlled using a query schedule (e.g., a client wants to be informed every hour) or trigger-controlled (e.g., a client wants to be informed if new information about an item of interest is available) [45].

The EPCIS standard defines four different event types [184]. Table 2.1 presents the event types including respective attributes.

- An ObjectEvent $oe \in OE$ indicates that one or more uniquely identified items passed a reader $r \in R$ without being modified. The first ObjectEvent occurs when the item i is equipped with it's unique identifier id_I. This is indicated by the read event action "ADD". Once the unique identifier id_I is removed from the item i, the last read event in the item's lifecycle is generated. It has the action "DELETE". M includes optional attributes (see Table 2.1) as well as further company-specific attributes.
- Given the fact that item-level granularity is not always needed, a QuantityEvent only includes item type and quantity like in traditional barcode scanning. QuantityEvents might be used to conduct inventory management, for example.
- A TransactionEvent links an EPC to a business transaction like a purchase order.
- The fourth event is an AggregationEvent $ae \in AE$. It describes that the hierarchical packaging relationship $hpr \in HPR$ was changed. The items that are added to or removed from a container are referenced to as *childEPCs*. The container is identified as the *parentEPC*. Either an item was packed into another entity such as a container, which is indicated by an event attribute action "ADD" or it was unpacked from a container, which is indicated by the action "DELETE". Again, M includes the optional attributes (see Table 2.1) as well as further company-specific attributes. The standard also describes an AggregationEvent with the action "OBSERVE" for situations where the aggregation is observed but not changed [45, p. 45]. Like [184], I do not follow this recommendation. If an item is observed and not changed, it is an ObjectEvent, from my point of view.

Object Name Service Standard

The idea of the Object Name Service (ONS) [49] is derived from the Domain Name System (DNS) and, given an EPC, is able to point to the EPCIS server of the respective EPC manager encoded in the EPC's company code or manager code, respectively.

Given the fact that read events RE are distributed and locally stored at various supply chain participants P, the ONS is not sufficient. A discovery service is needed to find all read events for an item of interest. Such a discovery service is not defined by EPCglobal yet but first steps in the process of defining it are taken. The content of the present dissertation will be made available to EPCglobal for consideration with regard to a future discovery service definition.

Table 2.1 EPC information services event types and attributes [45, 184]

		ObjectEvent	AggregationEvent	QuantityEvent	TransactionEvent	
When?	eventTime	●	●	●	●	Time of event observation
	recordTime	○	○	○	○	Time of event registration
	eventTimez.Offset	●	●	●	●	Time zone information
What?	epcList	●			●	List of observed EPCs
	parentEPC		●		○	Containing object ID
	childEPCs		●			Contained object IDs
	epcClass			●		Product type
	quantity			●		Number of observed objects
	action	●	●			Life-cycle phase of the EPCs
Where?	readPoint	○	○	○	●	Reader name
	bizLocation	○	○	○	○	Location name
Why?	bizStep	○	○	○	○	Business process step
	disposition	○	○	○	○	State of the objects
	bizTransactionList	○	○	○	●	Associated transaction

● = mandatory; ○ = optional

2.2 Approaches to Retrieve Track and Trace Information Without Discovery Services

Before simply accepting discovery services as the only and ultimate solution to retrieve all read events related to an item of interest, alternatives to a discovery service shall be analyzed. Discussed alternatives are:

- A central data store for each item,
- The daisy chain approach,
- The e-pedigree approach,
- Entry-Exit testing, and
- A federated database system comprised of read event repository databases.

The second and third approach can be found in literature. The fourth one resulted from research conducted by MIT. The first and fifth approach arose in discussions in academia.

I will briefly explain the idea behind these approaches and their suitability to replace the introduction of a discovery service for the EPC Network.

2.2.1 A Central Data Store for Each Item

A straightforward approach to collect all read events for a uniquely identified item $i \in I$ could be a central data store. Each $i \in I$ would have a dedicated data store. The data store could be accessed by a subdomain, for example

http://123262414837.037191.7948144.sgtin.manufacturer.com.

Another possibility would be to encode the EPC directly in the URL, i.e.

http://www.manufacturer.com/urn/epc/id/sgtin/037191/123262414837.

The interaction with the item's data store could follow the REST-ful architectural style [64]. To retrieve the URL, the ONS could be used. However, discussions about the suitability of the ONS, especially security, are still ongoing [58, 60, 157, 166].

Although the idea of a central data store for each item is interesting, it falls short with regard to a very fundamental requirement. Read events are sensitive data because the complete supply chain can be reconstructed using this information. Thus, each participant $p \in P$ stores the read events RE_p happening at p in it's own read event repository. This is the only way to ensure data ownership of the read events RE_p. Thus, a central data store for where all read events are collected is not feasible from a data ownership point of view.

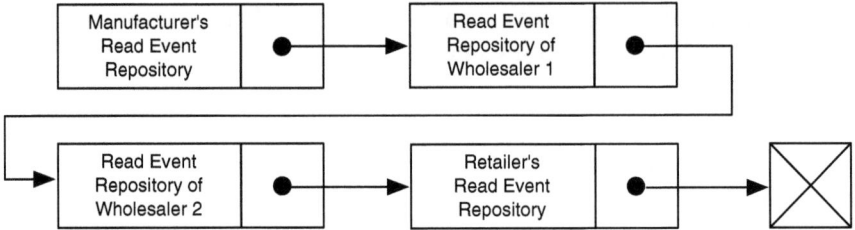

Fig. 2.5 Example of a singly-linked list in the daisy chain approach

2.2.2 Daisy Chain Approach

In a supply chain, a supplier's customer is the next customers' supplier etc. The daisy chain approach leverages the fact that all supply chain partners are arranged in a chain. In this approach, their read event repositories are explicitly connected.

Each supplier could add the next supply chain partners' read repository URL to the respective read event when he ships goods [78]. This creates a singly-linked list of read event repositories that contain track and trace information for an item $i \in I$ (see Fig. 2.5).

The identification of all read events for an item of interest would be conducted as follows [188]:

1. The legitimate client $c_{id}^L \in C$ interested in relevant read events about an item of interest $i \in I$ would scan the item using a reader device.
2. Using the unique identifier id_I, he would query the ONS.
3. The ONS would return id_{RER}, the URL of the read event repository of the item's manufacturer p_1.
4. The client would query rer_{P_1} with the unique identifier id_I.
5. rer_{P_1} would return the relevant read events tti_i that are stored in rer_{P_1} and the URL of rer_{P_2}, with p_2 being the participant that received the item i from the manufacturer p_1.
6. The client would query rer_{P_2} to receive read events and the URL of p_2's customer etc. until no further read event repository URL is returned.

Assuming that the client could somehow determine the read event repository URL of the participant where he received the item, he could query the manufacturer's read event repository rer_1 and the other known read event repository rer_N in parallel. This could be leveraged in a doubly-linked list. To create such a doubly-linked list, each participant stores the suppliers' read event repository URL at goods receipt (see Fig. 2.6).

According to the EPCIS standard, the daisy chain approach would use optional attributes to add the attributes *nextEPCISServerURL* for the singly-linked list and, in addition, *previousEPCISServerURL* for the doubly-linked list [45]. This, the daisy chain approach is feasible.

2.2 Approaches to Retrieve Track and Trace Information Without Discovery Services

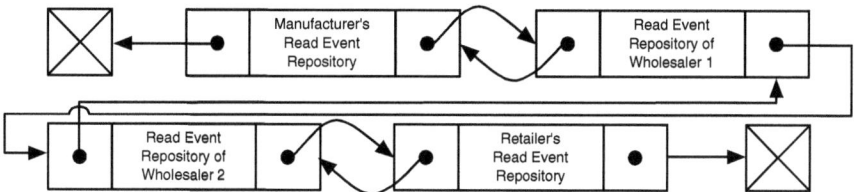

Fig. 2.6 Example for a doubly-linked list in the daisy chain approach

The major vulnerabilities of the daisy chain approach are that it is fragile due to its structure and slow given the fact that requests sequentially have to process the chain. It is not possible to query all relevant read event repositories in parallel.

If only one single read event repository of any supply chain participant for a given $i \in I$ is not available or the participant owning the read event repository cannot or does not want to answer a query, the remaining read events cannot be determined. In the doubly-linked list daisy chain approach, read events cannot be identified completely if two read event repository requests fail.

Assuming a supply chain with five supply chain partners and an average response time of 500 ms per request, a client trying to retrieve the read events for an item of interest would have to wait at least 2.5 s per item. Even if one assumes that the doubly-linked daisy-chain approach could work, the response time for one item is at least 1.25 s. Taking hierarchical packaging into consideration, even more requests would have to be stated, resulting in a substantial waiting time which is neither wanted by customers nor acceptable for transportation or other industrial processes. Thus, I conclude that the daisy chain approach is too slow and fragile.

Another disadvantage of the daisy-chain approach is its inability to execute selective queries, e.g., a query requesting only those events captured within a certain time frame. A client requesting all events captured after a certain point in time would still have to start with the manufacturer's read event repository, traversing its path through all read event repositories that have information about this respective item.

2.2.3 E-Pedigree

In some areas, especially pharmaceutical supply chains, documenting papers have to be shipped together with the goods. This is enforced by pedigree laws, for example in some U.S. states, Belgium, and Italy [46, 178]. The manufacturer creates and signs a so called pedigree document and all successive supply chain partners add their information to this document and sign it [96].

This concept is adopted for a digital e-pedigree document [46, 82]: The manufacturer creates a digital e-pedigree document including information about the item of interest. Then, he certifies the e-pedigree document with his digital signature and sends it to his customer together with the physical shipment. The customer receives

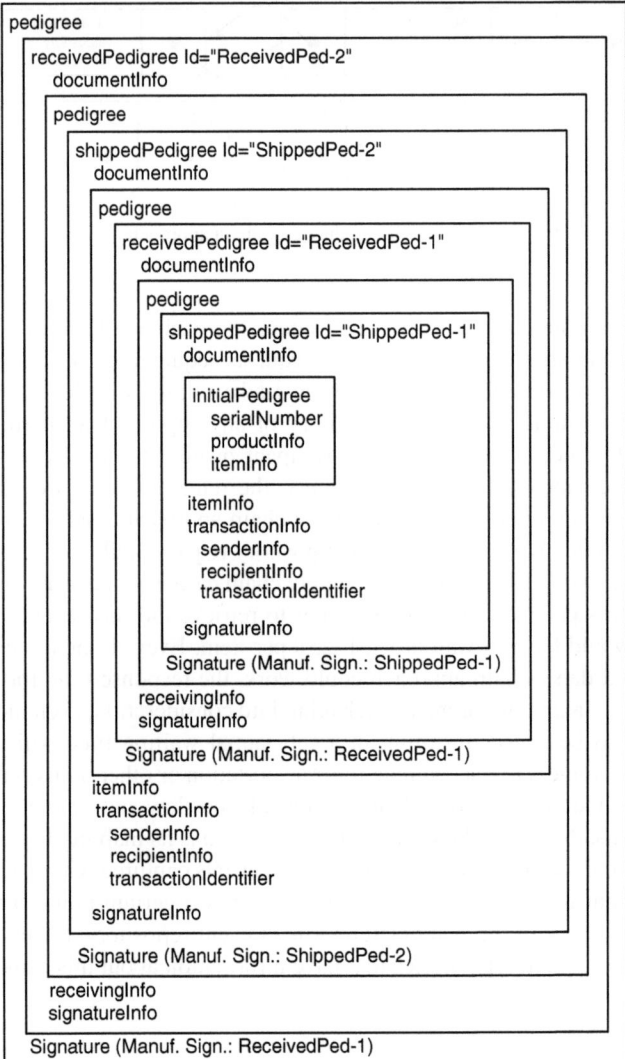

Fig. 2.7 Simplified example E-pedigree document (adopted from [46])

the shipment and the e-pedigree document, authenticates the digital signature of the sender, conducts a goods inwards inspection, and signs the e-pedigree document with his digital signature stating that he received the item. These steps are conducted by all supply chain partners in the supply chain.

Thus, the route taken through the supply chain can be digitally tracked (see Fig. 2.7 for an example e-pedigree document), while still being compliant to paper-based pedigree laws.

2.2 Approaches to Retrieve Track and Trace Information Without Discovery Services

The e-pedigree document can be either stored on a server or on the RFID tag itself, if rewritable RFID tags with sufficient storage capacity are used. Common RFID tags with 96 bit storage capacity are not sufficient [52]. For a discussion about data-on-tag versus data-on-network, the interested reader is referred to Diekmann, Melski, and Schumann [41].

The main disadvantages of this approach are that it only aims at fighting counterfeits and that only the company in possession of the item has the latest tracking information because no plan for sharing this information is included in the e-pedigree standard. Other use cases such as real-time supply chain visibility or product recalls cannot be supported by the e-pedigree approach. Furthermore, rewritable RFID tags are much more expensive than passive RFID tags or data matrices.

2.2.4 Entry-Exit Testing

In entry-exit testing, items are equipped with unique identifiers by the manufacturer at the point of entry into the supply chain. The manufacturer maintains a database with all unique identifiers $i \in I$ that were issued [95]. At the point of exit, the recipient can verify whether this serial number was issued by the manufacturer or not. This basic concept is used by Philip Morris International and Roche India [95]. It is very cost efficient and provides a basic protection against counterfeiting and smuggling.

Nevertheless, it cannot be used for supply chain visibility, product recalls, or other more complex use cases because the path of an item through the supply chain is not covered by the tracking system. Although, companies could start with entry-exit testing and add track and trace functionality later on. Furthermore, especially when using data matrix codes, counterfeiters easily can copy the data matrix code. Thus, the basic protection of this system would be broken because the manufacturer's database would confirm that this serial number was issued and the product is no counterfeit.

2.2.5 A Federated Read Event Repository Database System

A discovery service acts mainly as a pointer to additional data that is stored in participants' read event repositories. As the discovery service replicates and centralizes selected data from these read event repositories, it can be interpreted as a view on the underlying read event repositories of all participants in the unique identifier network.

A system managing distributed, heterogeneous, and autonomous databases is referred to as federated database system [169]. It is composed of autonomous and possibly heterogeneous database systems that are cooperating. A Federated Database Management System (FDBMS) is characterized by the three orthogonal dimensions distribution, heterogeneity, and autonomy. In the case of a FDBMS for a discovery service, data could be distributed from the read event repositories RER to the discovery service or the data could reside at the repositories only. For a discovery service in the context of a FDBMS, data would have to be replicated into the discovery service database. Otherwise, latency would be too high when the discovery service database would have to query all read event repositories to retrieve respective read events. Furthermore, if the data would not be replicated, the discovery service would not know which read event repository has information about a certain item of interest. Thus, this would result in querying each and every read event repository for each query stated against the discovery service. As companies are not homogeneous, the databases would not be heterogeneous, either. This relates to differences in hardware and underlying software.The different read event repositories would stay autonomous, even in the case of a federated discovery service database. Each participant would retain control of their part of the database and operate it independently. In addition to this, selected data would be shared with the discovery service, as it is necessary for the discovery service to reconstruct the lifecycle of an item of interest.

To reconstruct an item's lifecycle, the discovery service needs to be informed about ObjectEvents OE at least. For each ObjectEvent $oe \in OE$, the unique identifier id_I, the time t of the read event, and the URL of the read event repository id_{RER} that stores detailed information about this read event oe has to be submitted to the discovery service D. For a discovery service that resolves containment hierarchies, data about AggregationEvents AE need to be propagated, too. This includes the unique identifier of the childEPCs, the parentEPC, time, and URL of the respective read event repository.

A possible concept for a federated discovery service database is depicted in Fig. 2.8. The example shows this process for the database table "ObjectEvents" only. As not all read events of a participant $RE_p \in RE$ are to be shared with the discovery service, the database field *publish_to_discovery_service* is introduced. Hence, read events that shall not be shared with other participants can be stored in the read event repository but are not shared with a discovery service. If a read event is to be shared with the discovery service, the respective field is set to '1'. Otherwise, a NULL value is inserted. The concept for AggregationEvents would be similar but more sophisticated as it includes a 1:n relationship between the parent EPC and the involved child EPCs. The federation concept of [169] could be adopted for ObjectEvents as follows:

1. Each read event repository rer_1 to rer_N can have its own local schema. This is transformed into an export schema once, which is the same for all read event repositories $rer \in RER$.
2. For the sake of federation, the read events to be shared with the discovery service are chosen by applying a selection (σ) checking whether the field *publish_to_discovery_service* is set to '1'.
3. A projection (π) is applied and only the field's *event_time* and *epc* are filtered.
4. Each tuple is joined ($\bowtie$) with the respective read event repository URL as it is not included in the source data set.
5. The accordingly prepared data of all read event repositories is united ($\cup$) into the discovery service database as the external schema.
6. The external schema is used to construct the local schema at the discovery service.

2.2 Approaches to Retrieve Track and Trace Information Without Discovery Services

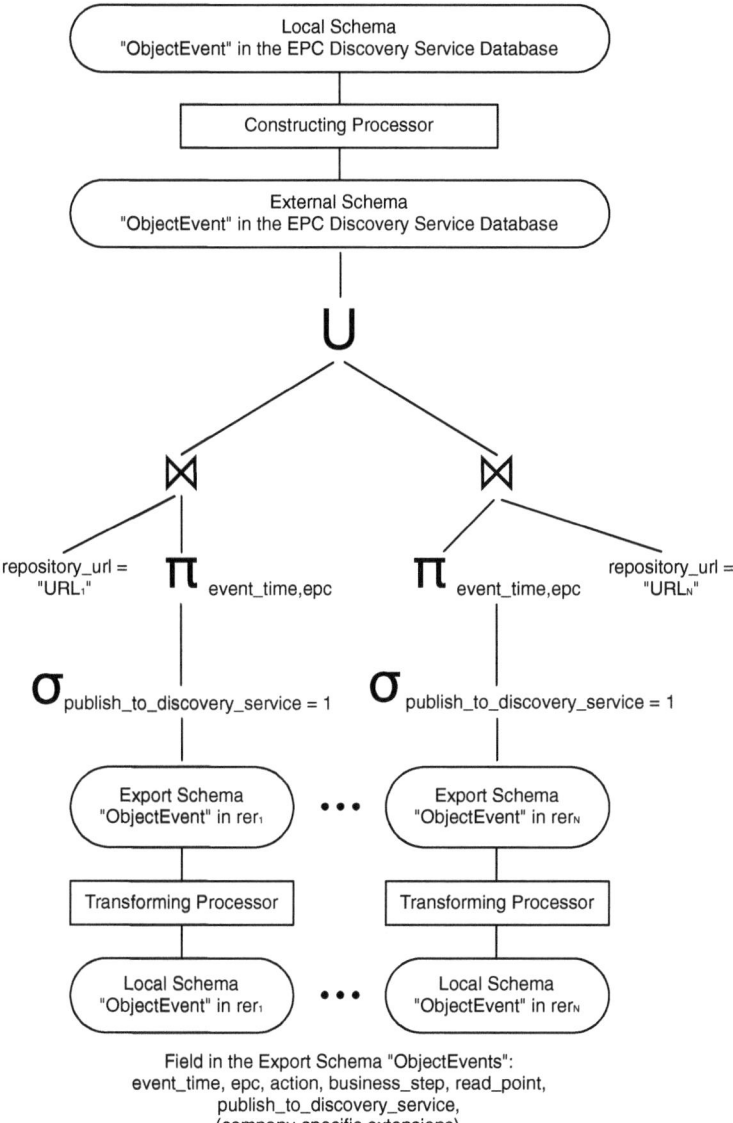

Fig. 2.8 Simplified concept for a federated discovery service database (database table "ObjectEvents" only)

After having developed a concept for a federated discovery service database, I discuss its advantages and disadvantages. The advantages are that:

- The FDBMS inherently takes care of distributing the data to the discovery service.

- The FDBMS also supports design autonomy of the database as long as the format of the export schema is met.

The disadvantages are that:

- FDBMSs are not well-adopted. Hundred thousands of companies will operate their read event repositories using different database systems. They would likely choose a database vendor that does not support FDBMSs or that the FDBMSs would be incompatible.
- The data is duplicated and, therefore, the FDBMs-based approach is inferior to other approaches with regard to space consumption.
- FDBMS include much overhead such as global transaction management and sophisticated techniques to ensure data integrity. These are not needed when read event repositories and discovery service are designed as two separate systems that interact with each other on the application layer.
- It must be ensured for security reasons that each read event repository owner is only allowed to view discovery service data that he submitted.
- The effort and complexity to add or remove a participant to/from the FDBMS is huge as the distribution concept has to be updated and redeployed.
- The scalability and stability for a FDBMS with hundreds of thousands participants would have to be ensured. This is more challenging for one complex FDBMS.

The disadvantages outweigh the advantages by far for this specific use case. In general, FDBMS are not well-adopted [146]. Rather than using FDBMS to integrate applications on the database layer, companies either leverage parallel databases to distribute data or, as in our case, if two separate systems are affected, each system gets its own database. The term federated database today mainly refers to the concepts of vertical and horizontal partitioning [27, 115, 135]. This means that the data is distributed amongst several database instances but the database has only a single interface and all data resides within one physical database.

2.2.6 Summary

The above-mentioned alternatives for a discovery service have their advantages and disadvantages. A detailed requirements analysis is conducted in Sect. 2.3.2. Nevertheless, the discovery service alternatives are now evaluated based on the description in the last sections using four requirements:

- *Performance*: Is the performance sufficient to support use cases like checkout at a pharmacy or conducting a verification using a mobile device?
- *Track and Trace Information*: Is sufficient track and trace information available to increase supply chain visibility?
- *Data Ownership*: Is data ownership respected such that each participant $p \in P$ is in full control of the read events RE_p generated at their facilities?
- *Feasibility*: Is the discovery service alternative technically feasible?

Table 2.2 Evaluation of discovery service alternatives (● = complete fulfillment, ◐ = partial fulfillment, ○ = requirement not fulfilled, ? = cannot be evaluated yet)

	Performance	Track & trace inform.	Data ownership	Feasibility
Central data store	●	●	○	●
Daisy chain	○	◐	◐	●
E-Pedigree	●	○	◐	●
Entry–Exit testing	●	○	●	●
Federated database	◐	●	●	○
Discovery service	?	●	?	●

The whole purpose of a discovery service is to provide track and trace information. As premature discovery service approaches already exist, the implementation of a discovery service is supposed to be feasible. Details about discovery services will be discussed in the next chapters. The resulting evaluation is presented in Table 2.2.
As no alternative can fulfill all stated requirements, it makes sense to evaluate alternative concepts, such as a discovery service. Prior to that, the next section presents assumptions made in this dissertation.

2.3 Related Work on Discovery Services

This section presents related work on discovery services. It is divided into four subsections. Sect. 2.3.1 identifies and classifies related work. This classification is used as the basis for a requirements elicitation in Sect. 2.3.2. Existing discovery services are presented in Sect. 2.3.3 and evaluated in Sect. 2.3.4.

2.3.1 Literature Review

This section conducts a literature review. To this end, relevant literature is identified and classified.

Identification of Relevant Literature

The applied process of literature identification follows the advice of Webster and Watson [195]. Firstly, an initial search is conducted. The references of the resulting relevant papers are analyzed to identify former relevant work (going backwards in time). In this sense, relevant means that studying the paper contributes to understanding the present thesis. This step is repeated until no prior work can be found. After that, key papers are identified. These key papers are used as a starting point to search for contributions that are based on these key papers (going forward in time). The newly identified papers are analyzed again in terms of "whom do they cite?" and "who cites them?". Finally, in addition to the advices of Webster and Watson, I apply a social approach to answer the question if I missed any relevant work. All research results were confirmed on April 11, 2011.

Initial Search

The central term for this dissertation and the related research area is the "discovery service". Thus, the main scientific databases for computer science and related disciplines are queried using this term. As searching for the plural term "discovery services" might lead to a different search result, this term is also searched for. The literature databases are: IEEE Xplore [84], ACM Portal [3], and SpringerLink [176]. In addition, CiteSeer and GoogleScholar are used to incorporate papers published by other publishing houses. When the search result is too large to analyze it manually, the additional terms "electronic product code" and eventually "epcglobal" are used. The "electronic product code" is the most established unique identifier standard and likely to be mentioned in respective papers. "epcglobal" is the leading standardization organization with regard to unique identifiers.

Initially, IEEE Xplore is searched for "discovery service". This results in 153 hits. A selection based on title and abstract results in five relevant papers: [11, 23, 57, 126, 200]. The search for "discovery services" comes up with 42 hits, from which three additional papers are relevant: [22, 25, 82].

Searching for "discovery service" at the ACM portal results in 413 results with one relevant paper: [177]. The search for "discovery services" at the ACM portal results in 147 results without additional relevant papers.

The search for "discovery service" at CiteSeer produces in 1,997 results. Thus, the search is narrowed down to "discovery service" AND "electronic product code". The search results in 19 papers, none of them being relevant for the present literature identification. The same result comes up for "discovery services" AND "electronic product code".

The search for "discovery service" at SpringerLink leads to 1,031 results. Thus, the search is narrowed down to "discovery service" AND "electronic product code" again. This search results in 32 hits including three new and relevant articles: [76, 105, 154]. The search for "discovery services" AND "electronic product code" reveals 37 publications without new relevant ones.

Using GoogleScholar to search for "discovery service" leads to about 31,000 search results. Thus, the search is again narrowed down to "discovery service" AND "electronic product code". This search reveals 309 results, from which two are new and relevant papers: [6], and [110].

Searching GoogleScholar for "discovery services" AND "electronic product code" results in 305 results, four of them relevant and new: [12, 109, 201, 204].

Searches for "discovery service" AND "epcglobal" and "discovery services" AND "epcglobal" at IEEEXplore, ACM, and GoogleScholar reveal [92].

2.3 Related Work on Discovery Services

In the course of studying the papers, the synonyms "lookup service", "directory service", and "naming service" occurred [154]. Thus, I also search for these terms but no additional papers are found.

Going Backwards in Time

After having read these 19 identified papers, I conclude that [76, 82, 177, 204] are not relevant as related work on discovery services. Thus, these papers are excluded from the literature review.

In a next step, the citations of each paper are analyzed to identify relevant prior work. This reveals eight new relevant contributions: [4, 38, 75, 156, 185, 186, 188, 189, 203].

The citations of these papers are analyzed again etc. until no new relevant papers can be identified. After reading the papers, I decide to exclude [38] from the literature review on discovery services as this work is focussing on other aspects than discovery services and does not contribute to this dissertation.

The resulting papers are summarized in Table 2.3.

Identification of Key Articles

Based on the citations for each paper shown in Table 2.3, I define the Top five papers with the most total citations or the most related citations to be "key papers". Following these criteria, these are: [6, 12, 23, 25, 75, 105, 185, 186, 188, 189, 203].

Going Forward in Time

In the following, I search for papers citing the identified key articles. This reveals four relevant papers: [70, 116, 133, 194].

Going Backward and Forward Again

The analysis of whom the authors of these papers cite and by whom they are cited reveals the publication [5].

Applying Social Approaches to Find Relevant Work

This set of papers was uploaded to CiteULike, a social researcher network [145]. Each researcher indicates, which papers he reads or finds relevant. Similar to product recommendations in online shops, CiteULike identifies additional papers that may

Table 2.3 Overview of related papers identified by going backward

Year	Authors	Title	C_T	C_R	ID
2006	Beier et al.	Discovery services–enabling RFID traceability in EPC global networks	24	4	[12]
2006	Agrawal et al.	Towards traceability across sovereign, distributed RFID databases	33	1	[6]
2007	Cao et al.	PTSP: A lightweight EPCDS platform to deploy traceable services between supply-chain applications	5	4	[25]
2007	BRIDGE	Requirements document of serial level lookup service for various industries	20	7	[189]
2007	BRIDGE	High level design for discovery services	24	8	[188]
2008	Lee et al.	Discovery architecture for the tracing of products in the EPC global network	4	3	[110]
2008	Kürschner et al.	Discovery service design in the EPC global network	18	4	[105]
2008	Cantero et al.	Traceability applications based on discovery services	6	5	[23]
2008	BRIDGE	Working prototype of serial-level lookup service	9	5	[75]
2008	Rezafard	Extensible supply-chain discovery service problem statement	5	2	[156]
2008	Afilias	Afilias discovery services	2	1	[4]
2008	Yough	Extensible supply-chain discovery service concepts	10	4	[203]
2008	Thompson	Extensible supply-chain discovery service commands	8	4	[185]
2008	Thompson	Extensible supply-chain discovery service schema	8	5	[126]
2009	Müller et al.	An aggregating discovery service for the EPC global network	1	0	[22]
2009	Burbridge and Harrison	Security considerations in the design and peering of RFID discovery services	2	1	[22]
2009	Barchetti et al.	Implementation and testing of an EPCglobal-aware discovery service for item-level traceability	1	1	[11]
2009	Le Moulec et al.	Discovery services interconnection	0	0	[109]
2009	Kang et al.	A development of traceability services in EPC global network environment	0	0	[92]
2010	Yan et al.	Pseudonym-based RFID discovery service to mitigate unauthorized tracking in supply chain management	0	0	[201]
2010	Evdokimov et al.	Comparison of discovery service architectures for the internet of things	0	0	[57]
2010	Polytarchos et al.	Evaluating discovery services architectures in the context of the internet of things	0	0	[154]
2010	Worapot et al.	Design and implement of the EPC discovery services with confidentiality for multiple data owners	0	0	[200]
2010	Cantero et al.	A design for secure discovery services in the EPC global architecture	0	0	[24]

(C_T = number of citations in total; C_R = cited by identified related work)

be interesting to a researcher based on what other researchers find relevant. For the uploaded set of papers, no recommendations were shown.

Thus, to the best of the author's knowledge, all relevant literature has been identified. The resulting papers for the literature review, in addition to the papers listed in Table 2.3, are listed in Table 2.4.

2.3 Related Work on Discovery Services

Table 2.4 Overview of papers in the literature review

Year	Authors	Title	ID
2007	Grummt et al.	Access control: Challenges and approaches in the internet of things	[70]
2010	Manzanarez-Lopez et al.	An efficient distributed discovery service for EPCglobal network in nested package scenarios	[116]
2010	Wang et al.	A novel RFID event data integration approach via EPC network	[194]
2010	Muñoz-Gea et al.	Implementation of traceability using a distributed RFID-based mechanism	[133]
2011	Afilias	How afilias discovery services works	[5]

Classification of Relevant Literature

As proposed by Webster and Watson, I analyze the relevant literature and classify it in a concept matrix [195]. This provides an overview of which papers contribute to which concepts and allows fast access with regard to contributions related to a concept of interest. The concepts for the concept matrix presented in Table 2.5 are extracted by analyzing the relevant literature and are:

- *Requirements (Req.)*: Does the paper state new requirements on a discovery service?
- *Discovery Service Approach (DS Approach)*: How do the authors see a discovery service? Is it based on the *Directory Lookup (DL)*, *Query Relay (QR)*, or *Fat Discovery Service* concept? Does the author deviate from these concepts and propose a *miscellaneous (Misc)* concept (see Sect. 2.3.3)?
- *Evaluation*: Do the authors present an *Implementation (Impl.)*? Do they *Benchmark (Bench.)* the implementation?

The papers [5, 185, 186, 201] do not contribute to any of the selected categories but discuss other aspects. Thus, they are excluded from the literature review.

2.3.2 Requirements Elicitation

At first glance, the Discovery Service Problem (DSP) appears to be trivial: read events re happening at several participants P are stored in participant-operated read event repositories rer and a central discovery service D is notified about the respective read events through notification messages N_{RE}. To retrieve an item's lifecycle information, a query is stated to the discovery service and the relevant read event repositories. Nevertheless, many challenges arise for a proper discovery service approach. The most relevant requirements are presented in this section.

To be successful, each software system or product has to be desired by the user, technically feasible as well as economically viable (see Sect. 2.3.2). In addition to

Table 2.5 Concept matrix of relevant literature (ordered by year ascending)

Articles	Req.	DS approach				Evaluation	
		DL	QR	Fat	Misc	Impl.	Bench.
Beier et al. [12]	●	●				●	
Agrawal et al. [6]		●	●	●		●	●
Cao et al. [25]		●					
BRIDGE [189]	●						
BRIDGE [188]		●	●	●	●		
Kürschner et al. [105]	●		●				
Cantero et al. [23]	●	●					
BRIDGE [75]		●	●			●	
Young [203]		●					
Grummt et al. [70]	●						
Lee et al. [110]		●				●	
Rezafard [156]	●						
Afilias [4]	●	●					
Müller et al. [126]					●	●	
Burbridge and Harrison [22]		●	●				
Barchetti et al. [11]		●				●	
Le Moulec et al. [109]							
Kang et al. [92]		●				●	
Evdokimov et al. [57]	●	●	●				●
Polytarchos et al. [154]		●	●			●	●
Worapot et al. [200]		●				●	
Cantero et al. [24]		●	●				
Manzanarez-Lopez et al. [116]	●					●	
Wang et al. [194]		●					
Muñoz-Gea et al. [133]		●				●	

these high-level requirements, I synthesize requirements on a discovery service stated in related work following the ISO/IEC 9126 standard [86].

The ISO/IEC 9126 standard describes software engineering product quality. It identifies three different product qualities: quality in use, external quality, and internal quality [86]. Quality in use considers the quality requirements by the user when the software is used. External quality is the set of software product characteristics from an external perspective when the software is executed. It can be derived from the system in use quality. Internal quality describes the rigor related to software design and construction of the software product. It can be derived from the external quality. As proposed in ISO/IEC 9126 [86], this classification can also be used for structuring requirements. Given the fact that general discovery service requirements rather than implementation details shall be considered, I will only incorporate requirements for the system in use and external requirements.

2.3 Related Work on Discovery Services 45

Desirability, Feasibility, and Viability

Without going into detail, I argue that a discovery service should pbe desirable, feasible, and viable [150]. To be desirable, it has to be easily consumable [12] and deliver an irreplaceable benefit for the respective user, among other aspects. Of course, the implementation and operation of a discovery service has to be feasible. Finally, the benefits have to be greater than the costs to make a discovery service viable. Costs include equipping products with unique identifiers, and operating the local read event repositories as well as the discovery service. Benefits are associated with better supply chain visibility, higher probability of therapeutic success due to fewer circulating counterfeit or smuggled products, reduction of lost sales, and the like. Discovery service plays an important role in a unique identifier network because many of the potential benefits such as these based on increased supply chain visibility cannot be leveraged without a proper discovery service. The more interested reader is referred to [118, 119, 131] for detailed discussions about economic viability.

Requirements on the Discovery Service in Use

The requirements stated in related work can be summarized to six properties:

- *Basic Functional Capabilities and Ease of Use*: A user will only interact with a discovery service if it fulfills the main requirements of storing event notifications and being able to query this data. Furthermore, its usage has to be convenient for the end user [12, 23, 156].
- *Performance*: To bring value to the user, a discovery service has to have a low latency (within a few seconds) from receiving a notification event to processing the data and being able to query it. In addition, the time to retrieve an item's lifecycle or its last location has to be low (within a few seconds) [4, 23, 156, 189]. This makes it a "real-time discovery service".
- *Security and Trustworthiness*: Security is a major concern because companies grant access to sensitive participant data. Thus, companies have to have full control over their data and access control policies need to be in place [12, 23, 70, 105, 156].
- *Completeness and Correctness*: Of course, a discovery service has to return complete and correct results, reflecting the latest client access rights [4, 105, 116, 156]. This is crucial because a client could gain access to sensitive information if the access rights are not properly reflected by the discovery service.
- *Reliability*: Given the fact that many companies will base their operations on a discovery service, it has to be reliable [156]. The discovery service is subject to high load and huge data volumes (up to 8,000 notification events per second; up to 2,000 queries per second; and about 35 billion read events per year stored for 5–10 years in the European pharmaceutical supply chain only, see Sect. 1.2).
- *Standardization*: Especially for discovery service operators and read event repositories, it is important that existing standards such as the EPCIS standard are

respected and a new standard for discovery services is defined. A discovery service should be seamlessly integrated into the existing infrastructure [4].

External Requirements

In this subsection, I refine each of the requirements on the discovery system in use and add further external requirements.

Basic Functional Capabilities and Ease of Use

To fulfill the basic functional requirements, the respective interfaces have to be present. In particular, these are:

- *Notification Interface*: To inform the discovery service about events that shall be shared, the notification interface is used [57, 156].
- *Query Interface*: In order to perform queries, a client uses a query interface [57, 156]. Three different kind of queries are most relevant:
  - *Lifecycle Query*: A client $c \in C$ is interested in the complete lifecycle of an item of interest [23, 189].
  - *Last-seen Query*: A client $c \in C$ queries the discovery service with regard to the latest position of an item of interest [23, 189].
  - *Standing Query*: A client $c \in C$ is interested in all events related to a certain item. Thus, he submits a standing query to the discovery service in order to get informed each time the discovery service gets notified about an event related to this item [189].

Further requirements with regard to ease of use are:

- *Synchronous Response*: A discovery service might reply to queries synchronously or asynchronously. A synchronous response is clearly preferred because this reduces the client complexity and also thin devices, e.g., point-of-sale terminals or mobile devices can easily query the discovery service [12, 189].
- *Access Control Maintenance*: The data stored in local read event repositories $rer \in RER$ and, potentially, at the discovery services is protected by means of access control. The maintenance of this access control rules and mechanisms should be minimal [105].
- *URL Changes*: URLs of the read event repositories might change. Thus, it must be possible to update the URLs stored at the discovery service [156].
- *Altering Data*: It should be able to update or delete records. In doing so, the original record should be reconstructable for auditing reasons [57].
- *Auditing*: A discovery service is subject to audits. Thus, it should be easy to conduct audits [4, 156].
- *Trust Relationship*: When a legitimate client queries the discovery service or a read event repository for the first time, it might be the case that no trust relationship has

2.3 Related Work on Discovery Services   47

been established yet. Even in such a situation, the client should be dynamically authorized and retrieve his query result [156].
- *Bootstrapping*: When a client wants to use a discovery service for the first time, he has to find out the correct URL of the discovery service to submit its query. This is called bootstrapping and has to be comfortable for the user [156].
- *Support of Thin Devices*: The usage of a discovery service should be simple. Thus, thin devices such as point-of-sale machines or mobile devices should be able to query the discovery service, i.e. requests to the discovery service must not rely on any client computing capabilities and the request has to be conducted within a couple of seconds.

Performance

The goal is to achieve low latency for notification messages to become visible (ideally only a few seconds) [4, 156, 189] and minimum response times of lifecycle and last-seen queries (within a few seconds) [4, 23, 156, 189]. As depicted in the scenario of the European pharmaceutical supply chain, a discovery service has to handle dozens of billion records per year and store them for multiple years. Some authors refer to trillions of records per year that have to be stored at the discovery service [156]. Thus, the discovery service has to be scalable to achieve the desired performance [12].

To achieve this, the external requirements are the following:

- *Minimum Data Storage at the Discovery Service*: To achieve such a high performance, the data stored at the discovery service should be minimal [23].
- *Low Complexity of Discovery Service Operations*: Performance is also affected by the complexity of the operations conducted by the discovery service. The simpler the tasks the discovery service has to conduct, the better the discovery service performs.
- *Data Aging*: In many situations, track and trace information is mainly interesting for "current" data [189]. For example, if a package of pharmaceuticals is sold or dispensed and a couple of months passed, it is likely that no additional request with regard to this package of pharmaceuticals will be issued. Nevertheless, all data needs to be available for exceptional situations, e.g. if any investigation with this type of pharmaceutical is conducted. The access time for this so called "passive" data can be a factor 10 slower [153, pp. 92].
- *Low Number of Messages and Network Traffic*: Depending on the discovery service approach, a considerable load might be put onto existing infrastructures due to the discovery of lifecycle information for single items. Thus, to work efficiently, the number of messages exchanged between client, discovery service, and read event repositories as well as the network traffic caused by the discovery service should be low [12, 82, 125].
- *Scale-up*: It should be possible to add resources such as Central Processing Units (CPUs) or memory to increase the discovery service performance.

- *Scale-out*: It should be possible to add computing nodes to an existing discovery service system to increase its performance. In addition, scale-out can be understood to add new discovery services by means of distributed discovery services [4, 156].

Security and Trustworthiness

EPC-related information needs to be protected because it is confidential and mining this data could compromise a companies' complete supply chain, i.e. it's suppliers and customers [12]. Although I excluded some security aspects from this thesis as this topic is sufficient for several dissertations in their own right, I include the most relevant requirements on a discovery service from a security point of view. Furthermore, I want to mention the rest of security-related requirements to give the reader a complete overview.

For a discovery service, the most relevant requirements are:

- *Fine-grained Access Control*: Participants shall be in full control of their data including read event repository URL and fine-grained access rights for each read event $re \in RE_p$ [4, 12, 23, 57, 70, 105, 156].
- *Access Control Updates*: Changes made to the local read event repository access control policies should be immediately active, also at the discovery service level.
- *Client Authentication*: Clients using the query interface need to be authenticated [156].

Further requirements are that communication needs to be secure [156]; a discovery service has to provide the ability to track the usage and requests upon its own data [105]; confidentiality of data publishers needs to be provided [105]; confidentiality of clients needs to be ensured [105]; the notification interface must only be used by authorized parties [70]; access control information has to be protected as it allows conclusions about the actual data to be protected [70]; and a discovery service has to be resistant to network attacks [156]. In addition, given the fact that about 35 billion read events appear each year in the European pharmaceutical supply chain alone, the probability is high that some of the read events get lost. Thus, a discovery service should be robust, even if read events are missing. Of course, track and trace information is suspicious if read events are missing and the consumer or regulatory parties have to be informed about potential issues with an item of interest. Nevertheless, from a technical point of view, the discovery service should be robust.

Completeness and Correctness

- *Storing ObjectEvents*: To be able to reconstruct a trace, ObjectEvents have to be stored at the discovery service [57, 156, 189].
- *Storing AggregationEvents*: In addition to ObjectEvents, AggregationEvents shall be recorded at the discovery service to be able to reconstruct the complete packaging hierarchy of an item of interest [57, 156, 189]. Some authors state that storing

2.3 Related Work on Discovery Services

AggregationEvents is optional assuming that an ObjectEvent happens at the same location where the AggregationEvent takes place [188].
- *Access Rights Enforcement*: A result set of the discovery service is only correct if it adheres to the respective access rights of the querying client [105].
- *Dealing with Refusals*: It might be the case that a read event repository $rer \in RER$ does not reply at all to a client request because of his access rights. A discovery service protocol has to make sure that a client knows how long to wait for a reply.
- *Business Steps*: One author claims that it would be useful to store business steps, i.e. what actually happened to the item of interest at that strategic point in the supply chain, at the discovery service level to be able to define more precise queries [189].
- *Relabeling*: In the course of its lifecycle, the identifier attached to an item might be relabeled. Thus, the discovery service needs to support relabeling activities [156].
- *Returnable Transport Items*: Returnable Transport Items (RTIs) pose special requirements because they can be in use for decades (e.g., a container). Thus, the result set of a query related to an RTI might be huge. It has to be filtered with regard to access control policies to protect the confidentiality of each RTI user [156].
- *Reverse Logistics*: A discovery service must be able to identify all locations where an item has been, independent of whether it is in a regular supply chain or on its way back to the manufacturer.

Reliability

In a productive environment, a discovery service has to be reliable with more than 99.99 % uptime [156, 189]. Without going into detail, measures to secure systems that are connected to the public Internet need to be implemented.

Standardization

To increase wide adoption, a discovery service should be based on open standards and compatible to the EPCIS standard [4]. Furthermore, multiple numbering authorities should be supported [4, 57, 156].

2.3.3 Existing Discovery Service Approaches

Two possibilities for discovery service structures exist: central or distributed. Most authors adhere to a central discovery service while some follow the concept of distributed discovery services (see Table 2.5).

The main characteristic that distinguishes discovery services is the interaction protocol, i.e. the message exchange pattern defined for the communication between client c, discovery service D, and read event repositories $rer \in RER$. All discovery

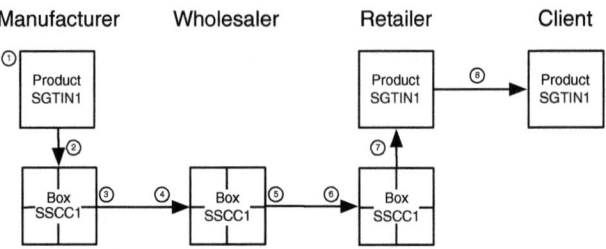

Fig. 2.9 Very simple supply chain used to exemplify principles of operation for different discovery service approaches

service protocols consist of the three phases *setup*, *discovery*, and *fulfillment* [188]. In the *setup phase*, the discovery service is notified about read events that took place at strategic points in the supply chain by notification messages. This happens within a short time frame after each read event was stored in a read event repository. The *discovery phase* starts when a client $c \in C$ queries a discovery service with an item of interest. It ends when all read event repositories containing read events about this item of interest or all read events itself are identified. The *fulfillment* phase comprises the requests to the identified read event repositories and their responses. After the fulfillment phase, the client receives all read events that are relevant for the item of interest, according to his access rights.

Three main discovery service approaches exist:

- Directory Look-up Approach
- Query Relay Approach
- Fat Discovery Service Approach

These three approaches and additional ones in related work (labeled as 'Misc' in Table 2.5) are presented in this subsection. An example with a very simple lifecycle (see Fig. 2.9) is used to exemplify the principle of operation of each discovery service approach. The example comprises three locations. Read events that happen in the item's lifecycle are indicated by ⊙. An item uniquely identified by $SGTIN1$ is produced (①), packed into a box identified by $SSCC1$ (②), and shipped (③) at a manufacturer. Goods receipt (④) and goods issue (⑤) happens at a wholesaler. Finally, the retailer receives the box (⑥), unpacks it (⑦), and sells the item to a customer (⑧).

Directory Look-up Approach

The directory look-up approach works as depicted in Fig. 2.10.

For each read event re happening at a strategic point in the supply chain, a notification message n_{RE} is published to the discovery service (①–⑧) [12]. The discovery service stores at least the EPC and the URL of the submitting read event repository for each combination of EPC and URL of the submitting read event repository server.

2.3 Related Work on Discovery Services

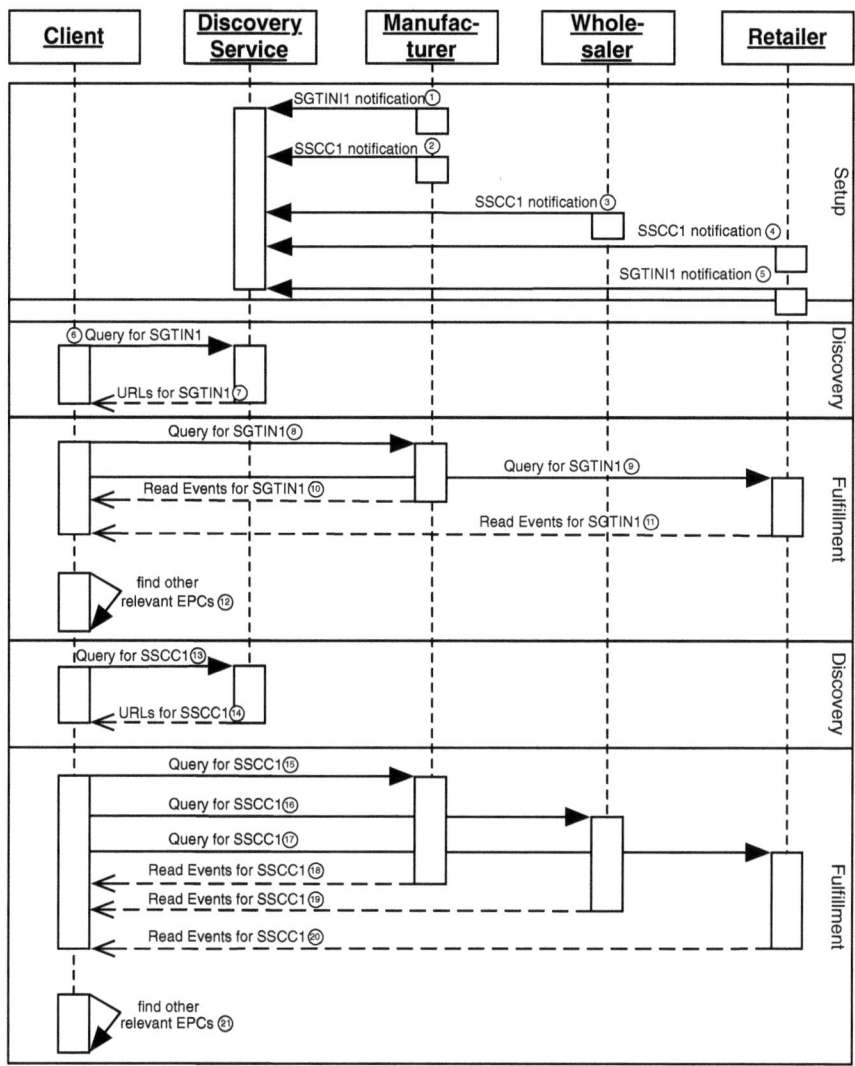

Fig. 2.10 Process of gathering lifecycle information following the directory look-up approach

If queried with the unique identifier of an item of interest (⑥), the discovery service responds with a list of relevant read event repository URLs, according to the client's access rights (⑦) [12]. Finally, the requester can query all relevant read event repositories by himself and receives respective responses (⑧–⑪) [116, 126, 133]. Due to hierarchical packaging, the client will have to analyze the read event repository responses (⑫) and query the discovery service (⑬ and ⑭) and read event repositories (⑮–⑰) again for each hierarchy level. The read event repositories' results are

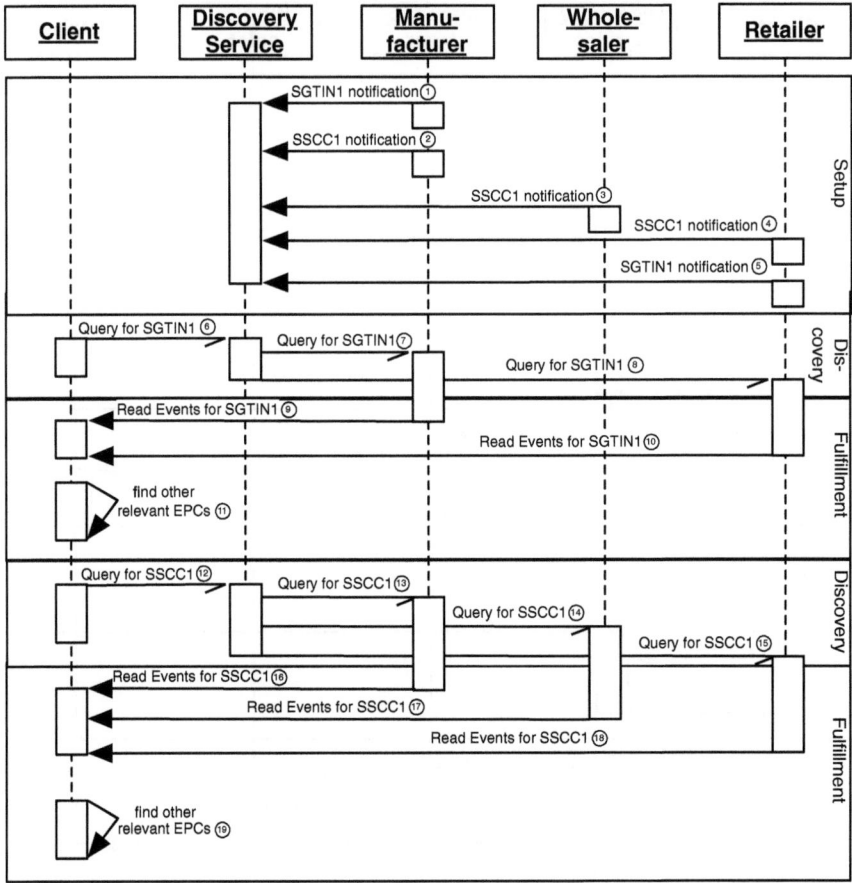

Fig. 2.11 Process of gathering lifecycle information following the query relay approach

retrieved (⑱–⑳) and analyzed again with regard to further changes in hierarchy levels (㉑), which are indicated by AggregationEvents.

The directory look-up approach has been initially presented and implemented by Beier et al. [12]. The majority of authors in this research area have picked up this type of discovery service [4, 6, 11, 22, 23, 24, 25, 57, 75, 92, 110, 133, 154, 188, 194, 200, 203]. It is also called 'Directory of Resources Approach' [188].

Query Relay Approach

The query relay approach mitigates the burden of fine-grained access control policies at the discovery service level (see Fig. 2.11).

2.3 Related Work on Discovery Services   53

Each read event happening at a strategic point in the supply chain is published to the discovery service (①–⑤). The discovery service is used as a relay that forwards incoming client queries (⑥) to all relevant read event repositories (⑦ and ⑧). The read event repositories reply directly to the requester, which has to offer a respective callback interface (⑨ and ⑩). Therefore, the read event repository URLs are not revealed to the requester if the respective participant decides not to reply to the query at all. The client has to wait for all incoming read event repository responses and then analyzes the resulting events with regard to changes in the packaging hierarchy (⑪). For each aggregation found in the read events, the discovery service is queried again (⑫), which forwards the query to all read event repositories that had possession of the item of interest (⑬–⑮). The read event repositories reply asynchronously (⑯–⑱). After having received the read event repository responses, the client again analyzes the read events for AggregationEvents (⑲).

This approach was partly presented by Agrawal et al. [6] and finalized by the BRIDGE project [188]. A first implementation was demonstrated by Kürschner et al. [105]. Other authors follow this type of discovery service in their contributions [22, 24, 57, 75, 154]. It is also known as 'Query Propagation Approach' [188].

Fat Discovery Service Approach

The fat discovery service approach, also known as the fat registry approach, follows the concept that data of all read event repositories RER is replicated at the discovery service D in order to facilitate the discovery service replying independently to each query without any read event repository interaction (see Fig. 2.12).

The participants send their event notifications to the discovery service in the setup phase (①–⑤). The client states its query to the discovery service (⑥) and receives all relevant read events including all attributes that are stored in the read event repositories like in all other discovery service approaches (⑦). The client analyzes the read events with regard to AggregationEvents (⑧) and queries the discovery service for each new container to which the item had been aggregated (⑨). The discovery service responds with the respective read events according to the client's access rights (⑩). This is repeated until the client no longer identifies any new AggregationEvents (⑪).

The idea was presented by Agrawal et al. [6] and has been adopted from the idea of one big database by Van Alstyne, Brynjolfsson, and Madnick [191]. The BRIDGE project included this approach in their contribution calling it 'Meta Resource Approach' [188].

Miscellaneous Approaches

Further discovery service approaches are proposed by the BRIDGE project and Müller et al. Their ideas are presented in the following.

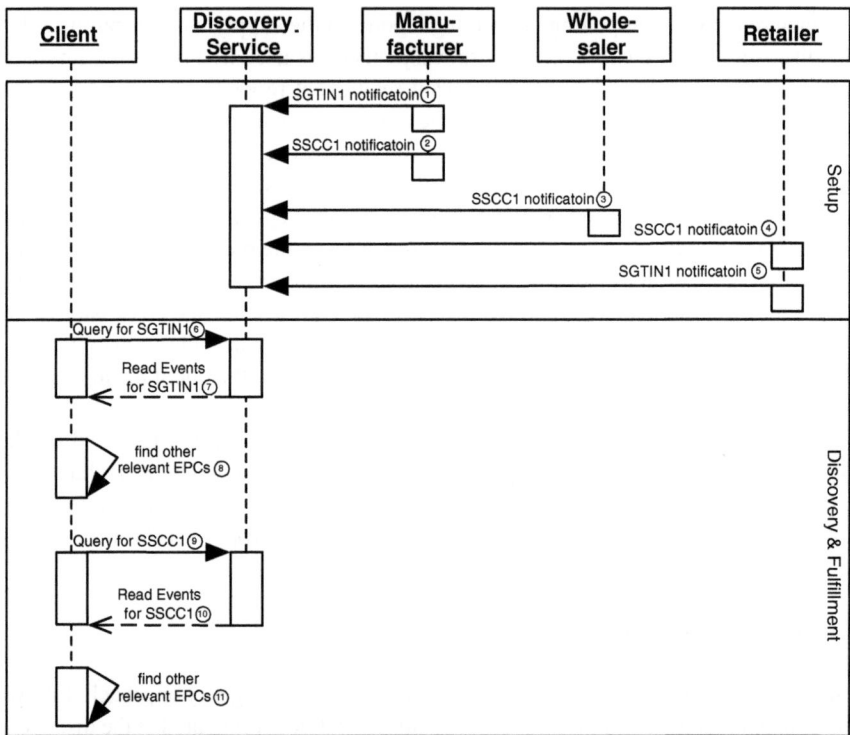

Fig. 2.12 Process of gathering lifecycle information following the fat discovery service approach

BRIDGE Project

In the BRIDGE project, several additional discovery service protocols are generated and evaluated [188]:

- *Directory of Clients*: Clients publish their interest in events related to EPCs to the discovery service. Instead of publishing read events to the discovery service, companies look up the EPCs of interest registered at the discovery service. If any EPCs match their current read event, the participant notifies the client, who then can query the companies' read event repository [188, Sect. B, pp. 13].
- *Notification of Resources*: Clients publish their interest in events related to EPCs to the discovery service. Participants do not publish their read events RE_P to the discovery service but send a list of available EPCs to the discovery service. The discovery service matches this list to the registered clients and forwards the identity of the companies' read event repository to the client if any EPCs match. The client can then submit its query to the read event repository and gets a response [188, Sect. B, pp. 15].
- *Notification of Clients*: Companies publish their read events to the discovery service. Clients notify the discovery service about their interest in certain EPCs. The discovery service forwards the client identity and EPCs of interest to read event

repositories that are in possession of read events related to these unique identifiers. The read event repositories then notify the client that relevant read events are available in their repository. Afterwards, the client queries the respective read event repositories [188, Sect. B, pp. 17].
- *Meta Client*: The client submits its request to the discovery service. For each read event, participants look up respective queries registered at the discovery service. If a read event is relevant for a query, the participant sends the read event to the client [188, Sect. B, p. 20].
- *Notification of Events*: A client sends his query to the discovery service. For each read event stored at a read event repository, all information is replicated to the discovery service. The discovery service analyzes, which queries are relevant for this new read event and replies to the queries accordingly [188, Sect. B, p. 21].

Hierarchical-Packaging-Aware Discovery Service

Parts of this dissertation have already been published. In [126], I present the first discovery service that explicitly leverages hierarchical packaging. A more detailed presentation is conducted in [127]. This discovery service D stores ObjectEvents OE and AggregationEvents AE. When queried by a client $c \in C$ with regard to the lifecycle of an item of interest, this discovery service analyzes the packaging hierarchy to identify where an item has been in what packaging context. After that, the discovery service queries the respective read event repositories, aggregates their responses and responds to the querying client synchronously. This response includes all read events TTI_i that happened in the item's lifecycle. No fine-grained access control policies are in place at the discovery service because access control is conducted at the read event repositories. The design and implementation of this discovery service is described in Chaps. 3, 4, 5, 6 of this dissertation.

2.3.4 Qualitative Evaluation

In this section, existing discovery service approaches are evaluated in order to determine how a discovery service for a unique identifier network could be designed and implemented.

The fulfillment of the requirements on a discovery service in use is substantial for a well-designed discovery service approach. It only makes sense to include requirements that are dependent on the discovery service approach in this evaluation. Thus, I select the following requirements for discussion:

1. *Basic Functional Capabilities and Ease of Use*: track and trace functionality, synchronous response, low access control maintenance effort, support of thin devices
2. *Performance*: minimum data storage at the discovery service, low complexity of discovery service operations, low number of messages, low network traffic

3. *Security and Trustworthiness*: confidentiality of data publishers
4. *Completeness and Correctness*: dealing with refusals, returnable transport items

Directory Look-up Approach

The directory look-up approach was presented in Sect. 2.3.3. It is evaluated as follows:

1. *Basic Functional Capabilities and Ease of Use*: The directory look-up approach is generally suited for track and trace functionality. Its response to a client query happens synchronously. Access rights have to be maintained at the discovery service level. Updating the potentially enormous amount of access rights results in a delay until the changes are applied. As the discovery service response being a list of read event repository URLs, the client has to query the respective read event repositories by himself. This adds complexity to the client application because the client has to implement necessary parallelization of requests and then aggregate the read event repository's responses.
2. *Performance*: Only a minimum of data is stored at the discovery service. Complexity of discovery service operations is medium because fine-grained access control policies have to be analyzed. The number of messages is high, network traffic is low.
3. *Security and Trustworthiness*: Fine-grained access control policies are in place to ensure confidentiality of data publishers. Due to potential faults in access control policies and update latency, the confidentiality is judged as medium.
4. *Completeness and Correctness*: The result of the discovery service following the directory look-up approach is complete and correct. If a read event repository does not reply, the client notices this immediately. Dealing with returnable transport items poses a challenge to the discovery service. If a client states a query with regard to an RTI, the size of the result set can be very large whereas the number of relevant read events for a respective client is very small. Nevertheless, access control policies for all returned read events will have to be analyzed. If a client uses an RTI more than once, the discovery service cannot distinguish which read events are relevant for the client.

Query Relay Approach

The query relay approach is presented in Sect. 2.3.3. It is evaluated as follows:

1. *Basic Functional Capabilities and Ease of Use*: The query relay approach uses asynchronous communication methods. No access control policies have to be in place at the discovery service level. Using thin devices is cumbersome because a query callback interface is needed.
2. *Performance*: The amount of data stored at the discovery service as well as the operation complexity are minimal. The number of messages is high and network traffic is low.

2.3 Related Work on Discovery Services   57

3. *Security and Trustworthiness*: Data publishers' confidentiality is ensured because no information is published by the discovery service.
4. *Completeness and Correctness*: A major concern arises with regard to refusals: A read event repository $rer \in RER$ might not answer a client's query because of access control policies. However, the discovery service might be overloaded or a participant's read event repository might be slow in replying to a client query. This leads to the permanent question for a client when following the query relay approach: How long do I wait for responses? Can I be certain that all results have come in? This halting problem makes the query relay approach impractical to use. Querying RTIs is not efficient either because all read event repositories that store information about the respective EPC, which might be thousands, would be notified about this query.

Fat Discovery Service Approach

The fat discovery service approach was depicted in Sect. 2.3.3. It is evaluated as follows:

1. *Basic Functional Capabilities and Ease of Use*: The fat discovery service approach uses synchronous responses. Access control maintenance is an issue because not only disclosure control on read events but each and every attribute of read events like in a read event repository has to be applied. Thin devices could leverage this discovery service approach.
2. *Performance*: Data is massively replicated from read event repositories as each and every read event is duplicated at the discovery service. Thus, together with cell-level disclosure control, the complexity is enormous. Network traffic is very high due to the data replication.
3. *Security and Trustworthiness*: Data publishers' confidentiality can only be ensured by access control policies.
4. *Completeness and Correctness*: The same holds true for situations with refusals. A query with respect to an RTI potentially results in a huge result set that has to be analyzed with respect to access control policies.

BRIDGE Project: Directory of Clients

The directory of clients discovery service approach was presented in Sect. 2.3.3. It is evaluated as follows:

1. *Basic Functional Capabilities and Ease of Use*: The directory of clients approach only supports standing queries. Thus, the response is asynchronous. Access control policies have to be in place, not for the published read events, but for the published queries. It is cumbersome to connect thin devices to this discovery service.

2. *Performance*: To fulfill the basic requirements of a discovery service, too little data is stored at the meta client discovery service. The operation complexity of the discovery service is medium because for each notification by a data publisher, all queries have to be analyzed with respect to access control policies. The number of messages and network traffic is high.
3. *Security and Trustworthiness*: Confidentiality of data owners is ensured.
4. *Completeness and Correctness*: Read event repositories can refuse to reply to a client. This usually happens if an unauthorized client c_i^U submits a query with regard to unique identifier i. Assuming that clients update their queries regularly, dealing with RTIs is not a problem.

BRIDGE Project: Notification of Resources

The notification of resources approach was described in Sect. 2.3.3. It is judged as follows:

1. *Basic Functional Capabilities and Ease of Use*: The notification of resources approach does not support one-off queries such as lifecycle queries or last-seen queries. The discovery service notifies the client once a matching notification of a participant arrives. This happens asynchronously to the initial query request by the client. Access control policies have to be in place to protect data publishers' confidentiality. Thin devices are not supported. Such a solution would not make sense, e.g. at a point-of-sale system, because the query had to be submitted before the actual read events occur, which is hardly possible in today's flexible and dynamic supply chains.
2. *Performance*: No actual references to read events are stored at the discovery service but it stores all queries from clients. This might easily be millions of queries and for each read event notification $n_{RE} \in N_{RE}$, the discovery service would have to search for matching queries. Many messages need to be exchanged and network traffic is high.
3. *Security and Trustworthiness*: Access control policies are used at the discovery service level.
4. *Completeness and Correctness*: In case a client is not supposed to be informed about a respective read event, this needs to be defined in access control policies. Assuming that clients regularly update their standing queries, RTIs can be handled in this approach.

BRIDGE Project: Notification of Clients

The notification of clients discovery service approach was presented in Sect. 2.3.3. It is evaluated as follows:

1. *Basic Functional Capabilities and Ease of Use*: The notification of clients approach could be used for track and trace purposes. Nevertheless it is cumber-

2.3 Related Work on Discovery Services   59

some because two queries (the first is asynchronous, the second is synchronous) are stated in order to retrieve any read event. It is not necessary to implement fine-grained access control at the discovery service level because no information is revealed to clients by the discovery service. Given the fact that the availability notifications from the read event repositories are asynchronous, it is hard to use thin devices together with the notification of clients discovery service approach.

2. *Performance*: The data stored at the discovery service is minimal, as is the operation complexity. The number of messages is very high. Caused network traffic is medium.
3. *Security and Trustworthiness*: Confidentiality of data publishers is met because each participant can decide to not reply to a query.
4. *Completeness and Correctness*: Data owners can protect their data just by not answering the client query. The client just does not recognize the refusal. If a client queries the discovery service with regard to an RTI, all read event repositories that hold information about this RTI are informed about this query. This is a huge overhead.

BRIDGE Project: Meta Client

The meta client discovery service approach was presented in Sect. 2.3.3. It is judged as follows:

1. *Basic Functional Capabilities and Ease of Use*: The meta client does not fulfill basic track and trace requirements because no one-off queries can be stated. It is completely designed for asynchronous communication. It has to deal with fine-grained access control maintenance effort at the discovery service because only authorized companies are allowed to access the queries stated by clients. This has to be ensured because client's confidentiality has to be ensured as well. Thin devices cannot handle asynchronous responses. In addition, according to the meta client discovery service, a client has to aggregate and analyze all incoming read event repository responses.
2. *Performance*: To fulfill the basic requirements of a discovery service, too little data is stored at the meta client discovery service. The operations conducted at the discovery service are simple. The number of messages is medium and network traffic is low.
3. *Security and Trustworthiness*: Client confidentiality is ensured using access control policies.
4. *Completeness and Correctness*: Refusals are no problem because companies can decide which query they respond to. Assuming that companies regularly update their access control policies, RTIs can be handled in this approach.

Hierarchical-Packaging-Aware Discovery Service

The hierarchical-packaging-aware discovery service was presented in Sect. 2.3.3. The evaluation is as follows:

1. *Basic Functional Capabilities and Ease of Use*: This discovery service approach is able to fulfill basic track and trace requirements. The response happens synchronously. No access control maintenance effort exists because all access control is conducted at the read event repositories $rer \in RER$. Thin devices are inherently supported because all relevant read events TTI_i are directly included in the discovery service response if a lifecycle query is invoked.
2. *Performance*: The data volume stored at the discovery service is minimal. No access control information is stored at all. Instead, all AggregationEvents are stored. The complexity of the operations at the discovery service is high. The number of messages and network traffic is low.
3. *Security and Trustworthiness*: The confidentiality of data publishers is perfectly protected at the discovery service as the data owner himself decides to reveal or not to reveal information at its read event repository.
4. *Completeness and Correctness*: Given the fact that the discovery service is trusted by all participants, read event repositories can decline to respond without revealing their secret if they have or do not have information related to an item of interest to the client. In this discovery service approach, the context of the client request is maintained. Thus, it is easy to identify the relevant RTIs for a respective client request.

Evaluation Summary

A summary of the discovery service discussion is given in Table 2.6. For readers' convenience, the requirements are repeated to introduce the abbreviations used in Table 2.6:

1. *Basic Functional Capabilities and Ease of Use (Basics)*: track and trace functionality (B_1), synchronous response (B_2), low access control maintenance effort (B_3), support of thin devices (B_4)
2. *Performance*: minimum data storage at the discovery service (P_1), low complexity of discovery service operations (P_2), low number of messages and network traffic (P_3)
3. *Security and Trustworthiness (Security)*: confidentiality of data publishers (S_1)
4. *Completeness and Correctness (C&C)*: dealing with refusals (CC_1), returnable transport items (CC_2)

The remainder of this dissertation deals with the ○ of the hierarchical-packaging-aware discovery service at P_2: How can the obviously complex operation of analyzing the lifecycle of an item of interest be designed in a way to ensure performance and scalability.

2.3 Related Work on Discovery Services

Table 2.6 Fulfillment of selected requirements by different discovery service approaches (● = complete fulfillment, ◐ = partial fulfillment, ○ = requirement not fulfilled)

	Basics				Performance			Security	C&C	
	B_1	B_2	B_3	B_4	P_1	P_2	P_3	S_1	CC_1	CC_2
Directory look-up	●	●	○	◐	●	◐	◐	◐	●	○
Query relay	●	○	●	○	●	●	◐	●	○	○
Fat discovery service	●	●	○	●	○	○	○	◐	●	○
Directory of clients	○	○	○	○	◐	◐	○	●	●	●
Notification of resources	○	◐	○	○	○	○	○	◐	●	●
Notification of clients	●	◐	●	○	●	●	○	●	●	○
Meta client	○	○	○	○	◐	◐	●	●	●	●
Hierarchical-packaging-aware	●	●	●	●	●	○	●	●	●	●

Chapter 3
An In-Memory Hierarchical-Packaging-Aware Discovery Service: Overview and Communication Protocol

This chapter introduces the main contribution of this thesis, the Hierarchical-Packaging-aware Discovery Service (HPDS). It gives an overview in Sect. 3.1 and presents the communication protocol in Sect. 3.2. This content is partially published in [127].

3.1 Overview of the Hierarchical-Packaging-Aware Discovery Service

An overview of the HPDS is given in Fig. 3.1 using Fundamental Modeling Concepts notation [100]. From bottom to top, the *read event repositories* submit notification messages $n_{RE} \in N_{RE}$ indicating that read events $re \in RE$ took place and are stored in the database of the respective EPCIS server. These notification messages are preprocessed and loaded into the *Discovery Service Database* in near real-time via bulk loading. When a *Client* states a query, a *Search Algorithm* is invoked. The search algorithm is efficient but not always exact. Thus, a *Filter Algorithm* is introduced. In order to make the search algorithm and filter algorithm more robust, modifications of the algorithms are developed, which also leads to a *Reverse Filter Algorithm*. In addition to these components, the communication protocol between discovery service D, clients C, and read event repositories RER is a main contribution of this thesis.

3.2 A Novel Discovery Service Communication Protocol

As shown in Sect. 2.3.3. which dealt with related work, the communication protocol is the main differentiator between discovery service approaches. This chapter describes the communication protocol of the HPDS.

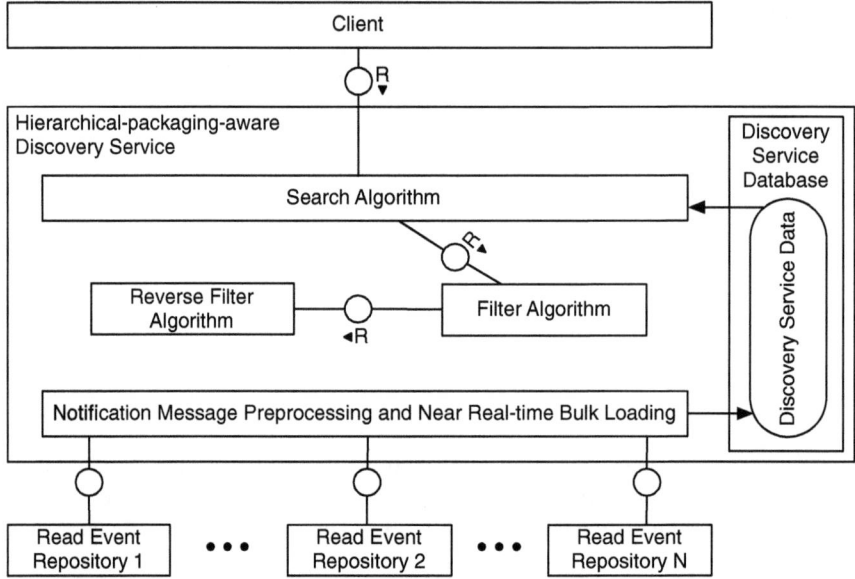

Fig. 3.1 Overview of the hierarchical-packaging-aware discovery service

The idea of the hierarchical-packaging-aware discovery service is to:

1. Retrieve a query from a client,
2. Identify all relevant read event repositories and, for each read event repository, the respective EPCs for which the read event repository can provide information,
3. Query all identified read event repositories in parallel,
4. Aggregate the read event repositories' responses, and
5. Respond synchronously to the client request.

Given the fact that the HPDS is informed about ObjectEvents and AggregationEvents, it can immediately resolve hierarchical packaging relationships $hpr \in HPR$ in which an EPC was involved throughout its lifecycle. Thus, all involved read event repositories can be queried exactly once with all relevant EPCs, without the need of analyzing each read event repositories' response and, after that, state a next query etc. This is supposed to mean 'efficient' with regard to a discovery service communication protocol. The most prominent type of queries is lifecycle queries, which are stated either as one-off queries or as standing queries. I present the communication protocol using lifecycle queries in Sect. 3.2.1 and how last-seen queries are processed in Sect. 3.2.2.

3.2.1 Processing Lifecycle Queries

The communication protocol is depicted in Fig. 3.2 using the same example supply chain presented in Sect. 2.3.3. The setup phase is the same as in other discovery

3.2 A Novel Discovery Service Communication Protocol

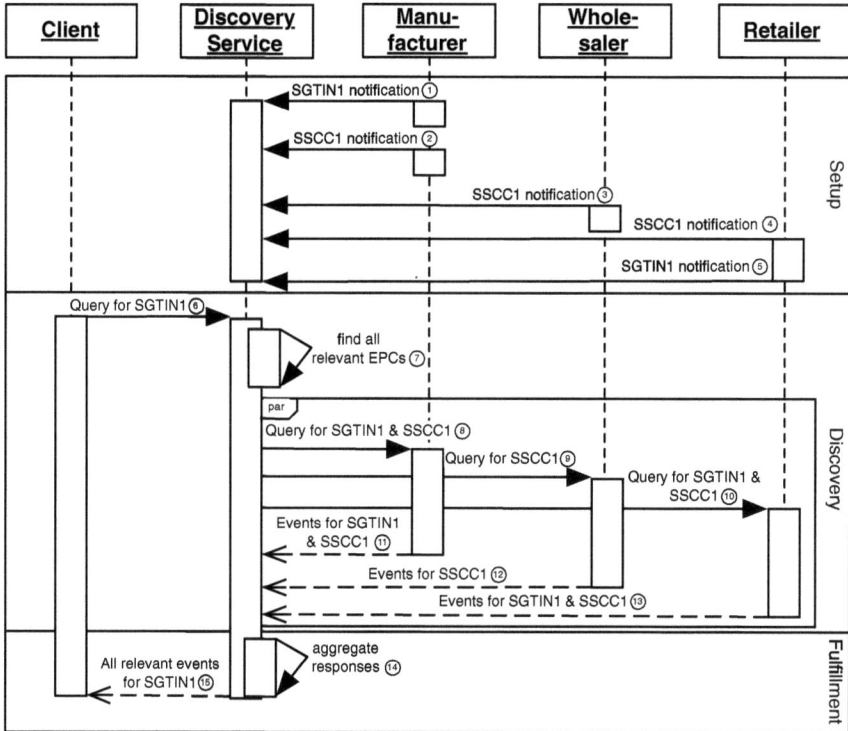

Fig. 3.2 Process of gathering lifecycle information following the hierarchical-packaging-aware discovery service approach

service approaches: the discovery service is notified about all read events that appear in the supply chain (①–⑤). Once the hierarchical-packaging-aware discovery service is queried with a lifecycle query (⑥), it first analyzes the route taken through the supply chain to identify relevant read event repositories and EPCs (⑦). Then, each affected read event repository is queried exactly once with all relevant EPCs they can provide information for (⑧–⑩). The responses are collected (⑪–⑬), aggregated (⑭), and a synchronous response is sent to the client (⑮).

In contrast to all existing discovery service approaches, the hierarchical-packaging-aware discovery service combines a synchronous response to the client with the capability of deriving complete lifecycle information about an item of interest on the fly. This simultaneously reduces client complexity, brings low response latency, delivers complete and correct information for the requester, ensures data ownership and confidentiality for the information holder, and avoids the need for fine-grained access control replicated at discovery service level. In addition, the number of messages exchanged is reduced in contrast to other approaches. In this analysis, I omit the setup phase, because it is composed of the same number of messages in each approach. Thus, only messages from the client to the discovery service and the discovery service to read event repositories as well as the message(s) needed to transfer the responses to the client are counted. Responses from read event repositories to the discovery service and the discovery service to the client are also counted.

Let l be the length of the supply chain sc_i, i.e. the number of participants the item of interest i passed in its lifecycle. I assume that each participant operates exactly one read event repository. Furthermore, let a be the number of different transport containers $tc \in TC$ in which the item of interest was involved. I assume that no repackaging takes place, i.e. the number of AggregationEvents is $2a$.

In the HPDS, the number of messages in the discovery phase contain the client query and a query to each of the l read event repositories that have to be queried in order to retrieve all read events (see Fig. 3.2). Thus, including the responses from the read event repositories, the number of messages that are necessary in the discovery phase is $1 + 2l$. The fulfillment consists of 1 message to the client (see Fig. 3.2). In total, this results in $2l + 2$ messages to retrieve the complete lifecycle of an item of interest. a does not influence the number of messages because the respective packaging hierarchy information is stored and evaluated at the HPDS.

In the directory look-up approach, $2 \times (1 + a) = 2a + 2$ messages occur in the discovery phase because the client has to submit a query for the item of interest and a query for each different transport container $tc \in TC$ to the discovery service and receive the response from it (see Fig. 2.10). In the worst case, all l read event repositories have to be queried by the client for each of the $1 + a$ discovery service responses. Including the read event repositories' responses, this results in $2 \times l \times (1 + a) = 2la + 2l$ messages in the fulfillment phase. In total, this is $2a + 2 + 2la + 2l = 2la + 2a + 2l + 2$ messages.

In the query relay approach, $2 \times (1+a) = 2a+2$ messages occur between client and discovery service because the client has to query the discovery service for every transport container $tc \in TC$ (see Fig. 2.11). In the worst case, the discovery service sends a message to each of the l read event repositories for the item of interest and each transport container. Thus, $2a+2+l \times (1+a) = la+2a+l+2$ messages occur in the discovery phase. Correspondingly, the client receives $l \times (1 + a) = la + l$ messages from the read event repositories in the fulfillment phase. This results in $la + 2a + l + 2 + la + l = 2la + 2a + 2l + 2$ messages in total.

The fat discovery service approach uses $1 + a$ client requests for the discovery phase and $1+a$ corresponding discovery service responses for the fulfillment phase, resulting in $2a + 2$ messages in total (see Fig. 2.12).

Table 3.1 gives an overview of the number of messages needed in order to retrieve lifecycle information about an item of interest.

After having shown how lifecycle queries are processed, the next section describes how last-seen queries are handled.

3.2.2 Processing Last-Seen Queries

For a last-seen query, the algorithm to find relevant EPCs just returns the latest event record associated to the item of interest. The communication protocol for processing

3.2 A Novel Discovery Service Communication Protocol

Table 3.1 Overview of the number of messages necessary to retrieve lifecycle information about an item of interest

Approach	Discovery	Fulfillment	Total
Directory look-up approach	$2a + 2$	$2la + 2l$	$2la + 2a + 2l + 2$
Query relay approach	$la + 2a + l + 2$	$la + l$	$2la + 2a + 2l + 2$
FatDS approach	$a + 1$	$a + 1$	$2a + 2$
HPDS	$2l + 1$	1	$2l + 2$

l = Length of the supply chain; a = Number of different transport containers

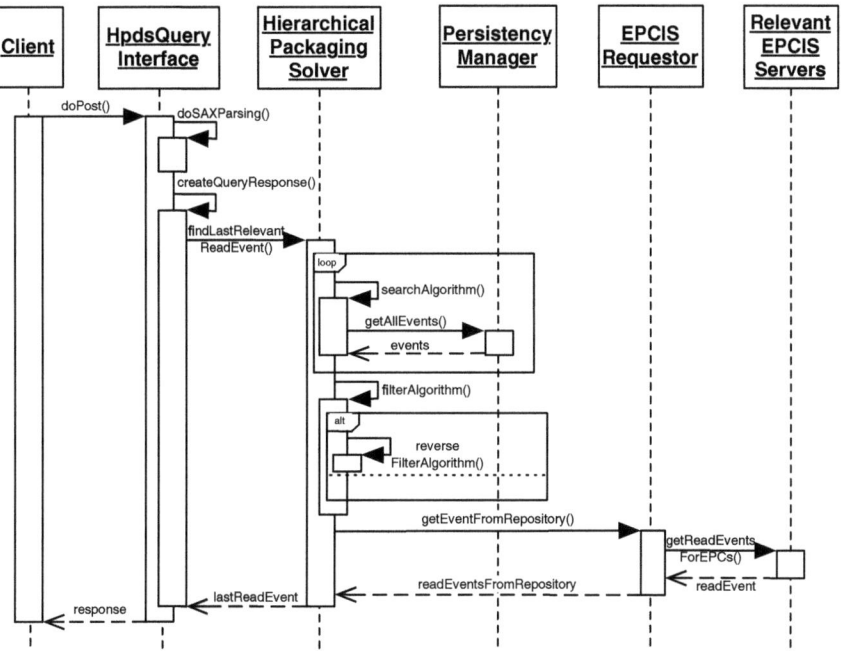

Fig. 3.3 Process of gathering last-seen information about the item of interest following the hierarchical-packaging-aware discovery service approach

last-seen queries is depicted in Fig. 3.3 using the same example supply chain as in the previous section. The setup phase is the same as in other discovery service approaches (①–⑤). When querying a last-seen query (⑥), the hierarchical-packaging-aware discovery service analyzes the path an item i took through the supply chain sc_i to identify the last relevant read event repository and EPC (⑦). Then, the affected read event repository is queried exactly once with the identified EPC (⑧). The response is retrieved (⑨) and a synchronous response is sent to the client (⑩).

As seen in Fig. 3.3, only the relevant read event repository is queried. In the directory look-up approach and query relay approach, all read event repositories would have to be queried and the client would have to submit multiple queries to the discovery service.

Table 3.2 Example values for the number of messages necessary to retrieve last-seen information about of item of interest

Approach	Discovery	Fulfillment	Total
Directory look-up approach	$2a + 2$	$2la + 2l$	$2la + 2a + 2l + 2$
Query relay approach	$la + 2a + l + 2$	$la + l$	$3la + 2a + 2l + 2$
FatDS approach	$a + 1$	$a + 1$	$2a + 2$
HPDS	1	3	4

l = Length of the supply chain; a = Number of different transport containers

			Number of Different Transport Containers			
			4	6	8	10
Length of the Supply Chain	4	DL	50	70	90	110
		QR	66	94	122	150
		FatDS	10	14	18	22
		HPDS	Lifecycle:10 Last-seen: 4	Lifecycle:10 Last-seen: 4	Lifecycle:10 Last-seen: 4	Lifecycle:10 Last-seen: 4
	8	DL	90	126	162	198
		QR	122	174	226	278
		FatDS	10	14	18	22
		HPDS	Lifecycle:18 Last-seen: 4	Lifecycle:18 Last-seen: 4	Lifecycle:18 Last-seen: 4	Lifecycle:18 Last-seen: 4
	12	DL	130	182	234	286
		QR	178	254	330	406
		FatDS	10	14	18	22
		HPDS	Lifecycle: 26 Last-seen: 4	Lifecycle: 26 Last-seen: 4	Lifecycle: 26 Last-seen: 4	Lifecycle: 26 Last-seen: 4
	16	DL	170	238	306	374
		QR	234	334	434	534
		FatDS	10	14	18	22
		HPDS	Lifecycle: 34 Last-seen: 4	Lifecycle: 34 Last-seen: 4	Lifecycle: 34 Last-seen: 4	Lifecycle: 34 Last-seen: 4
	20	DL	210	294	378	462
		QR	290	414	538	662
		FatDS	10	14	18	22
		HPDS	Lifecycle: 42 Last-seen: 4	Lifecycle: 42 Last-seen: 4	Lifecycle: 42 Last-seen: 4	Lifecycle: 42 Last-seen: 4

Fig. 3.4 Example values for the number of messages necessary to retrieve last-seen information about an item of interest

The number of messages exchanged is furthermore reduced in the scenario of last-seen queries: In the HPDS, the number of messages in the discovery phase only comprises the last-seen query from the client (see Fig. 3.3). The fulfillment consists

3.2 A Novel Discovery Service Communication Protocol

of a message to the identified read event repository, the respective response, and the response to the client. In total, this results in 4 messages to retrieve the last position of an item of interest. In all other approaches, the number of messages does not change (see Table 3.2).

Realistic numbers are between 5 and 20 for l as well as 4 to 10 for a. A comparison for different supply chain lengths and number of aggregation events is presented in Fig. 3.4. For the HPDS, the values for lifecycle queries and last-seen queries are shown. It is obvious that the hierarchical-packaging-aware discovery service is superior to all other approaches with regard to the number of messages exchanged for last-seen queries.

Only the fat discovery service approach requires fewer messages to be sent because it does not conduct any requests to the read event repositories. The huge number of disadvantages indicate the superiority of the hierarchical-packaging-aware discovery service over the other approaches.

This chapter described how the communication between client, discovery service, and read event repositories should take place. This answers research question RQ_1.

In the hierarchical-packaging-aware discovery service approach, it is of utmost importance that the retrieval of all relevant EPCs (step ① in Fig. 3.2) is performed as fast as possible. To recall the example of the European pharmaceutical supply chain, up to 2,000 lifecycle requests are stated per second while up to 8,000 event notifications need to be processed. To achieve the respective performance for the lifecycle queries, a search algorithm was invented. It is described in the next chapter.

Chapter 4
A Recursive Search Algorithm to Find all Potentially Relevant Read Events

As indicated in the last chapter, the discovery service identifies the relevant read events TTI_i for an item of interest i including an analysis of packaging hierarchies the item was involved in. This computation needs to be very fast in order to guarantee the scalability of this approach as well as the ability to provide real-time information in a synchronous response. Furthermore, performance is of utmost importance from a desirability point of view because end users only use a verification service on their mobile device if the check is completed in sub-second response time [153, pp.9], [108]. Even at the point of sale, no customer wants to wait ten seconds for the verification of a medicinal product.

This chapter presents and discusses the search algorithm. To this end, the data structure the search algorithm is working on is presented in Sect. 4.1. After that, the basic search algorithm is depicted in Sect. 4.2. The mode of operation is exemplified in Sect. 4.3. Then, the search algorithm is applied to challenging situations: Sect. 4.4 describes how the search algorithm can be used with returnable transport items. In Sect. 4.5, modifications to the search algorithm are applied to make it more robust in situations with missing read events. Finally, Sect. 4.6 conducts a critical discussion with regard to the correctness of the search algorithm and Sect. 4.7 shows the limitations of the search algorithm. Parts of this content is already published in [127].

4.1 Data Structure for the Discovery Service

To reconstruct the route an item of interest i took throughout the supply chain sc_i, some data has to be stored at the discovery service. ObjectEvents have the mandatory attributes *eventTime*, *eventTimezoneOffset*, *epcList*, and *action* (see Table 2.1). AggregationEvents have mandatory attributes *eventTime*, *eventTimezoneOffset*, *parentEPC*, *childEPCs* and *action*.

Optional attributes for ObjectEvents and AggregationEvents are *recordTime*, *readPoint*, *bizLocation*, *bizStep*, *disposition*, and *bizTransactionList*.

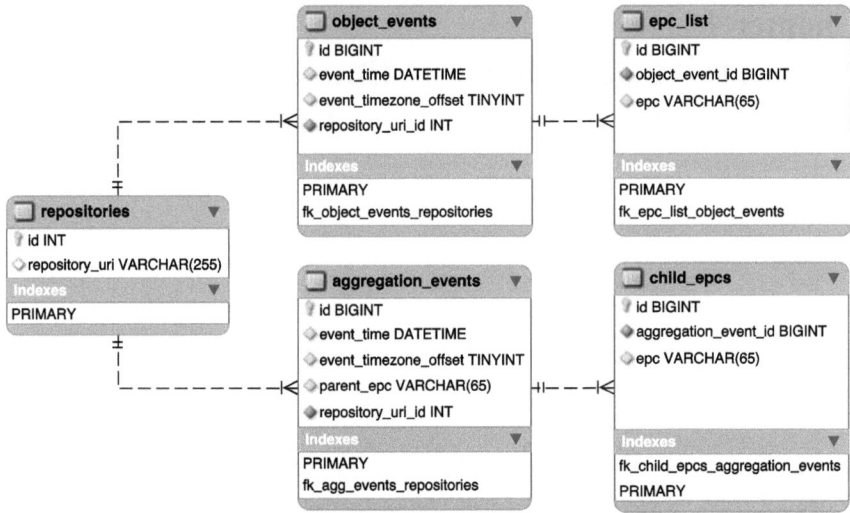

Fig. 4.1 Normalized database schema for the discovery service

The hierarchical-packaging-aware discovery service acts as a reference to read event repositories. In contrast to the discovery service, read event repositories store all attributes of a read event. Thus, it is sufficient to store only the information that is actually needed for recreating the route taken through the supply chain.

For ObjectEvents, I have decided to only store *eventTime*, *eventTimezoneOffset*, *epcList*, and *action*. The attributes *recordTime*, *readPoint*, *bizLocation*, *bizStep*, *disposition*, and *bizTransactionList* are omitted.

For AggregationEvents, I store *eventTime*, *eventTimezoneOffset*, *parentEPC*, and *childEPCs*. The attributes *recordTime*, *readPoint*, *bizLocation*, *bizStep*, *disposition*, and *bizTransactionList* are omitted.

In addition, the *repositoryURI* has to be stored in order to identifying the read event repository that stores the read event.

The attributes *epcList* and *childEPCs* can consist of multiple EPCs. Following good database design practices [28, 29], the data schema is normalized using an extra table for each of the 1:n relationships (see Fig. 4.1).

In total, five database tables are created. ObjectEvents and AggregationEvents are split up in a header table and a table with affected EPCs. The ObjectEvent header table "object_events" consists of

- A unique identifier "id" encoded as BIGINT,
- The time when the event happened "event_time" encoded as DATETIME,
- Time zone information "event_timezone_offset" encoded as TINYINT, and
- The URI of the read event repository "repository_uri" encoded as VARCHAR with a maximum length of 255 characters.

4.1 Data Structure for the Discovery Service

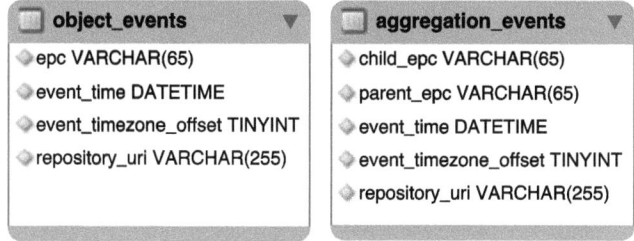

Fig. 4.2 Denormalized database schema for the discovery service with two tables

The "epc_list" table contains a unique identifier, a foreign key "object_event_id" to reference the respective ObjectEvent, and the affected EPC "epc", which is encoded as VARCHAR with a maximum length of 65 characters. The tables for AggregationEvents are specified accordingly with the exception that the header table has an additional attribute "parent_epc" for the parentEPC involved in the AggregationEvent. Indices are created for the unique identifiers and the foreign keys.

With a normalized database schema as shown in Fig. 4.1, a join has to be conducted to retrieve the complete event information. Furthermore, two queries need to be stated, one for ObjectEvents and another for AggregationEvents. Using a column-oriented in-memory database, the advantage of lightweight compression, such as dictionary compression is available [1, 2, 71, 111, 196]. Thus, redundancy does not come with the same disadvantages with regard to space consumption. Using the example data of the European pharmaceutical supply chain depicted in Sect. 1.2, on average about 2.1 EPCs are included in one read event. Thus, the 35 billion read events per year result in 73.5 billion database tuples per year. Nevertheless, by leveraging dictionary compression, I de-normalize the database schema to the schema shown in Fig. 4.2 while saving about 67% of space. In the combined tables, indices are no longer needed as the join is unnecessary. In addition, bulk loading can be easily conducted and the database state is always of integrity and consistent.

In the use case of a discovery service, no processing on single tuples is conducted. No delete or update operations are performed on the data. Thus, data management at the discovery service follows an insert-only approach [153, pp.111].

Obviously, the attributes *epc* / *child_epc*, *event_time*, *event_timezone_offset*, and *repository_uri* in the tables *object_events* and *aggregation_events* share a large portion of the distinct values that occur:

- Usually, each EPC that occurs in *aggregation_events* as a childEPC is already recorded in *object_events* as an EPC.
- As a design decision, the event time is only stored to the granularity of minutes. If more detailed data about the event time of a read event is needed, the respective read event repository has to be queried. Thus, with the average of 2,300 read events per second, $2,300 \times 60 = 138,000$ read events happen in the same minute.

By combining the tables, the total size of the dictionary for the attributes *epc* / *child_epc*, *event_time*, *event_timezone_offset*, and *repository_uri* can be reduced

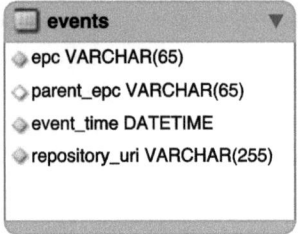

Fig. 4.3 Denormalized database schema for the discovery service with one table

by another 20%. For the *event_time*, this results in only one dictionary entry for on average 138,000 tuples. The number of distinct values is important because these values are stored in a dictionary when applying dictionary compression [1, 111, 196]. Details about in-memory data management applied in the discovery service are given in Chap. 6. Another advantage of combining the two tables is that only one query to the database is needed in order to retrieve all relevant read events for an item of interest.

Given the mass of read events per second and the requirement of 'near real-time', read events will be collected for a couple of seconds, e.g. three, and then inserted as a bulk.

Furthermore, the separate handling of *event_time* and *event_timezone_offset* can be mitigated by choosing a master timezone and store all event times in this time zone. Thus, a fixed but arbitrary time zone like Coordinated Universal Time (UTC) is used and the *event_time* is combined with the *event_timezone_offset* such that it corresponds to UTC [99]. The calculation happens in the process of preparing the notification messages for being bulk loaded into the discovery service database. Finally, this leads to a data structure depicted in Fig. 4.3.

The attribute *epc* stores either an entry of the epcList (for ObjectEvents) or an entry of the childEPCs. *parent_epc* is *NULL* for ObjectEvents and stores the *parentEPC* in case an AggregationEvent is recorded. This attribute can be used to distinguish ObjectEvents and AggregationEvents. It is the only attribute which is allowed to contain a *NULL* value (indicated by the blank diamond in front of the attribute name). The meaning of the attributes *event_time* and *repository_uri* is obvious. From now on, a row in this table is called "event record". One read event $re \in RE$ can contain multiple associated EPCs. For each EPC embodied in a read event, a single event record $er \in ER$ is created.

4.2 Description of the Search Algorithm

I developed a search algorithm that efficiently leverages the packaging hierarchy to retrieve all read events with regard to an item of interest. 'Efficiently' in this case means that as few event records as possible are scanned through while evaluating which EPC at what read event repository is relevant for a given item of interest.

4.2 Description of the Search Algorithm

The core of this algorithm is a recursive method to find all events related to an item of interest by traversing the packaging hierarchy information. Pseudo code of the algorithm is shown in Listing 4.1. The input parameters are (see lines 3–4, Listing 4.1):

1. The unique identifier id_I of the item of interest i, which is stated as 'epc_of_interest',
2. A timestamp describing the lower boundary for the search algorithm, and
3. A timestamp describing the upper boundary for the search algorithm.

Firstly, a new list called *event_list* is created (see line 6). This list will store the identified read events. After that, all ObjectEvents with regard to the item of interest as well as all AggregationEvents where the item of interest was involved as a childEPC in the given time span (lower timestamp up to upper timestamp) are identified from the discovery service database using Structured Query Language (SQL) (see line 7). If an item was packed and unpacked multiple times to/ from the same transport container $tc \in TC$, only the first packing event and the last unpacking event for each childEPC-parentEPC combination is respected for further analysis of packaging hierarchies. These read events are referred to as 'distinct AggregationEvents'. If an item i was packed into a transport container tc, the lifecycle analysis has to take into account what happened to tc while p was on that transport container. Thus, for each packaging level, the search algorithm is called again with the unique identifier id_{TC} of the transport container (parentEPC) as the new 'EPC of interest' (see lines 9–13, Listing 4.1). Thus, it is a recursive algorithm. The lower boundary is identified as the timestamp of the packing event. The upper boundary is defined as the timestamp of the corresponding unpacking event. 'Corresponding' in this sense means that the aggregation event consists of the same childEPC and the same parentEPC. If no corresponding unpacking event can be found, the item is not unpacked yet and the upper boundary is set to the previous input value of the upper boundary. The result of the method call is added to *event_list* (see line 14). Finally, the event list is returned including all read events that are relevant for the lifecycle of the item of interest (see line 15).

The complexity of the search algorithm is dominated by the number of different transport containers that an item of interest was involved in. These can be determined by the AggregationEvents $AE^{ADD}_{i\_distinct}$ with the action 'ADD' and distinct parent_epcs an item i was involved in. Thus, the complexity of the search algorithm is $\mathcal{O}(|AE^{ADD}_{i\_distinct}|)$ with $|AE^{ADD}_{i\_distinct}|$ being the cardinality of $AE^{ADD}_{i\_distinct}$ (see [101][35, pp.43], for the $\mathcal{O}$ notation).

The mode of operation is shown in the next section using a simple supply chain.

4.3 Mode of Operation Exemplified with a Simple Supply Chain

In this section, all read events that are to be identified with regard to the item's lifecycle are sketched by a circle with white background and black text (◯). The read events presented by a circle with black background and white text (⬛) must not be

```
1   SearchMethod: Traverse packaging hierarchy information and retrieve all relevant events
2   Input parameters:
3       1. epc_of_interest
4       2. lower_boundary
5       3. upper_boundary
6   Create a new empty list event_list and add the result of
7       the following query to it
8   SELECT epc, parent_epc, repository_uri, event_time
9       FROM events
10      WHERE epc = epc_of_interest
11      AND event_time >= lower_boundary
12      AND event_time <= upper_boundary
13      ORDER BY event_time
14  Create a new empty list aggregation_events, iterate through event_list, and store the first and
        last AggregationEvent for each childEPC−parentEPC combination so that all
        AggregationEvents with the same childEPC and parentEPC are stored consecutively,
        ordered by time.
15  FOR all AggregationEvents that have an odd position in the list DO /* this are packing events
        */
16      Invoke this search method again using
17          1. the parentEPC as the EPC input parameter,
18          2. the timestamp of the AggregationEvent as the lower_boundary input parameter,
19          3. the timestamp of the corresponding AggregationEvent that is an unpacking event as the
                upper_boundary input parameter,
20          and add the return value to event_list
21  END
22  Return the event_list
```

Listing 4.1 Search algorithm to retrieve read events for an item of interest

returned by the discovery service because they are not related to the item of interest. This notation will also be used in the remainder of the thesis.

Figure 4.4 shows a simple supply chain where the item identified by $SGTIN1$ is produced (①) and packed into a box identified by $SSCC1$ (②). This box is packed into a container with the identifier $SSCC2$ (③). Finally, the manufacturer ships the container to the first wholesaler (④ and ⑤). The first wholesaler unpacks the box from the container, packs it on the container again and sends it to the second wholesaler (⑥–⑨). The second wholesaler receives the container, unpacks the box, and ships the box to the retailer (⑨–⑫). The retailer receives the box, unpacks the item, and gives it to the client (⑫–⑭)

The timestamps indicating the lower and upper boundaries help to reduce the search space in each search iteration as shown in Fig. 4.4. Initially, the boundaries are set to '1970-01-01' as the lower boundary and '9999-12-31' as the upper boundary.

Data stored in the discovery service database for this supply chain could look as shown in Table 4.1.

In the remainder of this thesis, the querying client is assumed to be a legitimate client for $SGTIN1$. If this client c^L_{SGTIN1} states a lifecycle query with regard to the unique identifier $SGTIN1$, all events ①–⑭ should be identified by the search

4.3 Mode of Operation Exemplified with a Simple Supply Chain

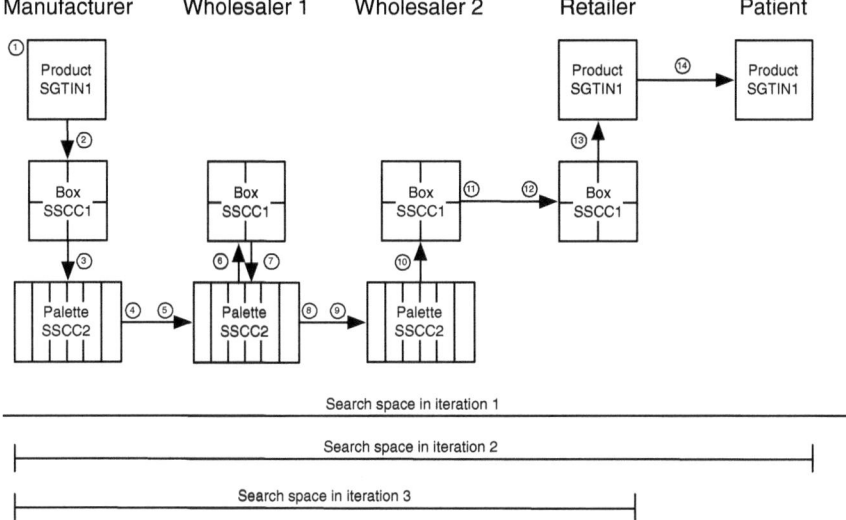

Fig. 4.4 Leveraging lower and upper boundaries to limit the search space

Table 4.1 Example data that could be stored at the discovery service for the simple supply chain shown in Fig. 4.4

Event	EPC	ParentEPC	Event Time	Repository URI
①	SGTIN1	NULL	2012-01-01 09:00	https://epcis.manufacturer.com
②	SGTIN1	SSCC1	2012-01-01 10:00	https://epcis.manufacturer.com
③	SSCC1	SSCC2	2012-01-01 10:30	https://epcis.manufacturer.com
④	SSCC2	NULL	2012-01-01 12:00	https://epcis.manufacturer.com
⑤	SSCC2	NULL	2012-01-03 09:30	https://epcis.wholesaler1.com
⑥	SSCC1	SSCC2	2012-01-03 13:00	https://epcis.wholesaler1.com
⑦	SSCC1	SSCC2	2012-01-03 13:30	https://epcis.wholesaler1.com
⑧	SSCC2	NULL	2012-01-03 16:00	https://epcis.wholesaler1.com
⑨	SSCC2	NULL	2012-01-05 07:00	https://epcis.wholesaler2.com
⑩	SSCC1	SSCC2	2012-01-05 14:00	https://epcis.wholesaler2.com
⑪	SSCC1	NULL	2012-01-06 09:00	https://epcis.wholesaler2.com
⑫	SSCC1	NULL	2012-01-07 11:00	https://epcis.retailer.com
⑬	SGTIN1	SSCC1	2012-01-07 20:00	https://epcis.retailer.com
⑭	SGTIN1	NULL	2012-01-10 10:00	https://epcis.retailer.com

algorithm. Thus, the desired solution set is $\mathbb{L}^{des}$ ={ ①, ②, ③, ④, ⑤, ⑥, ⑦, ⑧, ⑨, ⑩, ⑪, ⑫, ⑬, ⑭}.

Firstly, the search algorithm is called with $SGTIN1$ as the EPC of interest, '1970-01-01' as the lower boundary and '9999-12-31' as the upper boundary. This results in the query "SELECT epc, parent_epc, repository_uri, event_time FROM events WHERE epc = 'SGTIN1' AND event_time >= '1970-01-01' AND event_time <=

'9999-12-31' ORDER BY event_time" (line 7 in Listing 4.1), which reveals the ObjectEvents ① and ⑭. In addition, the AggregationEvents ② and ⑬, are retrieved by the query because the $SGTIN1$ was involved as a childEPC. Thus, after the first iteration of the search algorithm, the solution set is $\mathbb{L}^1 = \{①, ②, ⑬, ⑭\}$. The list *aggregation_events* contains $\{②, ⑬\}$. ② is at the odd position and will be used in the FOR loop (line 9 in Listing 4.1). Let $t(②)$ be the point in time when read event ② happened. The search algorithm is called again with ②. $parent\_epc = SSCC1$ as the EPC of interest, $t(②) = $ '2012-01-01 10:00' as the lower boundary and $t(⑬) = $ '2012-01-07 20:00' as the upper boundary.

In the second iteration, the query is "SELECT epc, parent_epc, repository_uri, event_time FROM events WHERE epc = 'SSCC1' AND event time >= '2012-01-01 10:00' AND event_time <= '2012-01-07 20:00' ORDER BY event_time". ObjectEvents ⑩ and ⑫ are identified (see line 7, Listing 4.1). In addition, the AggregationEvents ③, ⑥, ⑦ and ⑩ are identified. The intermediate solution set is $\mathbb{L}^2 = \{①, ②, ③, ⑥, ⑦, ⑩, ⑪, ⑫, ⑬, ⑭\}$.

The list aggregation_events in this iteration contains ③ and ⑩. AggregationEvents ⑥ and ⑦ are omitted because only the first and last AggregationEvent for the same childEPC-parentEPC combination is stored. Due to AggregationEvent ③, the search algorithm is called again with $SSCC2$ as EPC of interest, $t(③) = $ '2012-01-01 10:30' as the lower boundary, and $t(⑩) = $ '2012-01-05 14:00' as the upper boundary.

This leads to the query "SELECT epc, parent_epc, repository_uri, event_time FROM events WHERE epc = SSCC2 AND event time >= '2012-01-01 10:30' AND event_time <= '2012-01-05 14:00'" and reveals read events ④, ⑤, ⑧ and ⑨. No AggregationEvent is found and the algorithm terminates. The solution set is $\mathbb{L} = \{①, ②, ③, ④, ⑤, ⑥, ⑦, ⑧, ⑨, ⑩, ⑪, ⑫, ⑬, ⑭\} = \mathbb{L}^{des}$.

The next section describes how the search algorithm is applied in the context of returnable transport items.

4.4 Handling Returnable Transport Items

Returnable Transport Items (RTIs) are usually in use for a long period of time, i.e. years and even decades. Thus, it is important that a discovery service can handle the frequent occurrence of respective EPCs. Fig. 4.5 shows a use case of a returnable transport item.

The box identified with $SSCC1$ is reused after the item of interest ($SGTIN1$) is removed from the box. In addition, another item identified by $SGTIN2$ is transported in the same box identified by $SSCC1$. Thus, read events ②, ④ and ⑭–⑰ must not be revealed by the search algorithm. Respective example data stored at the discovery service is depicted in Table 4.2. The desired solution set is $\mathbb{L}^{des} = \{①, ③, ⑤, ⑥, ⑦, ⑧, ⑨, ⑩, ⑪, ⑫, ⑬\}$.

In the first iteration, the search algorithm is called with $SGTIN1$ as the EPC of interest, '1970-01-01' as the lower boundary, and '9999-12-31' as the upper boundary. Thus, the query "SELECT epc, parent_epc, repository_uri, event_time FROM events

4.4 Handling Returnable Transport Items

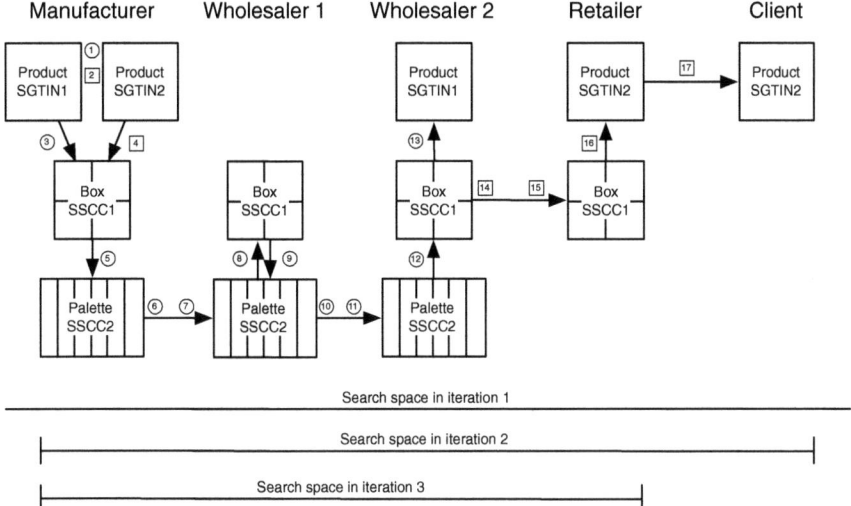

Fig. 4.5 Re-use of a box

Table 4.2 Example data that could be stored at the discovery service for the supply chain shown in Fig. 4.5

Event	EPC	ParentEPC	Event Time	Repository URI
①	SGTIN1	NULL	2012-01-01 09:00	https://epcis.manufacturer.com
②	SGTIN2	NULL	2012-01-01 09:05	https://epcis.manufacturer.com
③	SGTIN1	SSCC1	2012-01-01 10:30	https://epcis.manufacturer.com
④	SGTIN2	SSCC1	2012-01-01 10:30	https://epcis.manufacturer.com
⑤	SSCC1	SSCC2	2012-01-03 09:30	https://epcis.manufacturer.com
⑥	SSCC2	NULL	2012-01-03 13:00	https://epcis.manufacturer.com
⑦	SSCC2	NULL	2012-01-03 13:30	https://epcis.wholesaler1.com
⑧	SSCC1	SSCC2	2012-01-03 16:00	https://epcis.wholesaler1.com
⑨	SSCC1	SSCC2	2012-01-05 07:00	https://epcis.wholesaler1.com
⑩	SSCC2	NULL	2012-01-05 14:00	https://epcis.wholesaler1.com
⑪	SSCC2	NULL	2012-01-06 09:00	https://epcis.wholesaler2.com
⑫	SSCC1	SSCC2	2012-01-07 11:00	https://epcis.wholesaler2.com
⑬	SGTIN1	SSCC1	2012-01-07 20:00	https://epcis.wholesaler2.com
⑭	SSCC1	NULL	2012-01-10 10:00	https://epcis.wholesaler2.com
⑮	SSCC1	NULL	2012-01-12 14:00	https://epcis.retailer.com
⑯	SGTIN1	SSCC1	2012-01-12 18:00	https://epcis.retailer.com
⑰	SGTIN1	NULL	2012-01-22 09:30	https://epcis.retailer.com

WHERE epc = 'SGTIN1' AND event_time >= '1970-01-01' AND event_time <= '9999-12-31' ORDER BY event_time" is generated. It reveals the ObjectEvent ① as well as the AggregationEvents ③ and ⑬, resulting in the intermediate solution set $\mathbb{L}^1$ = {①, ③, ⑬}.

Based in read event ③, the search algorithm is called again using the parentEPC of ③ = $SSCC1$ as the EPC of interest, t(③) = '2012-01-01 09:00' as lower boundary, and t(⑬) = '2012-01-07 20:00' as upper boundary. The resulting query "SELECT epc, parent_epc, repository_uri, event_time FROM events WHERE epc = 'SSCC1' AND event_time >= '2012-01-01 09:00' AND event_time <= '2012-01-07 20:00' ORDER BY event_time" reveals the AggregationEvents ⑤, ⑧, ⑨ and ⑫. The intermediary solution set is $\mathbb{L}^2$ = {①, ③, ⑤, ⑧, ⑨, ⑫, ⑬}.

Based on the unique childEPC-parentEPC combination ⑤ and ⑫, the search algorithm is called again. The EPC of interest is $SSCC2$, the lower boundary is set to t(⑤) = '2012-01-03 09:30', and the upper boundary is set to t(⑫) = '2012-01-07 11:00'. The corresponding query "SELECT epc, parent_epc, repository_uri, event_time FROM events WHERE epc = 'SSCC2' AND event_time >= '2012-01-03 09:30' AND event_time <= '2012-01-07 11:00' ORDER BY event_time" identifies the ObjectEvents ⑥, ⑦, ⑩ and ⑪. As no AggregationEvents occur, the algorithm terminates. The final solution set is $\mathbb{L}$ = {①, ③, ⑤, ⑥, ⑦, ⑧, ⑨, ⑩, ⑪, ⑫, ⑬} = $\mathbb{L}^{des}$. The undesired read events are not included in the result set because the search algorithm does not query for event records related to $SGTIN2$ and the search boundaries are well-defined.

Other discovery service approaches would additionally return read events ⑭ and ⑮. The reason is that no search boundaries are respected. This shall be exemplified using the directory service approach:

1. The client queries the discovery service to retrieve information about $SGTIN1$.
2. The discovery service returns the read event repositories of the manufacturer and the second wholesaler.
3. The client queries the read event repositories and finds out that $SGTIN1$ was produced and packed into a box identified by $SSCC1$ at the manufacturer and unpacked again at the second wholesaler.
4. The client knows that the item was unpacked from the box at t(⑨) but a discovery service that follows the directory service approach cannot accept a time span [12]. Otherwise, it would be subject to espionage because detailed information about supply chains would be disclosed. Thus, the client sends a request to retrieve all read events associated with $SSCC1$, i.e. all ObjectEvents with id_I = 'SSCC1' and all AggregationEvents with id = 'SSCC1'.
5. The discovery service sends the read event repository URLs of the manufacturer, first wholesaler, second wholesaler, and retailer to the client. In a realistic setting, boxes could be used at thousands of companies, resulting in a large result set that discloses information to the client he should not be able to see, i.e. the client is not supposed to get to know that the box identified by $SSCC1$ was handled by the retailer.
6. The client queries the read event repositories with regard to $SSCC1$. The manufacturer, first wholesaler, and second wholesaler reply with the respective information. Given the assumption that proper access-control mechanisms are implemented at the read event repositories, the client will not get any results from the retailer because the retailer was not in possession of $SGTIN1$. Given the

responses, the client identifies that transport container $SSCC1$ was packed into container $SSCC2$.
7. The discovery service is queried by the client for $SSCC2$ and again returns the read event repository URLs of the manufacturer, the first wholesaler, and the second wholesaler. In reality, this probably would lead to many more read event repository URLs because containers are very often re-used.
8. The client queries the read event repositories again and finds out that no further aggregations exist.

In short, the disadvantages are that:

- Sensitive information might be disclosed.
- The client has to analyze whether more AggregationEvents are included in any read event in order to manually trace the path the item of interest took through the supply chain,
- The discovery service sends a large result set to the client, especially for transport containers $tc \in TC$ that are used for several years and therefore have many read events associated to them, in consequence. This could only be avoided by fine-grained access control on discovery service level, which would complicate the discovery service interaction and implementation and slow it down significantly. Another strategy would be to allow the definition of time spans in the discovery service interface. However, this could lead to espionage.
- No interactive usage of track and trace information is possible because of the cumbersome process of retrieving this information, e.g. the high number of messages to be exchanged.

The next sections deal with the situation of incomplete read event sequences.

4.5 Handling Situations with an Incomplete Read Event Sequence

Given the fact that 35 billion read events appear per year in the European pharmaceutical supply chain, it is obvious that read events can get lost. This might happen due to unavailability or imperfection of IT systems, network infrastructure, human errors, or intention. Such incomplete track and trace information would be flagged by the discovery service as being suspicious. Currently, the action a of a read event is not stored in the discovery service database. This is sufficient as long as the read event sequence of AggregationEvents is complete. Otherwise, the analysis of the packaging hierarchies cannot be successfully conducted.

The search algorithm relies on a complete read event sequence, meaning that a "packing" read event happens before each corresponding "unpacking" read event (childEPC–parentEPC combination). Following the current data structure, this is done without storing the event action ("OBSERVE", "ADD", or "DELETE"). Thus, the discovery service cannot distinguish AggregationEvents with the action "ADD" or "DELETE".

If, for some reason, one or multiple read events are lost, the read event sequence would be incomplete. Different situations might occur:

1. One missing packing read event.
2. One missing unpacking read event.
3. A missing pair of corresponding read events is missing.
4. Various missing corresponding read events.

These situations and the adjustment of the search algorithm are discussed in the next subsections in order to come up with a robust search algorithm that can technically handle missing read events as far as possible. To this end, in each case, the problem is described, the latest version of the search algorithm is applied and, if needed, the search algorithm is extended. Then, the extended version of the search algorithm is applied to the problem.

4.5.1 Missing Packing Read Events

A supply chain with a missing packing AggregationEvent is depicted in Fig. 4.6. The corresponding data is provided in Table 4.3.

In this situation, the desired solution set is $\mathbb{L}^{des} = \{①, ③, ④, ⑤, ⑥, ⑦, ⑧, ⑨, ⑩, ⑪, ⑫, ⑬, ⑭\}$.

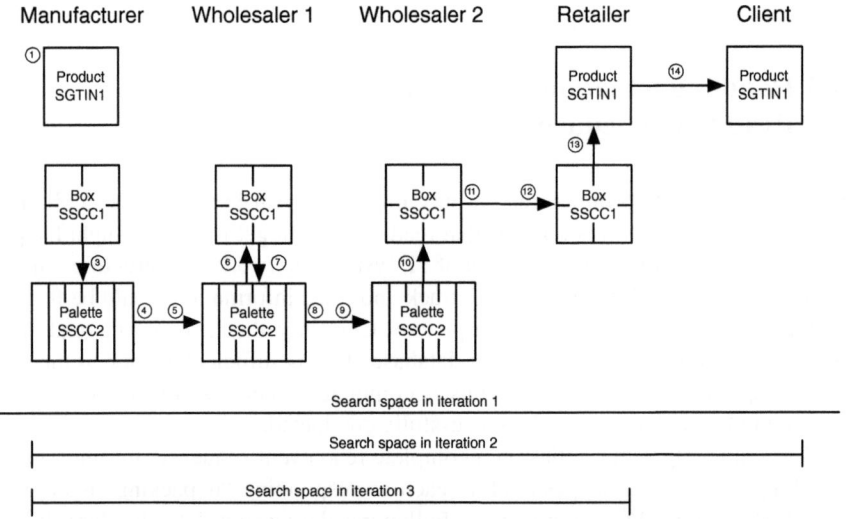

Fig. 4.6 Read events to be identified in a common supply chain with a missing packing AggregationEvent and desired behavior of the search algorithm with regard to search spaces

4.5 Handling Situations with an Incomplete Read Event Sequence

Table 4.3 Example data that could be stored at the discovery service for the simple supply chain shown in Fig. 4.6

Event	EPC	ParentEPC	Event Time	Repository URI
①	SGTIN1	NULL	2012-01-01 09:00	https://epcis.manufacturer.com
③	SSCC1	SSCC2	2012-01-01 10:30	https://epcis.manufacturer.com
④	SSCC2	NULL	2012-01-01 12:00	https://epcis.manufacturer.com
⑤	SSCC2	NULL	2012-01-03 09:30	https://epcis.wholesaler1.com
⑥	SSCC1	SSCC2	2012-01-03 13:00	https://epcis.wholesaler1.com
⑦	SSCC1	SSCC2	2012-01-03 13:30	https://epcis.wholesaler1.com
⑧	SSCC2	NULL	2012-01-03 16:00	https://epcis.wholesaler1.com
⑨	SSCC2	NULL	2012-01-05 07:00	https://epcis.wholesaler2.com
⑩	SSCC1	SSCC2	2012-01-05 14:00	https://epcis.wholesaler2.com
⑪	SSCC1	NULL	2012-01-06 09:00	https://epcis.wholesaler2.com
⑫	SSCC1	NULL	2012-01-07 11:00	https://epcis.retailer.com
⑬	SGTIN1	SSCC1	2012-01-07 20:00	https://epcis.retailer.com
⑭	SGTIN1	NULL	2012-01-10 10:00	https://epcis.retailer.com

Under these preconditions, the search algorithm (see Listing 4.1) works as follows: The initial input parameters are the same: $SGTIN1$ as the epc_of_interest, '1970-01-01' as the lower boundary, and '9999-12-31' as the upper boundary. The query "SELECT epc, parent_epc, repository_uri, event_time FROM events WHERE epc = 'SGTIN1' AND event time >= '1970-01-01' AND event_time <= '9999-12-31' ORDER BY event_time" reveals read events ①, ⑬ and ⑭. The intermediate solution set is $\mathbb{L}^1 = \{$ ①, ⑬, ⑭ $\}$.

The only AggregationEvent is ⑬. This read event is interpreted as a packing event. As no corresponding AggregationEvent is found, the search algorithm assumes that the item is not yet unpacked from this container. Thus, the epc_of_interest is set to $SSCC1$, the lower boundary is set to t(⑬), and the upper boundary is set to the previous upper boundary input parameter, i.e. '9999-12-31'.

The search algorithm is called again. The query parameters result to "SELECT epc, parent_epc, repository_uri, event_time FROM events WHERE epc = 'SSCC1' AND event_time >= '2012-01-07 20:00' AND event time <= '9999-12-31' ORDER BY event_time". The result of the query is ∅ because the 'wrong' lower boundary was chosen. Thus, the search algorithm is not able to identify read events ③–⑫ (see Fig. 4.7).

Thus, the search algorithm and underlying data structure should be adjusted in order to be more robust in the case of lost read events. In order to do so, an attribute *action* is added to the data structure (see Fig. 4.8).

Using this attribute, the read event actions ("ADD", "DELETE", or "OBSERVE") can explicitly be distinguished as follows:

$$action = \begin{cases} 0 & \text{read event action a} = ADD \\ 1 & \text{for read event action a} = DELETE \\ 2 & \text{read event action a} = OBSERVE \end{cases}$$

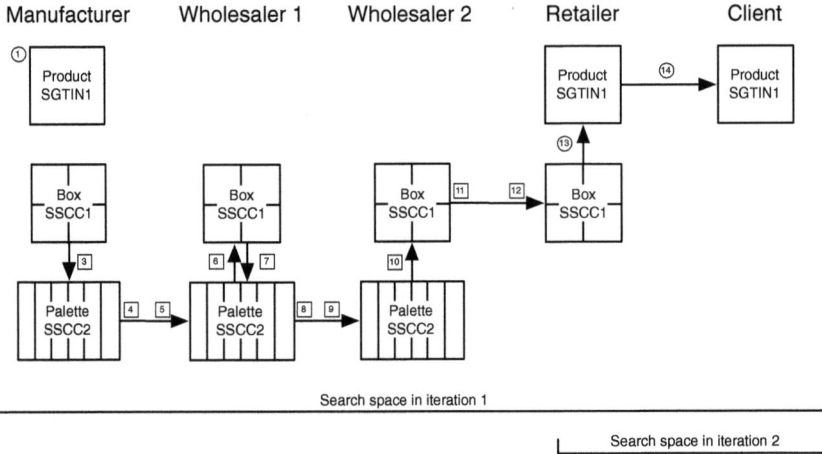

Fig. 4.7 Actual identified events in a common supply chain with a missing packing Aggregation-Event and respective search spaces

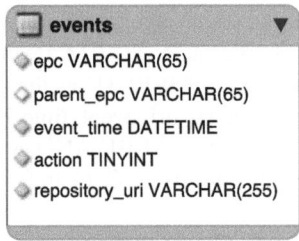

Fig. 4.8 Database schema for the discovery service with action field

For readers' convenience, I still use the textual version in the text and listings. In the database, the integer representation is used.

Now, the algorithm is extended in such a way that the current value of lower_boundary is maintained if the action of the first read event for a given parentEPC is "DELETE", meaning that a packing event that must have taken place is missing. The extended algorithm is described in Listing 4.2.

The adjusted search algorithm retrieves all relevant read events: The search algorithm is called with $SGTIN1$ as the EPC of interest, '1970-01-01' as the lower boundary and '9999-12-31' as the upper boundary. The first query again reveals read events ①, ⑬ and ⑭ which are stored in the list event_list. The list aggregation_events consists of {⑬}.

The entry ⑬, is a read event with the action "DELETE". The search algorithm is called again using

1. ⑬.$parent\_epc$, i.e. $SSCC1$, as the EPC of interest,

4.5 Handling Situations with an Incomplete Read Event Sequence

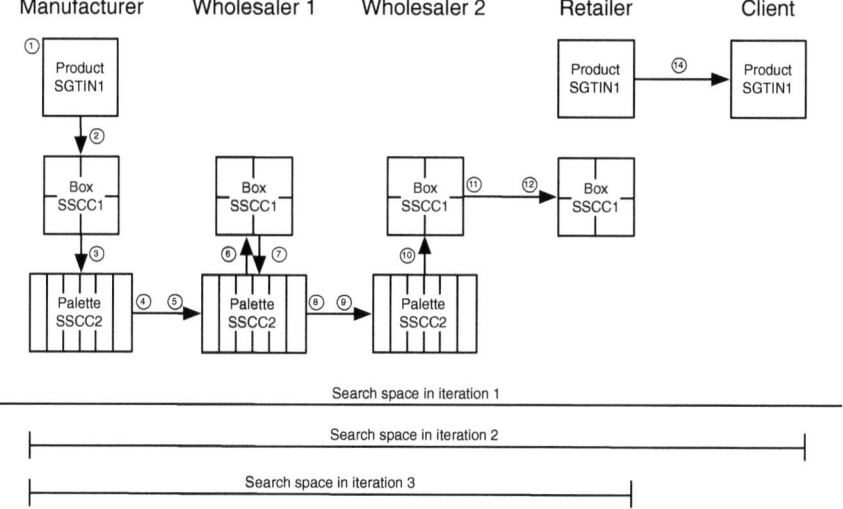

Fig. 4.9 Events to be identified in a common supply chain with a missing unpacking Aggregation-Event and desired behavior of the search algorithm with regard to search spaces

2. the current value of the lower boundary, i.e. '1970-01-01', as the lower boundary, and
3. t(⑬), i.e. '2012-01-07 20:00', as the upper boundary.

Then, the query "SELECT epc, parent_epc, event_time, action, repository_uri FROM events WHERE epc = 'SSCC1' AND event time >= '1970-01-01' AND event_time <= '2012-01-07 20:00' ORDER BY event_time" is executed and reveals read events ③, ⑥, ⑦ and ⑩. The list *aggregation_events* contains {③, ⑥, ⑦ and ⑩}. The action of the first event in the list, ③. *action*, is "ADD". Thus, the search method is called again using

1. ③.*parent_epc*, i.e. $SSCC2$, as the EPC of interest,
2. t(③), i.e. '2012-01-01 10:30', as the lower boundary, and
3. t(⑩), i.e. '2012-01-05 14:00', as the upper boundary.

The query "SELECT epc, parent_epc, event_time, action, repository_uri FROM events WHERE epc = 'SSCC2' AND event time >= '2012-01-01 10:30' AND event_time <= '2012-01-05 14:00' ORDER BY event_time" reveals read events ④, ⑤, ⑧ and ⑨. No AggregationEvents occur. Thus, the search method is not called again and the event_list is returned to the calling method etc. The solution set is $\mathbb{L} = \{①, ③, ④, ⑤, ⑥, ⑦, ⑧, ⑨, ⑩, ⑪, ⑫, ⑬, ⑭\} = \mathbb{L}^{des}$.

The next subsection shows how the search algorithm is adopted in order to ensure a correct search result even when an unpacking event is missing.

```
1   hierarchy information and retrieve all relevant events
2   Input parameters:
3     1. epc_of_interest
4     2. lower_boundary
5     3. upper_boundary
6   Create a new empty list event_list and add the result of the following query to it
7   SELECT epc, parent_epc, action, repository_uri, event_time
8     FROM events
9     WHERE epc = epc_of_interest
10    AND event_time >= lower_boundary
11    AND event_time <= upper_boundary
12    ORDER BY event_time
13  Create a new empty two-dimensional list aggregation_events. Store the parent_epcs in the 1st
        dimension (one entry per distinct parent_epc). The 2nd dimension is a list. Add all read
        events for the parent_epc stored in the first dimension to that list.
14  FOR all distinct parent_epcs in aggregation_events DO
15    /** all events refered to in this loop are the events in the 2nd dimension for the current
            parent_epc **/
16    /** Determine lower and upper boundary **/
17    IF the first event has the action 'ADD' DO
18      Set new_lower_boundary to the event_time of the first event
19    ELSEIF the first event has the action 'DELETE' DO
20      Set new_lower_boundary to lower_boundary
21    END
22
23    Invoke this search method again using
24      1. the parentEPC as the EPC input parameter,
25      2. new_lower_boundary as the lower_boundary input parameter,
26      3. the event_time of the last event in the list as the upper_boundary input parameter,
27         and add the return value to event_list
28  END
29  Return the event_list
```

Listing 4.2 Algorithm to retrieve the complete list of read events for an item of interest leveraging the action attribute for missing packing read events

4.5.2 Missing Unpacking Read Events

Just like a packing event might be missing, an unpacking event might be missing as well (see Fig. 4.9). Example data for a supply chain with a missing unpacking event is shown in Table 4.4.

In the first iteration, the query is "SELECT epc, parent_epc, event_time, action, repository_uri FROM events WHERE epc = 'SGTIN1' AND event time >= '1970-01-01' AND event_time <= '9999-12-31' ORDER BY event_time". This reveals read events ①, ② and ⑭. The list *aggregation_events* contains the event {②}, which has the action "ADD". Thus, the lower boundary for the next iteration is set to t(②) (line 13 in Listing 4.2). Because ② also represents the last event in the list, t(②) is also

4.5 Handling Situations with an Incomplete Read Event Sequence

Table 4.4 Example data that could be stored at the discovery service for the simple supply chain shown in Fig. 4.9

Event	EPC	ParentEPC	Event Time	Action	Repository URI
①	SGTIN1	NULL	2012-01-01 09:00	0	https://epcis.manufacturer.com
②	SGTIN1	SSCC1	2012-01-01 10:00	0	https://epcis.manufacturer.com
③	SSCC1	SSCC2	2012-01-01 10:30	0	https://epcis.manufacturer.com
④	SSCC2	NULL	2012-01-01 12:00	2	https://epcis.manufacturer.com
⑤	SSCC2	NULL	2012-01-03 09:30	2	https://epcis.wholesaler1.com
⑥	SSCC1	SSCC2	2012-01-03 13:00	1	https://epcis.wholesaler1.com
⑦	SSCC1	SSCC2	2012-01-03 13:30	0	https://epcis.wholesaler1.com
⑧	SSCC2	NULL	2012-01-03 16:00	2	https://epcis.wholesaler1.com
⑨	SSCC2	NULL	2012-01-05 07:00	2	https://epcis.wholesaler2.com
⑩	SSCC1	SSCC2	2012-01-05 14:00	1	https://epcis.wholesaler2.com
⑪	SSCC1	NULL	2012-01-06 09:00	2	https://epcis.wholesaler2.com
⑫	SSCC1	NULL	2012-01-07 11:00	2	https://epcis.retailer.com
⑬	SGTIN1	NULL	2012-01-10 10:00	1	https://epcis.retailer.com

		1ˢᵗ Event ① in the List	
		Packing Event	**Unpacking Event**
Nth Event Ⓝ in the List	**Packing Event**	new_lower_boundary = ①.event_time new_upper_boundary = current_upper_boundary	new_lower_boundary = current_lower_boundary new_upper_boundary = Ⓝ.event_time
	Unpacking Event	new_lower_boundary = ①.event_time new_upper_boundary = Ⓝ.event_time	new_lower_boundary = current_lower_boundary new_upper_boundary = current_upper_boundary

Fig. 4.10 Rules to determine lower boundary and upper boundary

used as the upper boundary (line 21 in Listing 4.2). The search algorithm is called again with $SSCC1$ as the EPC of interest and the aforementioned search boundaries.

This results in the following query: "SELECT epc, parent_epc, event_time, action, repository_uri FROM events WHERE epc = 'SSCC1' AND event_time >= '2012-01-01 10:00' AND event_time <= '2012-01-01 10:00' ORDER BY event_time". Because of the wrong upper boundary, no further events are revealed and the algorithm terminates with the solution set $\mathbb{L} = \{①, ② \text{ and } ⑬\}$.

In order to deal with missing unpacking events, the algorithm has to be extended. Only the first and last event in the list are relevant to determine whether a packing or unpacking event is missing. The situations that can occur are that the first event ① in list *aggregation_events* has the action "ADD" or "DELETE" and the last event Ⓝ in list *aggregation_events* "ADD" or "DELETE", resulting in a 2x2 matrix (see Fig. 4.10). If the first event is a packing event, the new lower boundary is updated

```
30   hierarchy information and retrieve all relevant events
31   Input parameters:
32      1. epc_of_interest
33      2. lower_boundary
34      3. upper_boundary
35   Create a new empty list event_list and add the result of the following query to it
36   SELECT epc, parent_epc, action, repository_uri, event_time
37      FROM events
38      WHERE epc = epc_of_interest
39      AND event_time >= lower_boundary
40      AND event_time <= upper_boundary
41      ORDER BY event_time
42   Create a new empty two-dimensional list aggregation_events. Store the parent_epcs in the 1st
        dimension (one entry per distinct parent_epc). The 2nd dimension is a list. Add all read
        events for the parent_epc stored in the first dimension to that list.
43   FOR all distinct parent_epcs in aggregation_events DO
44      /** all events reffered to in this loop are the events in the 2nd dimension for the current
           parent_epc **/
45      /** Determine lower and upper boundary **/
46      Set new_lower_boundary to lower_boundary
47      Set new_upper_boundary to upper_boundary
48      IF the first event has the action 'ADD' DO
49         Set new_lower_boundary to the event_time of the first event
50      END
51      IF the last event has the action 'DELETE' DO
52         Set new_upper_boundary to the event_time of the last event
53      END
54
55      Invoke this search method again using
56         1. the parentEPC as the EPC input parameter,
57         2. new_lower_boundary as the lower boundary,
58         3. new_upper_boundary as the upper boundary,
59         and add the return value to event_list
60   END
61   Return the event_list
```

Listing 4.3 Algorithm to retrieve the complete list of read events for an item of interest leveraging the action attribute for missing AggregationEvents

to t(①). Otherwise, if the first event is an unpacking event, the lower boundary is unchanged. The rules for the last event are directly reversed: if the last event is a packing event, the item is either not unpacked yet or at least one unpacking event is missing. Thus, the upper boundary is unchanged. If the last event is an unpacking event, the new upper boundary is tightened to t(⊘). Using these rules, the adopted search algorithm is presented in Listing 4.3.

Applying the extended algorithm to the example (Fig. 4.9) leads to the same situation in the first iteration: read events ①, ② and ⑭ are identified. ② is the only Aggregation-Event. The new lower boundary is set to t(②), i.e. '2012-01-01 10:00'. The upper boundary is set to the current value of the upper boundary, i.e. '9999-12-31'. With

4.5 Handling Situations with an Incomplete Read Event Sequence

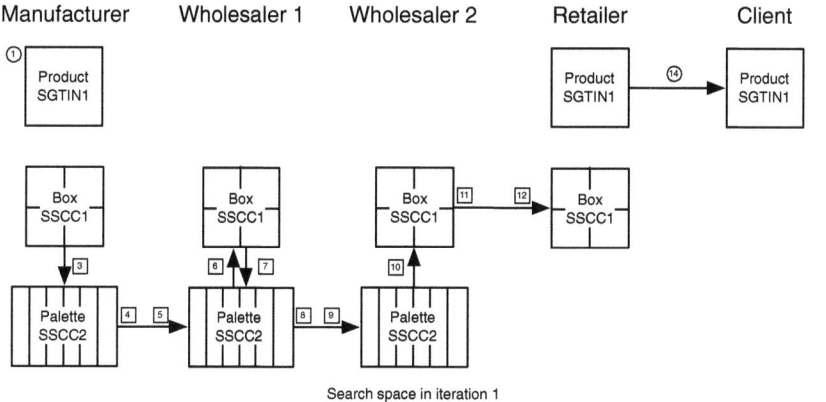

Fig. 4.11 Events in a supply chain with a missing pair of AggregationEvents

these search boundaries and $SSCC1$ as the EPC of interest, the search algorithm is called again.

This leads to the query "SELECT epc, parent_epc, event_time, action, repository_uri FROM events WHERE epc = 'SSCC1' AND event time >= '2012-01-01 10:00' AND event_time <= '9999-12-31' ORDER BY event_time", which reveals read events ③, ⑥, ⑦, ⑩, ⑪ and ⑫. The list $aggregation\_events$ contains {③, ⑥, ⑦ and ⑩}. Thus, the search method is called again using:

1. ②.$parent\_epc = SSCC2$ as the EPC of interest
2. t(①) as the lower boundary (line 15 in Listing 4.3), and
3. t(⑩) as the upper boundary (line 18 in Listing 4.3).

This identifies the remaining read events ④, ⑤, ⑧ and ⑨. The solution set is $\mathbb{L} = \{$①, ②, ③, ④, ⑤, ⑥, ⑦, ⑧, ⑨, ⑩, ⑪, ⑫, ⑭$\} = \mathbb{L}^{des}$.

This adjustment of the search algorithm also applies to situations where an item i is still packed into a transport container tc. Thus, situations with missing packing or missing unpacking events can now be handled by the search algorithm. Such results would be flagged by the search algorithm in order to enable the verification service to analyze the impact of missing read events on the decision wether an item is supposed to be genuine or counterfeit.

4.5.3 A Missing Pair of Corresponding Read Events

If a pair of corresponding AggregationEvents is missing, i.e. the childEPC and parentEPC of the missing read events are the same, a situation can occur that the trace cannot be reconstructed (see Fig. 4.11).

90   4 A Recursive Search Algorithm to Find all Potentially Relevant Read Events

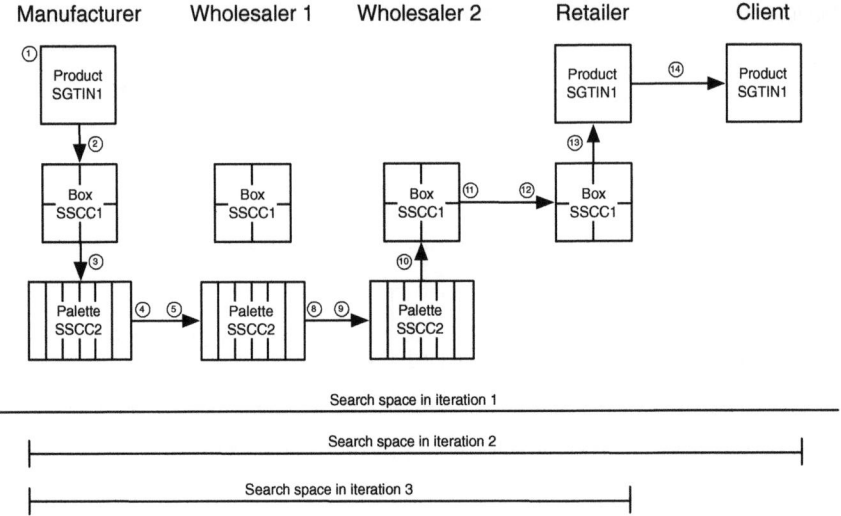

Fig. 4.12 A situation with a missing AggregationEvent pair but the trace can be completely reconstructed

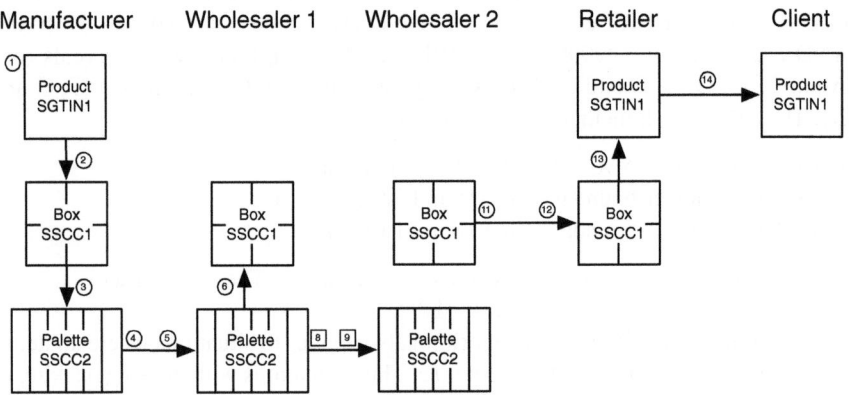

Fig. 4.13 A Situation with a Missing AggregationEvent Pair but the Trace can be Partly Reconstructed

However, if read events are missing that took place 'in the middle' of the item's lifecycle as depicted in Fig. 4.12, the trace can be reconstructed and a verification service could determine if the item is harmful or not. Obviously, the missing events cannot be reconstructed.

Another situation is depicted in Fig. 4.13. There, a corresponding pair of AggregationEvents got lost. Thus, the upper boundary in the third iteration is set to t(⑥) leading to a situation where events ⑧ and ⑨ are excluded from the set of relevant read events for the item of interest identified by $SGTIN1$. No rational adjustment of the algorithm can be made because important read events were lost.

4.5 Handling Situations with an Incomplete Read Event Sequence

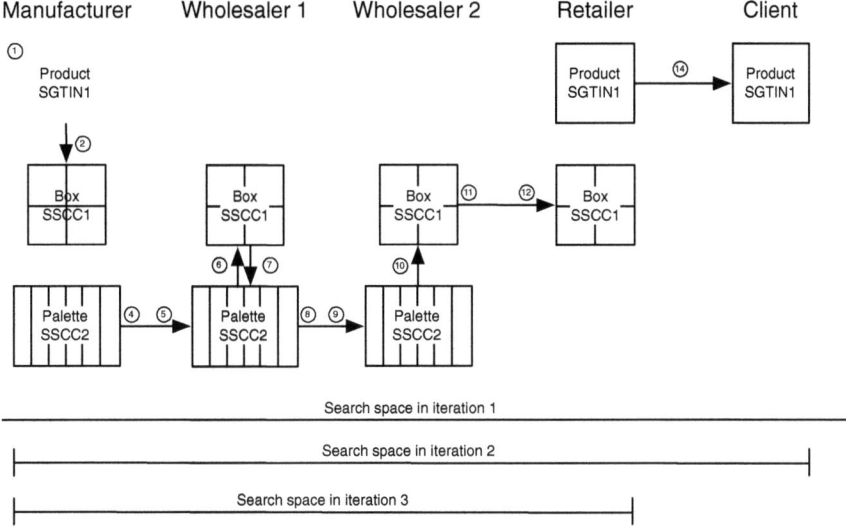

Fig. 4.14 Events in a common supply chain with two missing AggregationEvents affecting distinct pairs

Table 4.5 Example data that could be stored at the discovery service for the supply chain shown in Fig. 4.14

Event	EPC	ParentEPC	Event Time	Action	Repository URI
①	SGTIN1	NULL	2012-01-01 09:00	0	https://epcis.manufacturer.com
②	SGTIN1	SSCC1	2012-01-01 10:00	0	https://epcis.manufacturer.com
④	SSCC2	NULL	2012-01-01 12:00	2	https://epcis.manufacturer.com
⑤	SSCC2	NULL	2012-01-03 09:30	2	https://epcis.wholesaler1.com
⑥	SSCC1	SSCC2	2012-01-03 13:00	1	https://epcis.wholesaler1.com
⑦	SSCC1	SSCC2	2012-01-03 13:30	0	https://epcis.wholesaler1.com
⑧	SSCC2	NULL	2012-01-03 16:00	2	https://epcis.wholesaler1.com
⑨	SSCC2	NULL	2012-01-05 07:00	2	https://epcis.wholesaler2.com
⑩	SSCC1	SSCC2	2012-01-05 14:00	1	https://epcis.wholesaler2.com
⑪	SSCC1	NULL	2012-01-06 09:00	2	https://epcis.wholesaler2.com
⑫	SSCC1	NULL	2012-01-07 11:00	2	https://epcis.retailer.com
⑭	SGTIN1	NULL	2012-01-10 10:00	1	https://epcis.retailer.com

4.5.4 Various Missing Corresponding Read Events

If multiple AggregationEvents with different childEPCs and parentEPCs are missing (see Fig. 4.14 and Table 4.5 for respective example data), the search algorithm would still be able to retrieve potentially relevant read events.

In the first iteration, read events ①, ② and ⑭ are revealed. Leveraging ②, the search algorithm is called again with

1. ②.*parent_epc* = $SSCC1$ as the EPC of interest,
2. t(②) = '2012-01-01 10:00' as the lower boundary (line 15 in Listing 4.3),
3. '9999-12-31' as the upper boundary.

This reveals read events ⑥, ⑦, ⑨, ⑩, ⑪ and ⑫. The list *aggregation_events* contains {⑥, ⑦, ⑩}. Because the first event (⑥) is an unpacking event (action = "DELETE"), the lower boundary is set to the previous lower boundary (line 12 in Listing 4.3). As ⑩ also has the action "DELETE", the upper boundary is set to t(⑩) (line 18 in Listing 4.3). Thus, in the third iteration, the search algorithm is called again with

1. ②.*parent_epc* = $SSCC2$ as the EPC of interest,
2. t(②) = '2012-01-01 10:00' as the lower boundary,
3. t(⑩) = '2012-01-05 14:00' as the upper boundary.

All read events that could be revealed as relevant are actually identified and the algorithm terminates.

To sum up the discourse, it can be stated that event notifications to the discovery service should not be lost. However in some cases, all but the lost events can be retrieved as shown in the examples above. Given the fact that more than one read event is usually produced per item at each facility, all read events will be included in the respective responses of the read event repositories. Nevertheless, without a correct sequence of read events, meaning that events are lost, it is unrealistic to guarantee proper handling of the item of interest throughout its complete lifecycle, even if the trace can be (partly) reconstructed.

4.6 Critical Discussion of the Search Algorithm

In this section, I conduct a critical discussion with regard to the correctness of the search algorithm.

Given is a set of EventRecords ER. For the search algorithm, the relevant attributes of an event record *er* are an EPC *er.epc*, an event time *er.event_time*, and an action *er.action*. ER consists of a set of event records describing ObjectEvents OE and the set of event records describing AggregationEvents AE.

$$ER = OE \cup AE$$

Each event record either belongs to the set of ObjectEvents or to the set of AggregationEvents.

$$OE \cap AE = \emptyset$$

Each uniquely identified item i that shall be tracked has at least an initial ObjectEvent related to it. This initial read event is identified by the action "ADD". Without this event, no further events are valid for a given identifier.

4.6 Critical Discussion of the Search Algorithm

An item must be packed into a container before it can be unpacked again. Thus, an AggregationEvent with the action "ADD" must occur before an AggregationEvent with the action "DELETE" for the same childEPC and parentEPC. Each time an item is packed into or unpacked from a container, an AggregationEvent is generated with the item's EPC as the childEPC and the container's EPC as the parentEPC. For packing activities, the action is "ADD". For unpacking activities, the action is "DELETE".

AE.epc is the set of all childEPCs. AE.parent_epc is the set of all parentEPCs.

With regard to AggregationEvents, an EPC must occur as a parentEPC before it can occur as a childEPC. If an EPC is packed into a container (thus, occurs as a childEPC), it cannot occur again until it is unpacked (occurs as a childEPC again). Nevertheless, transport containers $tc \in TC$ can occur as ObjectEvents at any point in time.

If an item of interest was packed into a transport container tc_1 identified by $SSCCX$ and this transport container is packed into another transport container tc_2, the situation occurs that

$$container\_epc \in AE.parentEPC$$
$$\land$$
$$container\_epc \in AE.childEPC$$

When searching for an item of interest, four situations might occur:

1. No entries for a given item of interest are available at the discovery service.
2. The item of interest takes it's route through the supply chain without any packaging.
3. The item of interest is packed into a transport container and potentially unpacked again.
4. The item of interest is a transport container sheltering other items and being packed into a larger transport container.

These situations are evaluated with regard to the search algorithm's correctness in the following.

4.6.1 No Notification Messages at All

The unique identifier id_I (EPC of interest) is not known to the discovery service, meaning that

$$\forall oe \in OE : oe.epc \neq epc\_of\_interest$$

$$\forall ae \in AE : ae.child\_epc \neq epc\_of\_interest$$

$$\forall ae \in AE : ae.parent\_epc \neq epc\_of\_interest$$

No AggregationEvents can exist due to the missing prerequisite of the initial ObjectEvent. The search algorithm is valid as it returns ∅ because it does not find the EPC of interest in the database (line 7, Listing 4.3). Because no AggregationEvents are found, the search algorithm is not called again and the empty list is returned (lines 9–27, Listing 4.3). This represents the desired behavior.

4.6.2 No Packaging Read Events

In this case, the item of interest is never aggregated into a transport container. The EPC of interest is only available in ObjectEvents meaning that

$$\exists oe \in OE : oe.epc = epc\_of\_interest$$

$$\forall ae \in AE : ae.child\_epc \neq epc\_of\_interest$$

$$\forall ae \in AE : ae.parent\_epc \neq epc\_of\_interest$$

The search algorithm is valid in this situation due to the fact that all ObjectEvents with the EPC of interest are selected. If no AggregationEvents are present, they are not returned and no further call of the search algorithm is conducted. The list of all ObjectEvents with $oe.epc = epc\_of\_interest$ is returned.

4.6.3 No Hierarchical-Packaging Relationship

In this situation, the item of interest was packed into another transport container. It also might have been unpacked but it is not used as a transport container itself.

The EPC of interest is included in the set of ObjectEvents and in the set of AggregationEvents as a childEPC meaning that

$$\exists oe \in OE : oe.epc = epc\_of\_interest$$

$$\exists ae \in AE : ae.child\_epc = epc\_of\_interest$$

$$\forall ae \in AE : ae.parent\_epc \neq epc\_of\_interest$$

The ObjectEvents and AggregationEvents with the childEPC as the EPC of interest are identified as before (line 7, Listing 4.3).

Then, the distinct AggregationEvents AE' are identified. Here, the recursion of the search algorithm comes into play. The search algorithm iterates over all distinct parentEPCs in AE' and calls the search algorithm again using $ae'.parent\_epc$ as the EPC of interest. Now, the discovery service database is queried with $ae'.parent\_epc$

4.6 Critical Discussion of the Search Algorithm

analyzing whether it was involved in ObjectEvents or in AggregationEvents as a childEPC.

Given the present preconditions, no further elements are found. Thus, the search algorithm only returns the ObjectEvents where $oe.epc = epc\_of\_interest$ and the AggregationEvents with $ae.child\_epc = epc\_of\_interest$.

4.6.4 Hierarchical-Packaging Relationships

In this scenario, the item equipped with the EPC of interest is a transport container $tc \in TC$. Several items have been packed into that transport container tc_1 and the transport container tc_1 itself was packed into another transport container tc_2.

Thus, the EPC of interest is observed in ObjectEvents as well as in AggregationEvents as childEPC and parentEPC. The EPC of interest is included in the set of ObjectEvents and AggregationEvents meaning that

$$\exists oe \in OE : oe.epc = epc\_of\_interest$$

$$\exists ae \in AE : ae.child\_epc = epc\_of\_interest$$

$$\exists ae \in AE : ae.parent\_epc = epc\_of\_interest$$

In the first iteration of the search algorithm, all relevant ObjectEvents would be retrieved. In addition, the AggregationEvents AE' are retrieved as a subset of AE with the condition that $ae'.child\_epc = epc\_of\_interest$. Finally, for all $ae' \in AE'$, the search algorithm is called again and retrieves all AggregationEvents AE'' where $ae''.child\_epc = ae'.parent\_epc$ etc. Thus, the search algorithm delivers correct results.

For all cases, the search algorithm retrieves all read events that are potentially relevant as lifecycle information. Nevertheless, the next section highlights limitations of the search algorithm.

4.7 Limitations

Given the fact that the search algorithm reduces the number of database requests by just respecting the first and last AggregationEvent of the same childEPC–parentEPC combination, it is not exact in all situations. E.g., it cannot recognize the interim re-use of a box. This will be exemplified using the supply chain depicted in Fig. 4.15.

The item identified with the unique identifier $SGTIN1$ is produced (◯) and packed into a box identified by $SSCC1$ at the manufacturer (◉). After that, it is packed into a container with the identifier $SSCC2$ (◉) and shipped to the first wholesaler (◉). The first wholesaler receives the container (◉), unpacks the box (◉) and the

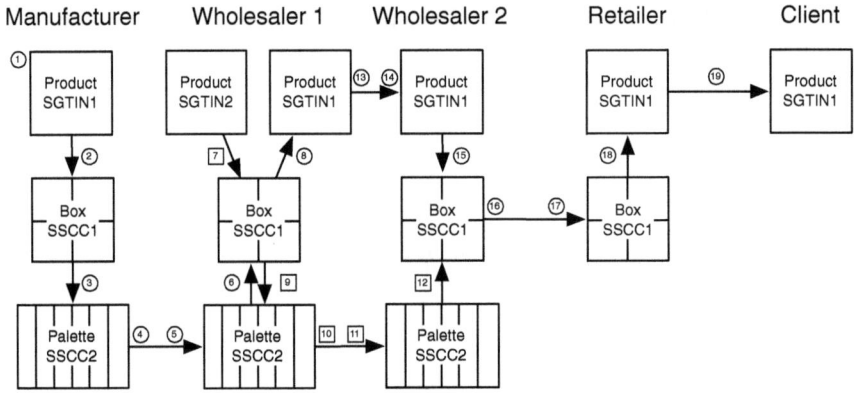

Fig. 4.15 Interim re-use of a box

item identified by $SGTIN1$ (⑥). The first wholesaler furthermore packs an item identified by $SGTIN2$ into the box (⑦), the box on the container again (⑨), and ships the container to the second wholesaler (⑩). The second wholesaler receives (⑪) and unpacks the box (⑫). In the meantime, the item identified by $SGTIN1$ was shipped to the second retailer on another route (⑬ and ⑭). Accidentally, the item identified by $SGTIN1$ is packed into the box with the unique identifier $SSCC1$ (⑮). The box is shipped to the retailer (⑯ and ⑰), who unpacks the item (⑱) and sells it to the client (⑲). Thus, the desired solution set is $\mathbb{L}^{des} = \{①, ②, ③, ④, ⑤, ⑥, ⑧, ⑬,$ ⑭, ⑮, ⑯, ⑰, ⑱, ⑲\}.

Now, the search algorithm (Listing 4.3) is applied. In the first iteration, the search algorithm identifies the ObjectEvents ①, ⑬, ⑭ and ⑲ as well as the AggregationEvents ②, ⑧, ⑮ and ⑱. The intermediate result set is $\mathbb{L}^1 = \{①, ②, ⑧, ⑬, ⑭, ⑮, ⑱, ⑲\}$.

In the second iteration, the ObjectEvents ⑯ and ⑰ are identified. Furthermore, the AggregationEvents ③, ⑥, [9] and [12] are retrieved. The intermediate result set is $\mathbb{L}^2 = \{①, ②, ③, ⑥, ⑧, [9], [12] ⑬, ⑭, ⑮, ⑯, ⑰, ⑱, ⑲\}$. The undesired events [9] and [12] are retrieved because the lower boundary is set to $t(②)$ and the upper boundary is set to $t(⑱)$ while the EPC of interest is set to $SSCC1$.

Finally, in the third iteration, the objects events ④, ⑤, [10] and [11] are identified. Thus, the final solution set is $\mathbb{L} = \{①, ②, ③, ④, ⑤, ⑥, ⑧, [9], [10], [11], [12] ⑬, ⑭, ⑮, ⑯, ⑰, ⑱, ⑲\}$. Obviously, it contains undesired read events.

To compensate this limitation, a filter algorithm is introduced to analyzing the identified events and removing undesired events from the solution set. The algorithm is described in the next chapter.

Chapter 5
A Filter Algorithm to Extract the Relevant Read Events

The worst thing that could happen in a unique identifier network is that confidential data is revealed to unauthorized clients. This would destroy trust in the complete unique identifier network and participants would stop sharing data with each other. Thus, a discovery service must only query read event repositories for read events that are really related to the item of interest. As shown in the previous chapter, the search algorithm might return read events that are not directly related to the item of interest. Therefore, I introduce a filter algorithm that processes all read events returned by the search algorithm and evaluates whether they are valid for a given item of interest or not. In parallel to that, I propose to include an 'analytical' interface to the discovery service that returns the unfiltered events. This can be used in exceptional situations to investigate the lifecycle of an event. Of course, a proper security and authorization concept must be in place, which is out of scope for this dissertation.

The remainder of this chapter is structured as follows: Section 5.1 describes the data structure used by the filter algorithm. The actual filter algorithm is described in Sect. 5.2. The mode of operation is exemplified with a simple supply chain in Sect. 5.3. The use case of RTIs is omitted because, as it will be shown throughout this chapter, the filter algorithm inherently supports this requirement. Section 5.4 describes how the limitations of the search algorithm are mitigated by the filter algorithm in a scenario of an interim re-usage of a box. Like the search algorithm, the filter algorithm has to be robust with regard to missing read events. Thus, the scenarios with missing read events are also applied to the filter algorithm in Sect. 5.5. Finally, a critical discussion is conducted in Sect. 5.6. In [127], I already describe parts of this content.

5.1 Data Structure for the Algorithm

The filter algorithm retrieves a list of all event records identified by the search algorithm. Each event record is represented by an object instance according to Fig. 5.1. It includes the attributes *epc*, *parent_epc*, *event_time*, *action*, and *repository_url*

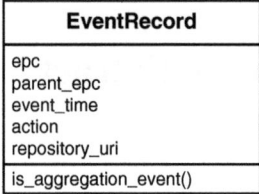

Fig. 5.1 Class diagram for events

as well as the method $is\_aggregation\_event()$. If $parent\_epc == NULL$, this method returns $false$. Otherwise, it returns $true$.

The filter algorithm leverages the analogy of a stack. A stack is a data structure that behaves like a Last-in First-out (LIFO) queue [144]. The filter algorithm uses the stack to evaluate EPCs. The methods used are: *push(String epc)*, *peek()*, *pop()*, and *search(String epc)* [144].

- *push(String epc)*: Adds the string *epc* to the top of the stack.
- *peek()*: Returns the topmost element from the stack without any modifications to the stack.
- *pop()*: Removes the topmost element from the stack and returns it as the return value.
- *search(String(epc))*: Searches for the string *epc* on the stack (top down) and returns its position. If the string is not found, -1 is returned.

Having set these preconditions, the filter algorithm is described in the next section.

5.2 Description of the Filter Algorithm

The filter algorithm validates which event records out of a given list of events are relevant concerning the route a certain item of interest i took through the supply chain sc_i. This is done by iterating through all event records, memorizing all packing and unpacking activities, and, based on the packaging information and the event record attributes, deciding whether the event record is valid or not. A stack is used to dynamically represent the packaging hierarchy with regard to the item of interest. The read events in the list of read events describe one of the following situations:

- *Initialization*: The unique identifier id_I is attached to the item of interest i. This is indicated by an ObjectEvent with the action "ADD".
- *Transport*: The item of interest i is transported through the supply chain sc_i. A read event with the action "OBSERVE" takes place.
- *Packing*: The item of interest is packed into a transport container. An AggregationEvent with id_I as the childEPC and the action "ADD" takes place.
- *Unpacking*: The item of interest is unpacked from a transport container. An AggregationEvent with id_I as the childEPC and the action "DELETE" takes place.

5.2 Description of the Filter Algorithm

```
1  FilterAlgorithm: Filter all relevant events
2    Input parameters:
3      1. event_list
4      2. epc_of_interest
5    Create a new empty list filtered_events_list to store the filtered events
6    Create a new empty stack hierarchy_stack to dynamically represent the packaging hierarchy
7    FOR all events in event_list DO
8      IF the action is 'ADD' DO
9        IF it is an ObjectEvent AND the EPC matches the epc_of_interest DO
10          Push the EPC of the current event onto the stack
11          Add the current event to the filtered_events_list
12        ELSEIF it is an AggregationEvent AND the childEPC matches the topmost element on the
              stack DO
13          Push the parentEPC of the current event onto the stack
14          Add the current event to the filtered_events_list
15        END
16      ELSEIF the action is 'DELETE' DO
17        IF it is an ObjectEvent AND the EPC matches the epc_of_interest DO
18          Remove the topmost EPC from the stack
19          Add the current event to the filtered_events_list
20        ELSEIF it is an AggregationEvent AND the parentEPC of the current event matches the
              topmost element on the stack DO
21          Remove the topmost EPC from the stack
22          Add the current event to the filtered_events_list
23        END
24      ELSE /** OBSERVE **/
25        IF the EPC of the current event is stored somewhere on the stack DO
26          Add the current event to the filtered_events_list
27        END
28      END
29    END
30    Return the filtered_event_list
```

Listing 5.1 Algorithm to filter exactly the related read events out of the initial event list

- *Destruction*: The item of interest is removed from the unique identifier network. A read event with id_I and the action "DELETE" takes place.
- *Undefined*: Read events other than the abovementioned can occur, i.e. another EPC is involved in the event record.

Once an aggregation took place, the algorithm has to respect that read events concerning the transport container are valid now. Nevertheless, id_I also can be read using RFID technology while it is packed into a transport container. Listing 5.1 describes the filter algorithm.

The input parameters are (see lines 3–4, Listing 5.1):

1. The list of read events retrieved by the search algorithm (sorted by event_time in ascending order).
2. The unique identifier of the item of interest (EPC of interest).

The output is a filtered list that only contains read events, which are really related to the item of interest. In the following, event records that successfully overcome the verification are called 'valid'. Otherwise, they are called 'invalid'. Firstly, a new list called *filtered_events_list* and a new stack called *hierarchy_stack* are created (lines 5–6, Listing 5.1). Then, all event records in the initial event record list are evaluated. They are distinguished by the read event actions ("ADD", "DELETE", and "OBSERVE").

If a read event has the action "ADD", only the following event records are valid. Event records that do not comply with these requirements are discarded.

- *Initialization*: The initial creation of the EPC of interest (ObjectEvent with the EPC matching the EPC of interest) or
- *Packing*: Packing an item into a transport container (AggregationEvent with the childEPC matching the current outermost container).

If it has the action "DELETE", only the event records fulfilling the following requirements are considered to be valid. All other events with the action "DELETE" are discarded.

- *Unpacking*: Unpacking an item from a transport container (AggregationEvent with the parentEPC matching the current outermost container) or
- *Destruction*: The final destruction of the EPC of interest (ObjectEvent with the EPC matching the EPC of interest).

If it has the action "OBSERVE", valid events are all events that refer to EPCs that are somewhere on the stack, i.e. the item of interest itself or a transport container the item of interest is transported in. All other events with the action "OBSERVE" are discarded.

The complexity of the filter algorithm is dominated by the number of read events in the event_list $|event\_list|$, thus $\mathcal{O}(|event\_list|)$.

5.3 Mode of Operation Exemplified with a Simple Supply Chain

This section exemplifies how the filter algorithm is applied. Figure 5.2 shows a simple supply chain already presented earlier in this thesis. The respective data stored at the discovery service is listed in Table 5.1.

The input for the filter algorithm is the event list similar to Table 5.1 and $SGTIN1$ as the EPC of interest. The item of interest is equipped with the EPC $SGTIN1$ in read event ①. The action is "ADD", it is an ObjectEvent, and the EPC matches the EPC of interest. Thus, line 9 in Listing 5.1 evaluates as true, which results in pushing the EPC onto the stack and storing the read event ① in the list of filtered read events (line 10, Listing 5.1). Figure 5.3 illustrates the current state of the algorithm execution.

The next read event again has the action "ADD", it is an AggregationEvent and the childEPC (= $SGTIN1$) matches the topmost element on the stack. Thus, this describes a valid packing event. The parentEPC (= $SSCC1$) is pushed onto the stack

5.3 Mode of Operation Exemplified with a Simple Supply Chain

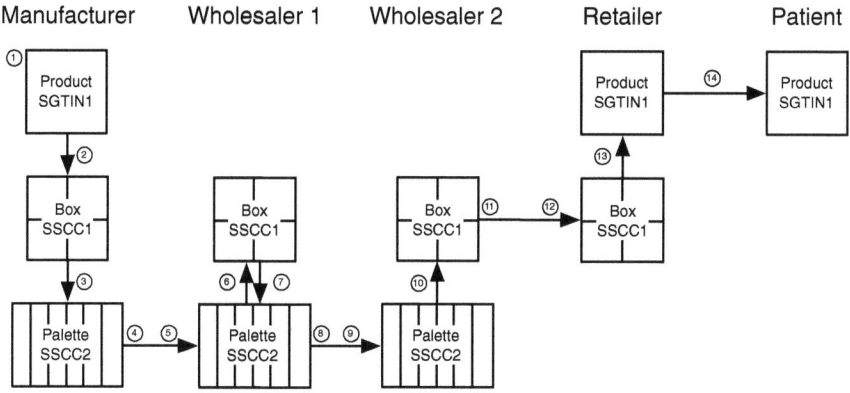

Fig. 5.2 A simple supply chain

Table 5.1 Example data that could be stored at the discovery service for the simple supply chain shown in Fig. 5.2

Event	EPC	ParentEPC	Event Time	Action	Repository URI
①	SGTIN1	NULL	2012-01-01 09:00	0	https://epcis.manufacturer.com
②	SGTIN1	SSCC1	2012-01-01 10:00	0	https://epcis.manufacturer.com
③	SSCC1	SSCC2	2012-01-01 10:30	0	https://epcis.manufacturer.com
④	SSCC2	NULL	2012-01-01 12:00	2	https://epcis.manufacturer.com
⑤	SSCC2	NULL	2012-01-03 09:30	2	https://epcis.wholesaler1.com
⑥	SSCC1	SSCC2	2012-01-03 13:00	1	https://epcis.wholesaler1.com
⑦	SSCC1	SSCC2	2012-01-03 13:30	0	https://epcis.wholesaler1.com
⑧	SSCC2	NULL	2012-01-03 16:00	2	https://epcis.wholesaler1.com
⑨	SSCC2	NULL	2012-01-05 07:00	2	https://epcis.wholesaler2.com
⑩	SSCC1	SSCC2	2012-01-05 14:00	1	https://epcis.wholesaler2.com
⑪	SSCC1	NULL	2012-01-06 09:00	2	https://epcis.wholesaler2.com
⑫	SSCC1	NULL	2012-01-07 11:00	2	https://epcis.retailer.com
⑬	SGTIN1	SSCC1	2012-01-07 20:00	1	https://epcis.retailer.com
⑭	SGTIN1	NULL	2012-01-10 10:00	1	https://epcis.retailer.com

and the read event ② is added to the list of valid events (line 13–14, Listing 5.1). The current state of the filter algorithm is visualized in Fig. 5.4.

Read event ③ is a valid packing event similar to read event ②. The parentEPC (= $SSCC2$) is pushed onto the stack and the read event ③ is added to the list of valid events (line 13–14, Listing 5.1).

The next read event describes the business step of goods issue for the transport container identified by $SSCC2$. It is an ObjectEvent with the action "OBSERVE". As the EPC $SSCC2$ is stored somewhere on the stack (more precisely, it is stored on top of the stack), line 25 of Listing 5.1 evaluates as true. As a consequence, read event ④ is added to the list of valid read events (line 26, Listing 5.1). The current state of the algorithm is depicted in Fig. 5.5.

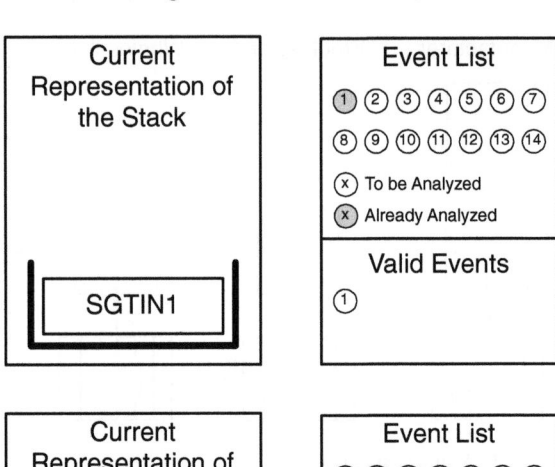

Fig. 5.3 State of the filter algorithm after read event ①

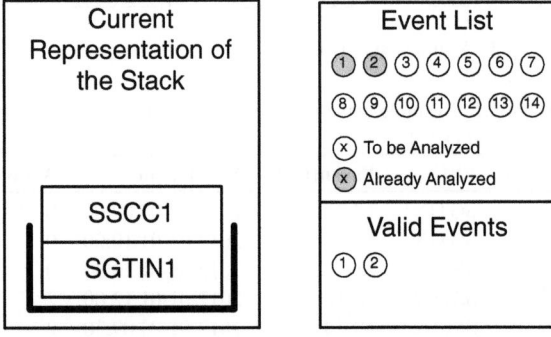

Fig. 5.4 State of the filter algorithm after read event ②

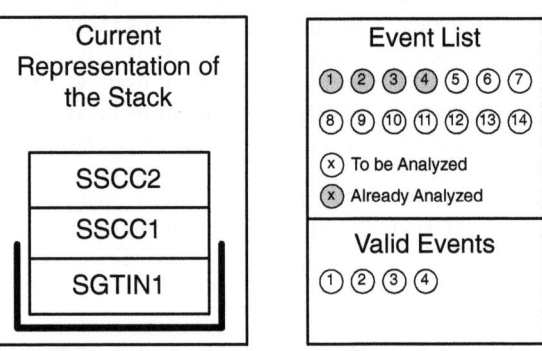

Fig. 5.5 State of the filter algorithm after read event ④

Read event ⑤ has the same attributes as the previous read event. Thus, it is added to the list of valid read events without any modifications to the stack.

The next read event describes the first read event with the action "DELETE". The parentEPC ($SSCC2$) matches the topmost element on the stack ($SSCC2$). Given these preconditions, line 20 of Listing 5.1 evaluates as true. $SSCC2$ is removed from the stack and read event ⑥ is added to the list of valid read events (lines 21–22, Listing 5.1). The current status of the filter algorithm is illustrated in Fig. 5.6.

5.3 Mode of Operation Exemplified with a Simple Supply Chain   103

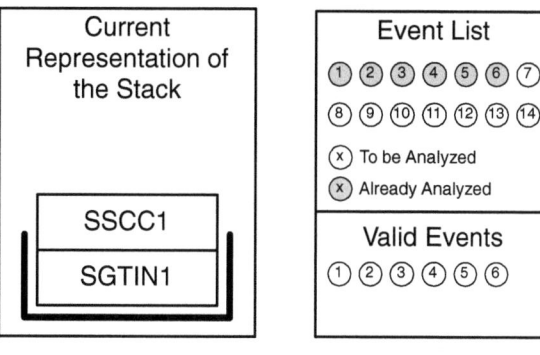

Fig. 5.6 State of the filter algorithm after read event ⑥

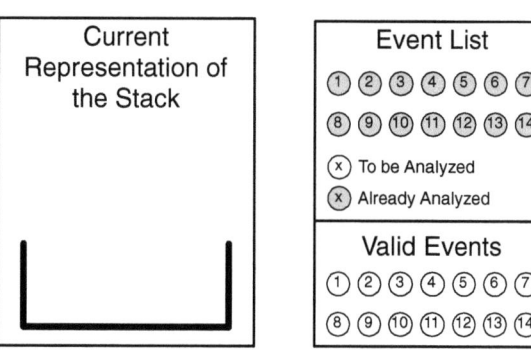

Fig. 5.7 State of the filter algorithm after read event ⑭

Read event ⑦ describes that the transport container identified by $SSCC1$ is packed into the transport container equipped with $SSCC2$, again. This equals to what happened in read event ③: $SSCC2$ is pushed to the stack and read event ⑦ is added to the list of valid read events.

Read events ⑧ and ⑨ are equal to read events ④ and ⑤ for this algorithm. Accordingly, they are added to the list of valid read events without modifications to the stack.

Read event ⑩ causes the removal of $SSCC2$ from the stack. The read event is added to the list of valid read events.

Read events ⑪ and ⑫ are ObjectEvents with the action "OBSERVE" and the EPC $SSCC1$. As the EPC $SSCC1$ is on the stack, both read events are added to the list of valid read events.

Read event ⑬ has the action "DELETE". As it is an AggregationEvent and the parentEPC ($SSCC1$) matches the topmost element on the stack ($SSCC1$), $SSCC1$ is removed from the stack and read event ⑬ is added to the list of valid read events.

The last read event has the action "DELETE" with the EPC $SGTIN1$. The EPC matches the EPC of interest. Thus, line 17 of Listing 5.1 evaluates as true, resulting in the removal of the topmost EPC from the stack and addition of read event ⑭ to the list of valid read events. The final state of the algorithm is shown in Fig. 5.7.

The search algorithm was not capable of retrieving only the relevant event records from the discovery service database in the case of an interim re-use of a box. Therefore, this use case is discussed in the next section.

5.4 Handling Interim Re-use of a Box

The need for the filter algorithm arose because of the limitation of the search algorithm to handle situations like the interim re-use of a transport container. For readers' convenience, the respective example supply chain is repeated in Fig. 5.8. The corresponding data stored at the discovery service is depicted in Table 5.2.

The speciality of this use case is that the EPC of interest $SGTIN1$ is unpacked from a box which is then used for other purposes. Later on, the EPC of interest is packed into this box again. This makes it impossible for the search algorithm to exclude the read events produced for the box in the time span the EPC of interest was not packed into that box.

As discussed in Sect. 4.7, the search algorithm returns a list *read_events* containing the read events $\{①, ②, ③, ④, ⑤, ⑥, ⑧, ⑨, ⑩, ⑪, ⑫, ⑬, ⑭, ⑮, ⑯, ⑰, ⑱, ⑲\}$. Now, the filter algorithm is supposed to discard the read events ⑨, ⑩, ⑪, and ⑫.

Until read event ⑥, the filter algorithm behaves as shown in the previous example (see Fig. 5.9 for the state of the filter algorithm after read event ⑥).

Read event ⑧ has the action "DELETE". It is an AggregationEvent and the parentEPC ($SSCC1$) matches the topmost element on the stack ($SSCC1$). Thus, $SSCC1$ is removed from the top of the stack and read event ⑧ is added to the filtered event list with valid read events. The state of the filter algorithm after read event ⑧ is illustrated in Fig. 5.10.

Read event ⑨ has the action "ADD". As it is an AggregationEvent but the childEPC ($SSCC1$) does not equal the topmost element on the stack ($SGTIN1$),

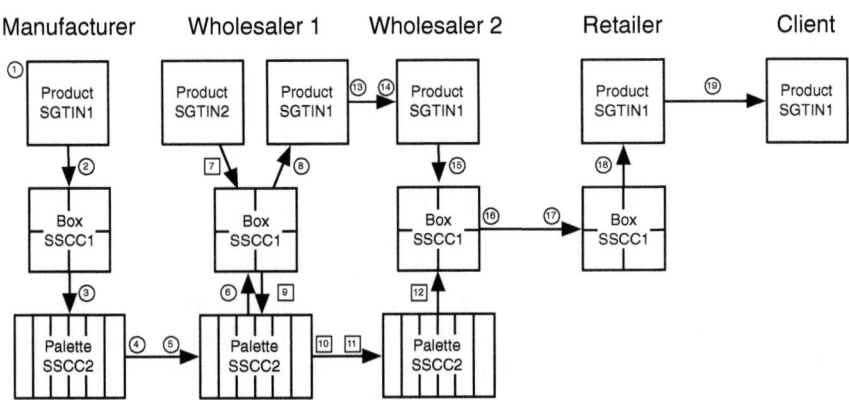

Fig. 5.8 Interim re-use of a box

5.4 Handling Interim Re-use of a Box

Table 5.2 Example data that could be stored at the discovery service for the supply chain shown in Fig. 5.8

Event	EPC	ParentEPC	Event Time	Action	Repository URI
①	SGTIN1	NULL	2012-01-01 09:00	0	https://epcis.manufacturer.com
②	SGTIN1	SSCC1	2012-01-01 10:00	0	https://epcis.manufacturer.com
③	SSCC1	SSCC2	2012-01-01 10:30	0	https://epcis.manufacturer.com
④	SSCC2	NULL	2012-01-01 12:00	2	https://epcis.manufacturer.com
⑤	SSCC2	NULL	2012-01-03 09:30	2	https://epcis.wholesaler1.com
⑥	SSCC1	SSCC2	2012-01-03 13:00	1	https://epcis.wholesaler1.com
⑦	SGTIN2	SSCC1	2012-01-03 13:10	0	https://epcis.wholesaler1.com
⑧	SGTIN1	SSCC1	2012-01-03 13:20	1	https://epcis.wholesaler1.com
⑨	SSCC1	SSCC2	2012-01-03 13:30	0	https://epcis.wholesaler1.com
⑩	SSCC2	NULL	2012-01-03 16:00	2	https://epcis.wholesaler1.com
⑪	SSCC2	NULL	2012-01-05 07:00	2	https://epcis.wholesaler2.com
⑫	SSCC1	SSCC2	2012-01-05 14:00	1	https://epcis.wholesaler2.com
⑬	SGTIN1	NULL	2012-01-05 15:00	2	https://epcis.wholesaler1.com
⑭	SGTIN1	NULL	2012-01-06 07:00	2	https://epcis.wholesaler2.com
⑮	SGTIN1	SSCC1	2012-01-06 08:00	0	https://epcis.wholesaler2.com
⑯	SSCC1	NULL	2012-01-06 09:00	2	https://epcis.wholesaler2.com
⑰	SSCC1	NULL	2012-01-07 11:00	2	https://epcis.retailer.com
⑱	SGTIN1	SSCC1	2012-01-07 20:00	1	https://epcis.retailer.com
⑲	SGTIN1	NULL	2012-01-10 10:00	1	https://epcis.retailer.com

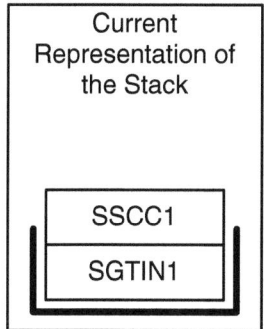 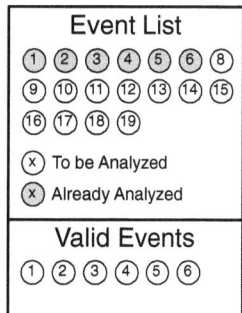

Fig. 5.9 State of the filter algorithm after read event ⑥

line 12 of Listing 5.1 evaluates as false. Consequently, no modifications to the stack are performed and read event ⑨ is discarded.

Read events ⑩ and ⑪ have the action "OBSERVE" with the EPC $SSCC2$. As $SSCC2$ is not stored on the stack, these read events are not added to the list of valid events (line 25 of Listing 5.1 evaluates as false).

The next read event has the action "DELETE" with the parentEPC $SSCC2$. Following line 20 of Listing 5.1 and the fact that $SSCC2$ does not match the topmost element on the stack ($SGTIN1$), the read event ⑫ is discarded. The state of the filter algorithm after read event ⑫ is depicted in Fig. 5.11.

Fig. 5.10 State of the filter algorithm after read event ⑧

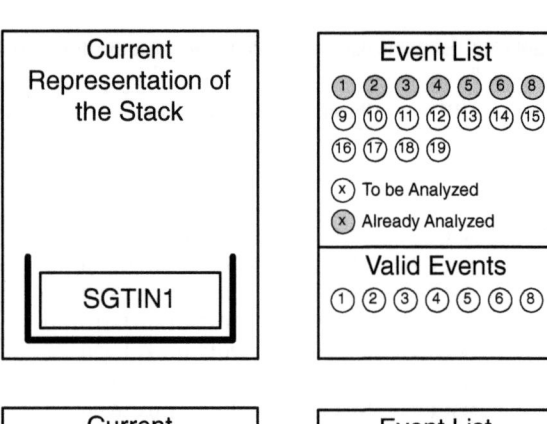

Fig. 5.11 State of the filter algorithm after read event ⑫

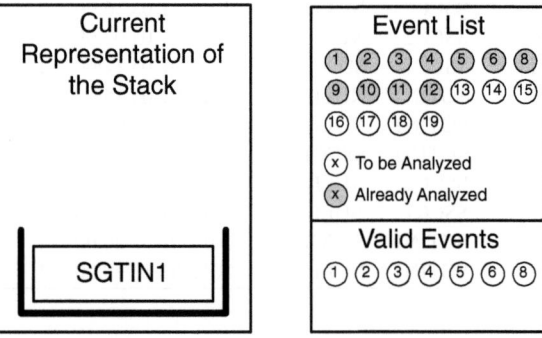

Fig. 5.12 State of the filter algorithm after read event ⑮

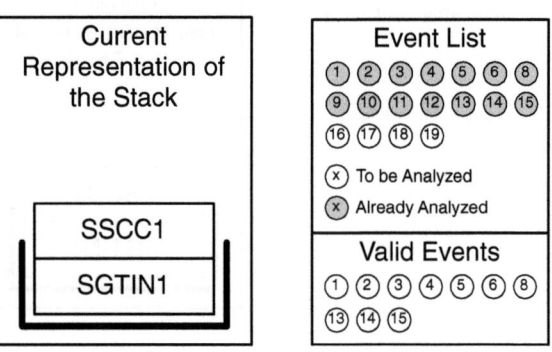

Read events ⑬ and ⑭ have the action "OBSERVE" and the EPC $SGTIN1$. As $SGTIN1$ is stored on the stack, line 25 of Listing 5.1 evaluates as true and the read events are added to the list of valid read events.

The next read event is an AggregationEvent with the action "ADD". As the childEPC of read event ⑮ matches the topmost element on the stack, the parentEPC $SSCC1$ is pushed onto the stack and read event ⑮ is added to the list of valid read events. The state of the filter algorithm after read event ⑮ is shown in Fig. 5.12.

5.4 Handling Interim Re-use of a Box

Fig. 5.13 Final state of the filter algorithm

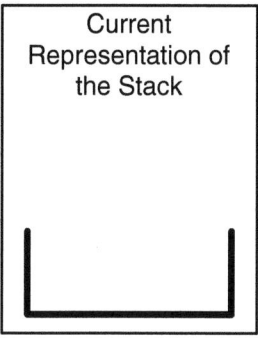
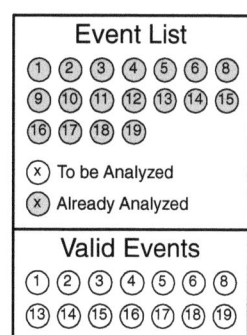

Read events ⑯–⑲ equal the read events ①–④ of the example in the previous section. ⑯ and ⑰ are read events with the action "OBSERVE". They are added to the list as their EPC ($SSCC1$) is stored on the stack. Read event ⑱ is a read event with the action "DELETE". As the parentEPC $SSCC1$ matches the topmost element on the stack, $SSCC1$ is removed and ⑱ marked as a valid read event. The last read event has the action "DELETE". It is an ObjectEvent and the EPC $SGTIN1$ matches the EPC of interest and equals the topmost element on the stack. Thus, $SGTIN1$ is removed from the stack and read event ⑲ is added to the list of valid events. The final state of the filter algorithm is illustrated in Fig. 5.13.

Obviously, the invalid read events ⑨, ⑩, ⑪, and ⑫ were discarded by the filter algorithm and the desired solution set of $\mathbb{L} = \{$①, ②, ③, ④, ⑤, ⑥, ⑧, ⑬, ⑭, ⑮, ⑯, ⑰, ⑱, ⑲$\}$ is returned.

The challenges for the search algorithm that were already discussed with regard to an incomplete read event sequence, also have to be discussed for the filter algorithm. Therefore, the next section is dedicated to discussing situations with missing read events.

5.5 Handling Situations with an Incomplete Read Event Sequence

Just like the search algorithm, the filter algorithm has to be adopted to be able to handle missing read events, too. Thus, the filter algorithm is confronted with the following situations with regard to missing read events:

1. One missing packing read event.
2. One missing unpacking read event.
3. A missing pair of corresponding read events is missing.
4. Various missing corresponding read events.

These situations and the necessary adjustments of the filter algorithm are discussed in the next subsections.

5.5.1 Missing Packing Read Events

In Subsect. 4.5.1, an adjustment of the search algorithm was made to make it more robust with regard to a missing packing event. The same challenge is addressed for the filter algorithm. For readers' convenience, the respective supply chain is shown again in Fig. 5.14. Corresponding example data is provided in Table 5.3. As discussed in Subsect. 4.5.1, the search algorithm returns the event list containing all events.

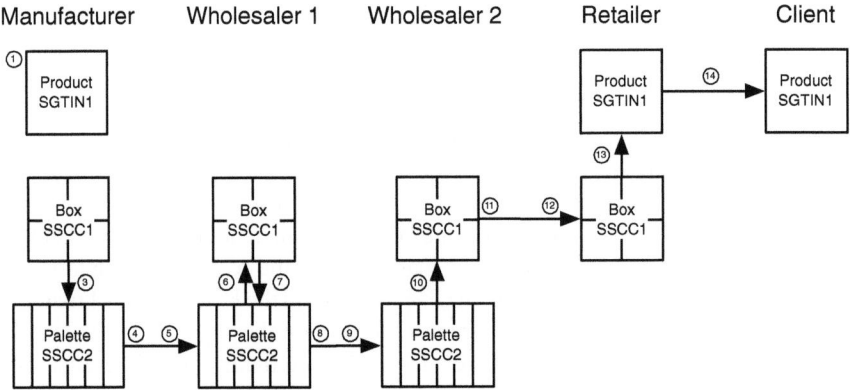

Fig. 5.14 Events to be identified in a common supply chain with a missing packing Aggregation-Event

Table 5.3 Example data that could be stored at the discovery service for the simple supply chain shown in Fig. 5.14

Event	EPC	ParentEPC	Event Time	Action	Repository URI
①	SGTIN1	NULL	2012-01-01 09:00	0	https://epcis.manufacturer.com
③	SSCC1	SSCC2	2012-01-01 10:30	0	https://epcis.manufacturer.com
④	SSCC2	NULL	2012-01-01 12:00	2	https://epcis.manufacturer.com
⑤	SSCC2	NULL	2012-01-03 09:30	2	https://epcis.wholesaler1.com
⑥	SSCC1	SSCC2	2012-01-03 13:00	1	https://epcis.wholesaler1.com
⑦	SSCC1	SSCC2	2012-01-03 13:30	0	https://epcis.wholesaler1.com
⑧	SSCC2	NULL	2012-01-03 16:00	2	https://epcis.wholesaler1.com
⑨	SSCC2	NULL	2012-01-05 07:00	2	https://epcis.wholesaler2.com
⑩	SSCC1	SSCC2	2012-01-05 14:00	1	https://epcis.wholesaler2.com
⑪	SSCC1	NULL	2012-01-06 09:00	2	https://epcis.wholesaler2.com
⑫	SSCC1	NULL	2012-01-07 11:00	2	https://epcis.retailer.com
⑬	SGTIN1	SSCC1	2012-01-07 20:00	1	https://epcis.retailer.com
⑭	SGTIN1	NULL	2012-01-10 10:00	1	https://epcis.retailer.com

Fig. 5.15 Final state of the filter algorithm

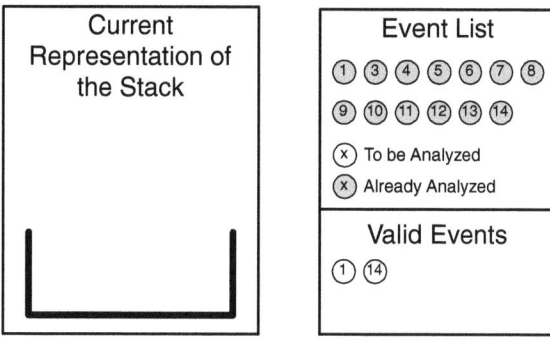

Under these preconditions, the developed filter algorithm (see Listing 5.1) works as follows:

Read event ① has the action "ADD" and the EPC $SGTIN1$, which is the EPC of interest. ① is an ObjectEvent and the EPC matches the EPC of interest. Thus, $SGTIN1$ is pushed onto the stack and ① is added to the list of valid read events (lines 10–11, Listing 5.1).

Read event ③ has the action "ADD". It is an AggregationEvent but the childEPC $SSCC1$ does not match the topmost element on the stack ($SGTIN1$). Therefore, the read event is discarded. The same happens with read events ④–⑬.

Read event ⑭ has the action "OBSERVE". It is an ObjectEvent and the EPC ($SGTIN1$) matches the EPC of interest as well as the topmost element on the stack. Hence, $SGTIN1$ is removed from the stack and read event ⑭ is added to the list of valid read events.

The result of the filter algorithm is illustrated in Fig. 5.15.

Only two out of 14 read events are validated by the filter algorithm. Thus, the filter algorithm has to be adjusted in order to be more robust. The idea is to apply the filter algorithm initially in its current version and, if read events are discarded, also in a reverse manner. The adjusted filter algorithm including the call to the reverse filter algorithm is presented in Listing 5.2. The reverse filter algorithm is shown in Listing 5.3.

The mode of operation of the adjusted filter algorithm and the reverse filter algorithm is shown using the same supply chain with the missing packing event. For readers' convenience, the supply chain is shown again in Fig. 5.16.

As only the end of the filter algorithm was adjusted, I continue where the original filter algorithm stopped: only two out of 14 read events were validated. Therefore, the reverse filter algorithm is called (line 31, Listing 5.2). The input parameters are the original event list containing read events ①, ③–⑬ and the EPC of interest ($SGTIN1$).

In the reverse filter algorithm, the sort order of the event list is inverted and the events are stored in a new list *event_list_desc*. In addition, a new empty list for the filtered read events as well as a new stack are created (line 5–6). The initial state of the reverse filter algorithm is shown in Fig. 5.17.

```
1   AdjustedFilterAlgorithm: Filter all relevant events. If events are
2   discarded, filter additionally in a reverse manner again
3     Input parameters:
4       1. event_list
5       2. epc_of_interest
6     Create a new empty list filtered_events_list to store the filtered events
7     Create a new empty stack hierarchy_stack to dynamically represent the packaging hierarchy of
          EPCs
8     FOR all events in event_list DO
9       IF the action is 'ADD' DO
10        IF it is an ObjectEvent AND the EPC matches the epc_of_interest DO
11          Push the EPC of the current event onto the stack
12          Add the current event to the filtered_events_list
13        ELSEIF it is an AggregationEvent AND the childEPC matches the topmost element on the
              stack DO
14          Push the parentEPC of the current event onto the stack
15          Add the current event to the filtered_events_list
16        END
17      ELSEIF the action is 'DELETE' DO
18        IF it is an ObjectEvent AND the EPC matches the epc_of_interest DO
19          Remove the topmost EPC from the stack
20          Add the current event to the filtered_events_list
21        ELSEIF it is an AggregationEvent AND the parentEPC of the current event matches the
              topmost element on the stack DO
22          Remove the topmost EPC from the stack
23          Add the current event to the filtered_events_list
24        END
25      ELSE /** OBSERVE **/
26        IF the EPC of the current event is stored somewhere on the stack DO
27          Add the current event to the filtered_events_list
28        END
29      END
30
31      IF the number of elements in filtered_event_list is smaller than the number of elements in the
              event_list DO /** at least 1 element was discarded **/
32        Call the reverse_filter_algorithm with the event_list and epc_of_interest
33        Add all returned elements that are not already in the list to filtered_event_list
34      END
35
36      Return the filtered_event_list
37   END
```

Listing 5.2 Adjusted algorithm to retrieve exactly the related read events

5.5 Handling Situations with an Incomplete Read Event Sequence

```
1   ReverseFilterAlgorithm: Filter all relevant events in a reverse
2   manner
3     Input parameters:
4       1. event_list
5       2. epc_of_interest
6     Order the elements in event_list descending by event_time and store them in a new list
          event_list_desc
7     Create a new empty list filtered_events_list to stores the filtered events
8     Create a new empty stack hierarchy_stack to dynamically represent the packaging hierarchy of
          EPCs
9     FOR all events in event_list_desc DO
10      IF the action is 'DELETE' DO
11        IF it is an ObjectEvent AND the EPC matches the epc_of_interest DO
12          Push the EPC of the current event onto the stack
13          Add the current event to the filtered_events_list
14        ELSEIF it is an AggregationEvent AND the childEPC matches the topmost element on the
              stack DO
15          Push the parentEPC of the current event onto the stack
16          Add the current event to the filtered_events_list
17        END
18      ELSIF the action is 'ADD'
19        IF it is an AggregationEvent AND the parentEPC matches the topmost element on the stack
              DO
20          Remove the topmost element from the stack
21          Add the current event to the filtered_events_list
22        ELSEIF it is an ObjectEvent AND the EPC matches the epc_of_interest DO
23          Remove the topmost element from the stack
24          Add the current event to the filtered_events_list
25        END
26      ELSE /** OBSERVE **/
27        IF the EPC of the current event is stored somewhere on the stack DO
28          Add the current event to the filtered_events_list
29        END
30      END
31    END
32    Return the filtered_event_list
```

Listing 5.3 Reverse algorithm to filter exactly the related read events out of the initial event list

Read event ⑭ is an ObjectEvent with the action "DELETE" and the EPC $SGTIN1$, which matches the EPC of interest (see Table 5.3 to comprehend the read event attributes). Thus, line 10 of Listing 5.3 evaluates as true, $SGTIN1$ is pushed onto the stack and read event ⑭ is added to the list of valid read events.

The next read event is ⑬. It also has the action "DELETE" but it is an AggregationEvent. As the childEPC ($SGTIN1$) matches the topmost element on the stack, line 13 of Listing 5.3 evaluates as true. The parentEPC ($SSCC1$) is pushed onto the stack and read event ⑬ is added to the list of valid read events.

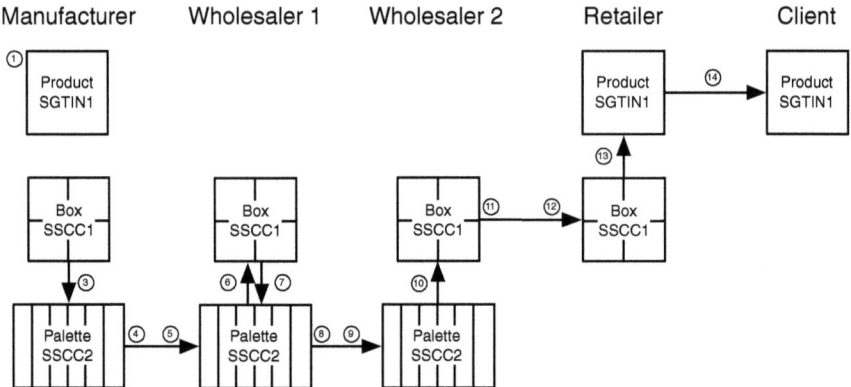

Fig. 5.16 Events to be identified in a common supply chain with a missing packing Aggregation-Event

Fig. 5.17 Initial state of the reverse filter algorithm

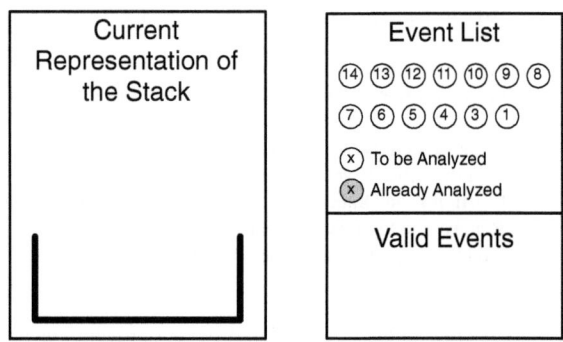

Read events ⑫ and ⑪ have the action "OBSERVE" and the EPC $SSCC1$. As the EPC is stored somewhere on the stack (more precisely, on top of the stack), the read events are added to the list of valid read events.

The next read event has the action "DELETE" again. As it is an AggregationEvent and the childEPC ($SSCC1$) matches the topmost element on the stack, the parentEPC ($SSCC2$) is pushed onto the stack and read event ⑩ is added to the list of valid read events.

Read events ⑨ and ⑧ have the action "OBSERVE" and the EPC $SSCC2$. As the EPC is stored somewhere on the stack, the read events are added to the list of valid read events. The status of the reverse filter algorithm after read event ⑧ is illustrated in Fig. 5.18.

Read event ⑦ has the action "ADD". It is an AggregationEvent and the parentEPC ($SSCC2$) matches the topmost element on the stack. Therefore, according to lines 19–20 of Listing 5.3, the topmost element is removed from the stack and read event ⑦ is added to the list of valid read events.

5.5 Handling Situations with an Incomplete Read Event Sequence

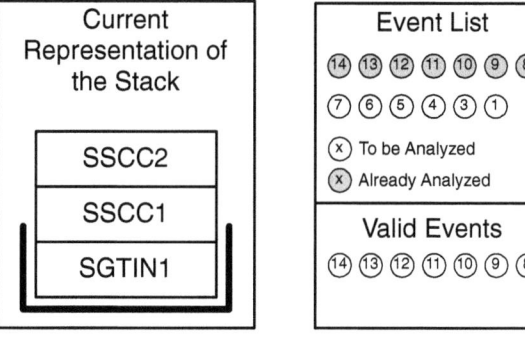

Fig. 5.18 State of the reverse filter algorithm after read event ⑤

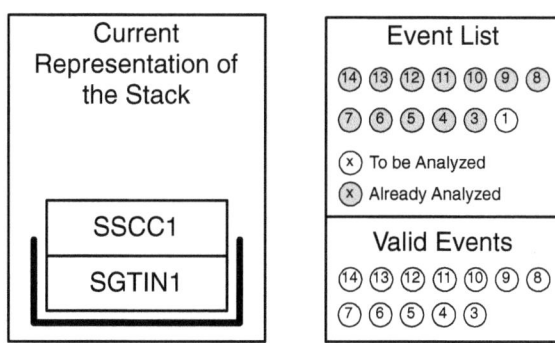

Fig. 5.19 State of the reverse filter algorithm after read event ③

The next read event has the action "DELETE". It is an AggregationEvent and the childEPC ($SSCC1$) matches the topmost element on the stack. Therefore, the parentEPC ($SSCC2$) is pushed onto the stack and read event ⑦ is added to the list of valid read events.

Read events ⑤ and ④ have the action "OBSERVE" and the EPC $SSCC2$. As the EPC $SSCC2$ is stored on the stack, the read events are added to the list of valid read events without any modifications to the stack.

The following read event ③ is an AggregationEvent with the action "ADD". The parentEPC matches the topmost element on the stack. Thus, the topmost element is removed from the stack and read event ③ is added to the list of valid read events. The state of the reverse filter algorithm after read event ③ is shown in Fig. 5.19.

The last read event ① is of type ObjectEvent with the action "ADD" and the EPC $SGTIN1$, which equals the EPC of interest. The topmost element on the stack, however, is $SSCC1$. Thus, read event ① is discarded by the reverse filter algorithm (line 21, Listing 5.3). Consequently, all read events but ① are marked as valid. This result is merged with the *filtered_event_list* of the adjusted filter algorithm. Finally, the desired result that all read events ① and ③–⑭ are identified as valid is reached because ① and ⑭ are identified by the adjusted filter algorithm. Then, ③–⑭ are identified by the reverse filter algorithm.

114   5 A Filter Algorithm to Extract the Relevant Read Events

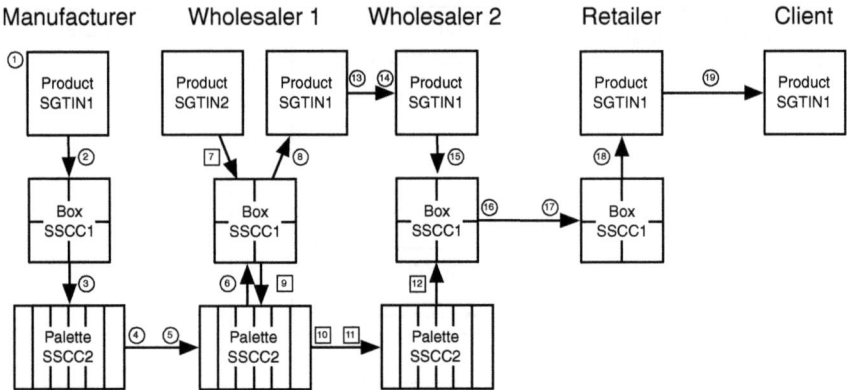

Fig. 5.20 Interim re-use of a box

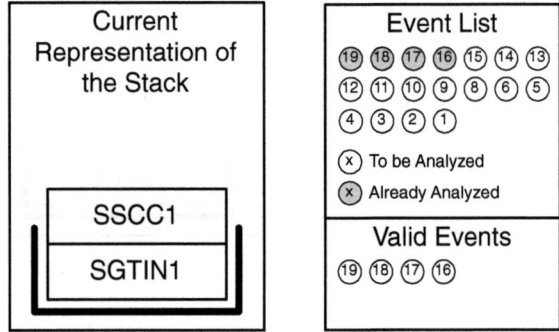

Fig. 5.21 State of the reverse filter algorithm after read event ⑯

Of course, the reverse filter algorithm must not mark invalid read events as valid. Thus, the supply chain with the interim re-use of a box is used again to validate the reverse filter algorithm. For readers' convenience, the supply chain is illustrated in Fig. 5.20 again. The respective table containing the read event attributes is Table 5.2. The mode of operation for read events ⑲–⑯ has already been exemplified with the help of the simple supply chain (see read events ⑭–⑪ there). The state of the reverse filter algorithm after read event ⑯ is depicted in Fig. 5.21.

Read event ⑮ is an AggregationEvent with the action "ADD", the childEPC $SGTIN1$, and the parentEPC $SSCC1$. Given these preconditions and the fact that the parentEPC matches the topmost element on the stack, line 18 in Listing 5.3 evaluates as true. Thus, the topmost element is removed from the stack and the current event is marked as valid.

The next read events ⑭ and ⑬ have the action "OBSERVE" with the EPC $SGTIN1$. As $SGTIN1$ is stored somewhere on the stack, the read events are marked as valid, too. The state of the reverse filter algorithm after read event ⑬ is shown in Fig. 5.22.

5.5 Handling Situations with an Incomplete Read Event Sequence

Fig. 5.22 State of the reverse filter algorithm after read event ⑬

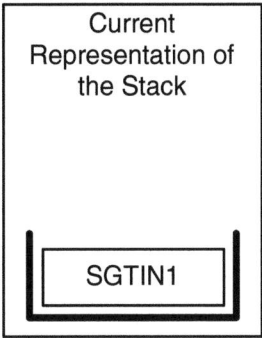
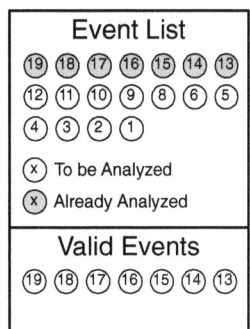

Read event ⑫ has the action "DELETE" and is an AggregationEvent. As the childEPC $SSCC1$ does not equal the topmost element on the stack ($SGTIN1$), the read event is discarded (line 13, Listing 5.3).

Read events ⑪ and ⑩ have the action "OBSERVE" and the EPC $SSCC2$. Given the fact that $SSCC2$ is not stored on the stack, the read events are also discarded (line 26, Listing 5.3).

The last undesired read event has the action "ADD". The parentEPC ($SSCC2$) does not equal the topmost element on the stack ($SGTIN1$). Therefore, the read event ⑨ is discarded (line 18, Listing 5.3).

Read event ⑧ is the next valid read event. It is an AggregationEvent with the action "DELETE". The childEPC $SGTIN1$ matches the topmost element on the stack. Thus, the parentEPC ($SSCC1$) is pushed onto the stack and read event ⑧ is added to the list of valid read events.

The handling of the remaining read events has already been described with the simple supply chain. Finally, all read events but ⑨–⑫ are identified as valid, as intended. As a result, I conclude that the filter algorithm returns valid results for these use cases.

The next challenge is a situation with a missing unpacking read event.

5.5.2 Missing Unpacking Read Events

For readers' convenience, the supply chain with a missing unpacking read event is depicted again in Fig. 5.23. The respective data stored in the discovery service can be found in Table 4.4.

The search algorithm returns all read events ①–⑫ and ⑭. The mode of operation of the adjusted filter algorithm has already been explained up to read event ⑬ in the previous subsection using the simple supply chain. The state after read event ⑬ is shown in Fig. 5.24.

Read event ⑭ has the action "DELETE" and the EPC $SGTIN1$. The EPC matches the EPC of interest but the topmost element on the stack is $SSCC1$. Therefore,

116 5 A Filter Algorithm to Extract the Relevant Read Events

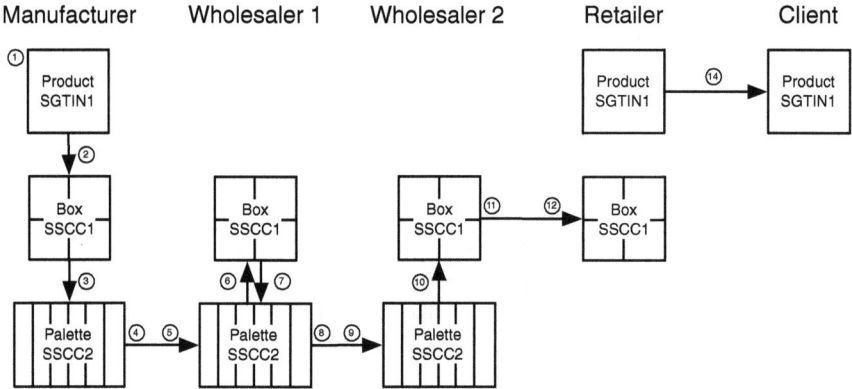

Fig. 5.23 A supply chain with a missing unpacking AggregationEvent

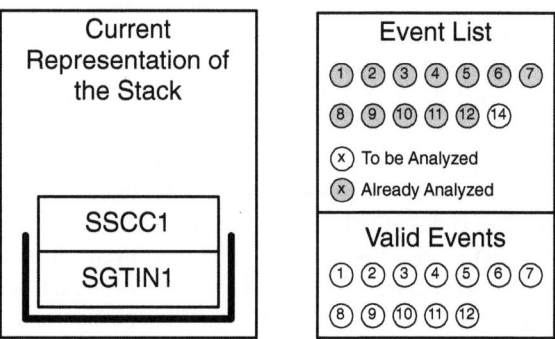

Fig. 5.24 State of the adjusted filter algorithm after read event ⑫

the read event is discarded (line 17, Listing 5.2). The number of events in the *filtered_events_list* is 12. This is less than the 13 events in the initial *event_list*. Thus, the reverse filter algorithm is called (line 31, Listing 5.2). Obviously, the reverse filter algorithm identifies ⑭ to be a valid read event. The read events ⑬–② are marked as invalid. Read event ① however is marked as valid again because it has the action "DELETE", it is an ObjectEvent, its EPC matches the EPC of interest, and the topmost element on the stack matches its EPC. Once the results are merged, all read events are marked as valid because ①–⑫ are identified to be valid by the adjusted filter algorithm and the missing read event ⑭ is validated by the reverse filter algorithm.

5.5.3 A Missing Pair of Corresponding Read Events

When recalling the challenge of missing corresponding read events (see Sect. 4.5.3), I state that the filter algorithm does not have any impact on the result. In the first use case, almost the complete supply chain was cut out. In the second use case, an intermediate pair of read events was missing. As the filter algorithm uses the search algorithms' output as its input, it cannot influence the search algorithms' result. All read events in the second use case for a missing pair of read events would be validated by the adjusted filter algorithm.

5.5.4 Various Missing Corresponding Read Events

The first use case for multiple missing read events affecting different corresponding read events was shown in Fig. 4.13. For readers' convenience, it is repeated in Fig. 5.25. The search algorithm returns read events ①–⑥ as well as ⑪–⑭. The adjusted filter algorithm validates read events ①–⑥. Then, the reverse filter algorithm is called and identifies read events ⑪–⑭ to be valid. Thus, this use case can be handled by the filter algorithms.

The next use case is depicted in Fig. 5.26. It describes a situation with two missing AggregationEvents affecting different hierarchy levels.

The adjusted filter algorithm marks read events ① and ② to be valid. The reverse filter algorithm identifies read event ⑭ as a valid read event. Read events ③–⑫ are discarded. Even though this situation could be handled by the search algorithm, I decide that too many read events are lost in such a situation with the consequence that the read events in the supply chain are not identified to be valid by the filter algorithm. The client only receives a limited number of read events and then could invoke the 'analytical' interface of the discovery service to investigate the cause of the elimination of these read events.

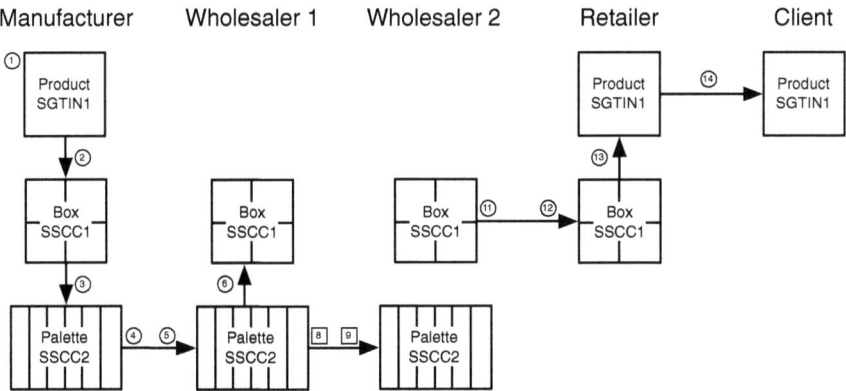

Fig. 5.25 A situation with a missing AggregationEvent pair but the trace can be partly reconstructed

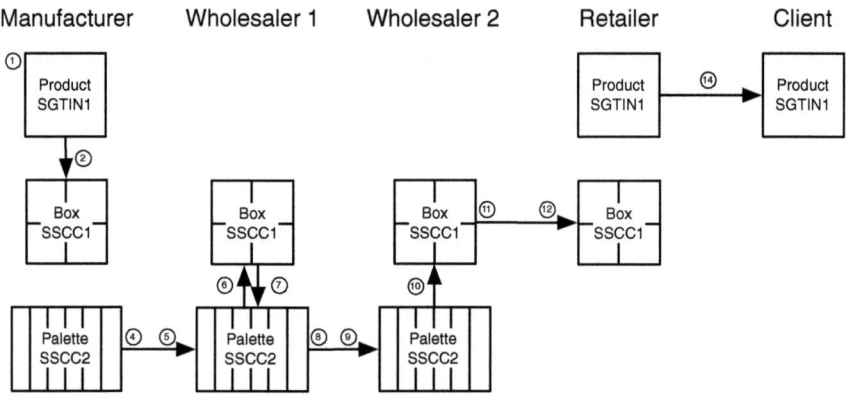

Fig. 5.26 Events in a common supply chain with two missing AggregationEvents affecting distinct pairs

5.6 Critical Discussion of the Filter Algorithm

In this section, I want to conduct a critical discussion with regard to the correctness of the filter algorithm. A central component of the filter algorithm is the stack that represents the packaging hierarchy. Thus, I first show that the stack representation matches the physical changes in packaging hierarchy indicated by the read events. The second vital part of the filter algorithm are the decisions made based on the current status of the stack and the read event attributes. Thus, I discuss these decisions afterwards. These discussions are conducted separately for the adjusted filter algorithm and the reverse filter algorithm.

5.6.1 Leveraging a Stack to Represent the Packaging Hierarchy

The stack has the purpose to dynamically represent the packing hierarchy the item of interest is involved in. The topmost element N on the stack always represents the outermost transport container. The bottommost element 1 of the stack represents the innermost item. Figure 5.27 represents all valid modifications to the stack that can take place. These are discussed in the following.

Prerequisites with Regard to the Stack

Initially, the stack s is empty. The size of the stack is 0:

$$s = \{\emptyset\}$$
$$s.size() = 0$$

5.6 Critical Discussion of the Filter Algorithm

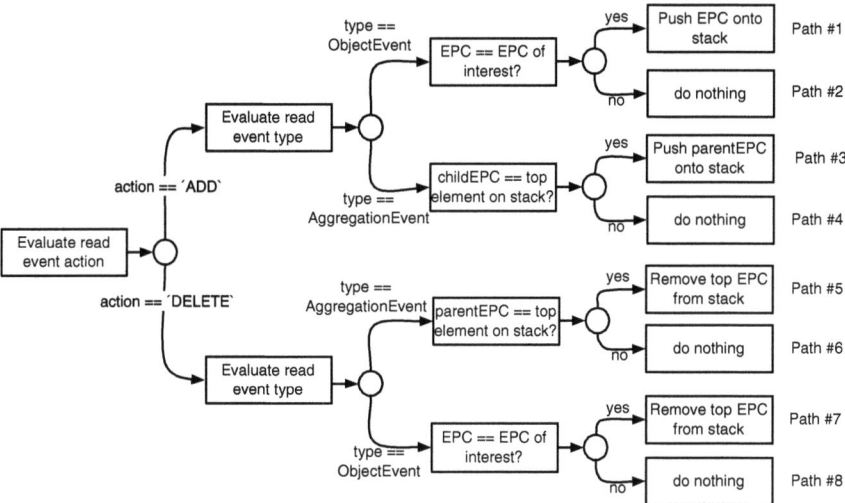

Fig. 5.27 Decision tree with regard to stack modifications

If an element e is added to the stack s, the size of s is increased by 1. For any given element f, the level on the stack can be determined by $s.search(f)$. The bottommost element on the stack has the level 0, the topmost element has the level $s.size() - 1$. If the element f is not stored on the stack, -1 is returned.

All read events that affect the packaging hierarchy have either the action "ADD" or "DELETE". Thus, read events with the action "OBSERVE" are omitted in this discussion.

Path #1 and Path #2

Path #1 in Fig. 5.27 describes a situation happening usually once in the lifecycle of the item of interest: the item is produced and equipped with a unique identifier. The characteristic is that the action equals "ADD", it is an ObjectEvent, and the EPC of the read event matches the EPC of interest. Thus, the EPC of the read event is pushed onto the stack (path #1). If the EPC does not equal the EPC of interest, no change in the stack representation is conducted because the read event does not affect the EPC of interest or related read events (path #2).

Path #3 and Path #4

If the action is "ADD" and it is an AggregationEvent, a potentially relevant packaging event takes place: the currently outermost container or item identified by childEPC is packed into another transport container identified by parentEPC. Of course, such a read event is only relevant if the *childEPC* matches the topmost element on the stack. Otherwise, some random transport container is packed into the transport container identified by *parentEPC*, which is not relevant for the EPC of interest. Applying this to the stack representation, this means that the size of the stack is increased by 1. In addition, the identifier of the new transport container (*parentEPC*) is pushed onto the stack as the topmost element (level $= N$). The prior outermost container identified by *childEPC* is still on the stack at the level $N - 1$ (path #3). If the *childEPC* does not match the top element on the stack, some other item than the currently outermost transport container is packed into a transport container, which is not relevant for the item of interest (path #4).

Path #5 and Path #6

Path #5 describes a situation where the item or transport container at level $N - 1$ is unpacked from the outermost transport container (level $= N$). The action matches "DELETE", it is an AggregationEvent, and the *parentEPC* of the read event matches the topmost element on the stack. Thus, as the stack always represents the current packaging hierarchy, the topmost element is removed from the stack (path #5). If the *parentEPC* of the read event does not match the topmost element on the stack, the read event describes that something is unpacked from any random transport container but not from the transport container the item of interest is associated with (path #6).

Path #7 and Path #8

At the end of it's lifecycle, the item's unique identifier might be destroyed or removed from the supply chain [45, 184]. This is represented by an ObjectEvent with the action "DELETE". Before the stack is modified, two validations take place. If the EPC of the read event does not match the EPC of interest, the read event is not relevant for the stack. If the EPC is not the topmost element on the stack, it has to be unpacked first in order to be removed from the supply chain. If these requirements are fulfilled, the EPC is removed from the stack (path #7). Otherwise, the stack is not modified (path #8).

The status of the stack for the common supply chain used at various places in this dissertation is illustrated in Fig. 5.28. Initially, the stack is empty. Read event ① causes $SGTIN1$ to be pushed onto the stack. $SSCC1$ is pushed onto the stack because of read event ②. After that, $SSCC2$ follows caused by read event ③. $SSCC2$ is removed from the stack by read event ⑥ and added again caused by read event ⑦. Later on, $SSCC2$ is removed again because of read event ⑩. Read event ⑬ causes $SSCC1$ to be removed from the stack. Finally, the remaining element $SGTIN1$ is removed from the stack by read event ⑭.

5.6 Critical Discussion of the Filter Algorithm

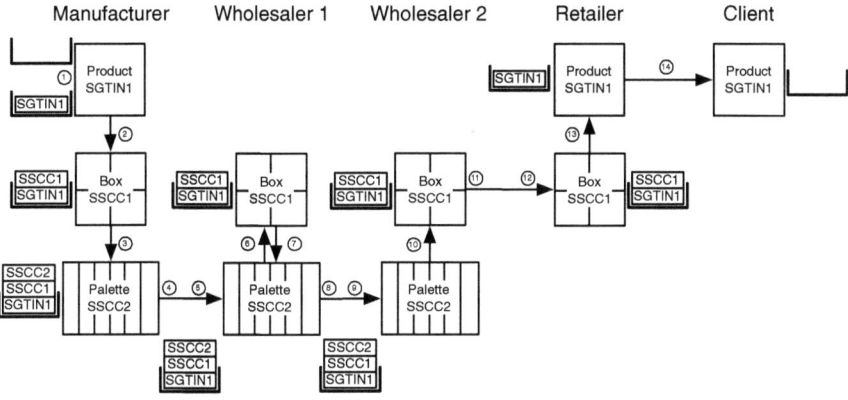

Fig. 5.28 Dynamic representation of the packaging hierarchy by the stack

5.6.2 Discussion of Filter Decisions

Having discussed the behavior of the stack, I continue with how an event is evaluated to be valid or not based on the current status of the stack and the read event attributes. Figure 5.29 shows the decision tree that is implemented by the adjusted filter algorithm.

A read event with the action "ADD" is only valid if it is either an ObjectEvent and the EPC is the EPC of interest (path #1) or it is an AggregationEvent and the childEPC is equal to the topmost element on the stack (path #3). A read event with the action "OBSERVE" is valid if the EPC is stored somewhere on the stack (path #5). A read event with the action "DELETE" is only valid if it is either an AggregationEvent and the parentEPC is equal to the topmost element on the stack (path #7) or it is an ObjectEvent and the EPC is the EPC of interest (path #9).

5.6.3 The Stack for the Reverse Filter Algorithm

The reverse filter algorithm (Listing 5.3) has a different underlying decision tree, which is shown in Fig. 5.30. The changes to the decision tree of the adjusted filter algorithm are marked in bold.

Given the fact that the sequence of read events is inverted, a read event e with the action "ADD" now indicates that a packaging hierarchy did not exist before t(e). Thus, if the $parentEPC$ of e matches the topmost element on the stack s, the top element on the stack has to be removed (path #3). This represents the packaging hierarchy because the $parentEPC$ is the outermost transport container from $t(e)$ onwards. Before $t(e)$, the element at level $s.search(parentEPC)$-1 was the topmost

5 A Filter Algorithm to Extract the Relevant Read Events

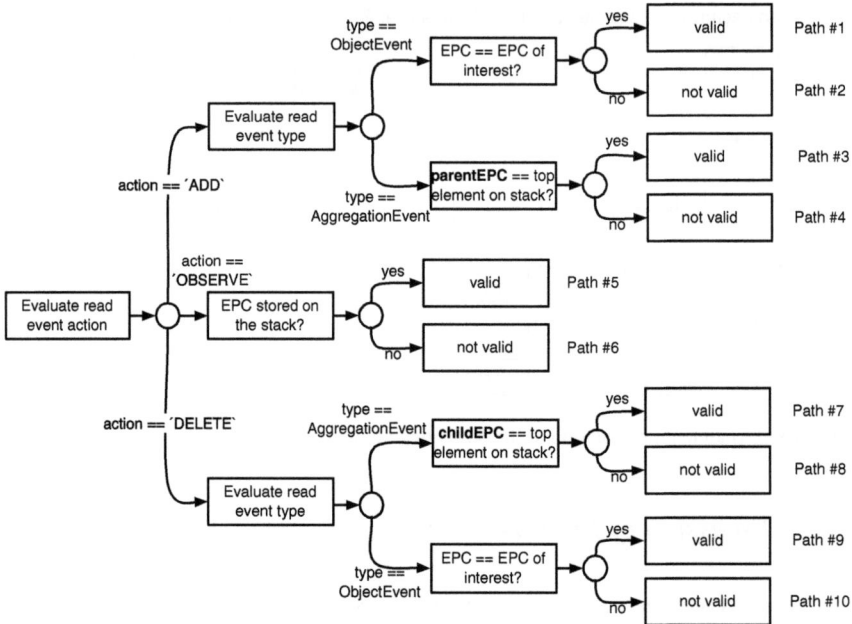

Fig. 5.29 Decision tree with regard to read event evaluations

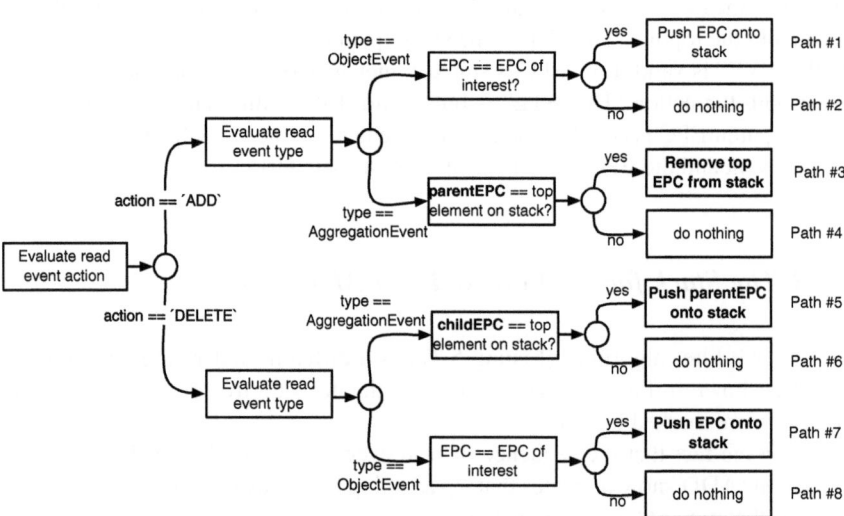

Fig. 5.30 Decision tree for the reverse filter algorithm with regard to stack modifications

5.6 Critical Discussion of the Filter Algorithm

element on the stack. Therefore, in path #3 and #4, the evaluation takes place with the *parentEPC* instead of the *childEPC*.

In addition, path #5 has changed: If the action of an AggregationEvent *ae* is "DELETE" and the *childEPC* matches the topmost element on the stack, the *parentEPC* is pushed onto the stack. The reasoning is analog to the one of path #3. Starting from the point in time where read event *ae* happened, *ae.childEPC* is the topmost element on the stack. When going backwards in time, the packaging hierarchy before $t(ae)$ is relevant for the stack. Before $t(ae)$, *ae.parentEPC* was the topmost element on the stack. Thus, the *parentEPC* is pushed onto the stack. In path #6, the evaluation is conducted with the *childEPC* instead of the *parentEPC*.

The last change occurred at path #7: An ObjectEvent *oe* with the action "DELETE" now results in pushing the respective EPC onto the stack. In the forward algorithm, the EPC was removed in such a constellation. Now, the contrary is conducted and the EPC is pushed onto the stack.

This, again, results in the stack representation depicted in Fig. 5.31. The result is the same but it was created by traversing all read events that are ordered by event time descending.

Initially, the stack is empty. Read event ⑭ results in pushing $SGTIN1$ onto the stack. In addition, $SSCC1$ is pushed onto the stack because of read event ⑬. Read event ⑩ causes $SSCC2$ to be pushed onto the stack. $SSCC2$ is removed from the stack because of read event ⑦ and added again caused by read event ⑥. It is finally removed from the stack given read event ③. Read event ② causes $SSCC1$ to be removed from the stack. Finally, $SGTIN1$ is removed from the stack because of read event ① and leaves an empty stack.

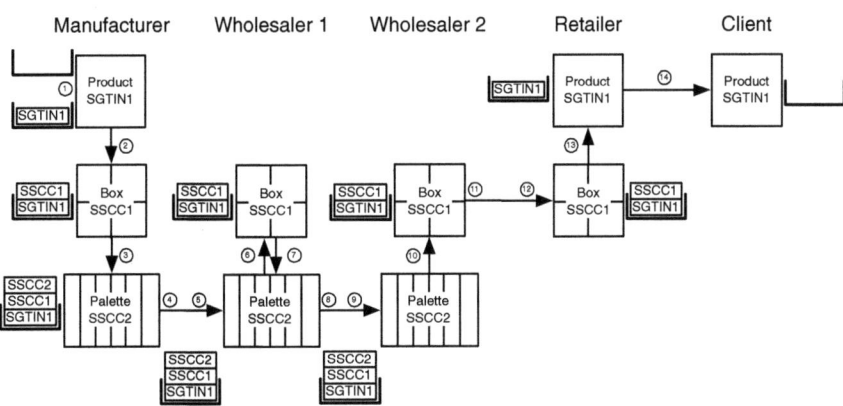

Fig. 5.31 Dynamic representation of the packaging hierarchy by the stack

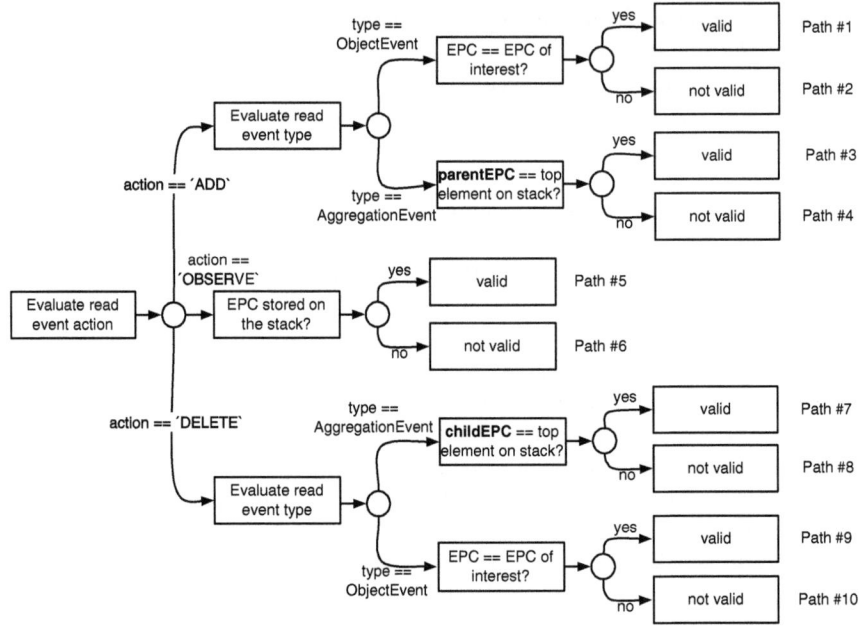

Fig. 5.32 Decision tree with regard to read event evaluations for the reverse filter algorithm

5.6.4 Discussion of Filter Decisions for the Reverse Filter Algorithm

Having discussed the behavior of the stack for the reverse filter algorithm, I continue with how an event is evaluated to be valid or not, based on the current status of the stack and the read event attributes. Figure 5.32 shows the decision tree that is implemented by the reverse filter algorithm.

A read event with the action "ADD" is only valid if it is either an ObjectEvent and the EPC is the EPC of interest (path #1) or it is an AggregationEvent and the parentEPC is equal to the topmost element on the stack (path #3). A read event with the action "OBSERVE" is valid if the EPC is stored somewhere on the stack (path #5). A read event with the action "DELETE" is only valid if it is either an AggregationEvent and the childEPC is equal to the topmost element on the stack (path #7) or it is an ObjectEvent and the EPC is the EPC of interest (path #9).

5.7 Summary

This chapter about the filter algorithm, together with the previous about the search algorithm, answered research question RQ_2: when the discovery service is queried with a unique identifier, it can use the search algorithm first, then apply the filter

5.7 Summary

algorithm and, if necessary, the reverse filter algorithm in order to identify exactly the relevant read events from the discovery service database.

The next chapter is dedicated to describing the system design and implementation considerations with regard to the prototypical implementation of the hierarchical-packaging-aware discovery service.

Chapter 6
System Design and Implementation Considerations

After having described the central concepts of the Hierarchical-Packaging-aware Discovery Service (HPDS), this chapter is dedicated to presenting the system design and implementation considerations. In order to evaluate the theoretical concepts developed in this dissertation, the HPDS is prototypically implemented using Java technology [39, 149]. As a Java servlet container [123], Apache Tomcat is used [183]. SAP HANA is chosen as the database of choice [153].

In the remainder of this chapter, I present the high-level design in Sect. 6.1, refer to bulk loading in Sect. 6.2, the in-memory data management in Sect. 6.3, and present the static structure of the discovery service in Sect. 6.4 as well as the dynamic behavior of the system in Sect. 6.5.

6.1 High-Level Design

The design of the hierarchical-packaging-aware discovery service prototype is depicted in Fig. 6.1.

Read event repositories submit notification messages $n_{re} \in N_{RE}$ about Object-Events $oe \in OE$ and AggregationEvents $ae \in Ae$ to the discovery service D using the *CaptureInterface*. As described in Sect. 6.2, the *Bulk Loading Manager* handles the process of inserting data into the discovery service's *SAP HANA* leveraging bulk loading. To this end, the *Persistency Manager* is used. The interested reader is referred to [153] with regard to in-memory technology. Throughout this thesis, the focus lies on the discovery service. Nevertheless, design decisions are made with the column-oriented in-memory database in mind.

Clients use the *Query Interface* to retrieve lifecycle information or perform last-seen queries about an item of interest. The *Query Interface* forwards the request to the *Hierarchical Packaging Solver* that executes the search algorithm and filter algorithm. After having determined which read event repositories to query for which EPCs, the *Requestor and Response Aggregator* is invoked. This component queries

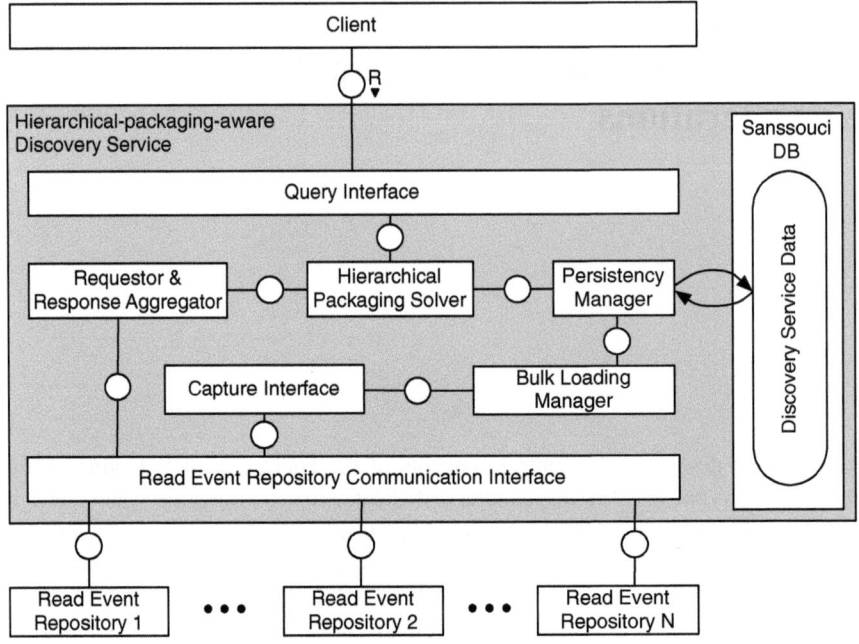

Fig. 6.1 Simplified architecture of the hierarchical-packaging-aware discovery service prototype

the relevant read event repositories. For a legitimate client c_{id}^L, it is assumed that all read events with regard to id are returned by the read event repositories. In contrast, an unauthorized client c_{id}^U would not receive any read events. The *Requestor and Response Aggregator* waits for the read event repository responses and concatenates them. Then, they are forwarded to the *Hierarchical Packaging Solver* and finally returned to the *Client* via the *Query Interface*.

The complexity with regard to notification messages is handled by the *Bulk Loading Manager*. Leveraging bulk loading, notification messages can be loaded in $\mathcal{O}(1)$ into the discovery service (see Sect. 6.2).

The complexity with regard to client queries is dominated by the *Hierarchical Packaging Solver*. It combines the complexity of the search algorithm $\mathcal{O}(|AE_{i\_distinct}^{ADD}|)$ and the filter algorithm $\mathcal{O}(length(event\_list))$.

The filter algorithm is called for each $ae \in AE_{i\_distinct}^{ADD}$ with the event list $event\_list_{ae}$.

Thus, the combined complexity is

$$\mathcal{O}(|AE_{i\_distinct}^{ADD}| + \sum_{j=1}^{|AE_{i\_distinct}^{ADD}|} |event\_list_{ae_j}|).$$

6.2 Bulk Loading Read Events into the Discovery Service

The previous chapters described how the hierarchical-packaging-aware discovery service can be queried. To this end, the communication protocol, search algorithm, and filter algorithm were introduced. On the other hand, data has to be inserted into the discovery service database, first. As stated in Sect. 2.3.2, up to 8,000 notification requests per second arrive at the discovery service. On average, a notification request is related to 2.1 read events. Thus, $8,000 \times 2.1 = 16,800$ event records have to be stored in the database per second, on average. Another requirement stated in Sect. 2.3.2 is that the data published to the discovery service should be visible within a few seconds. Therefore, if a query is stated to the discovery service a few seconds after having published a read event that is associated to that query, the particular read event should be included in the discovery service response.

As stated in the requirements, the notification messages N_{RE} sent to the discovery service need to become visible within a short period of time but not immediately. Thus, having this continuous stream of read events at hand, it makes sense to leverage bulk loading for the respective notification messages. Otherwise, each and every $n_{RE} \in N_{RE}$ would be processed individually, resulting in a complexity of $\mathcal{O}(|N_{RE}|)$.

The involved activities for bulk loading are shown in Fig. 6.2. A legitimate client $c_{id}^L \in C$ sends a notification message n_{re}, which is received by the discovery service D. The message is validated. If no error occurs, the message is decomposed to single event records according to the representation in the data-

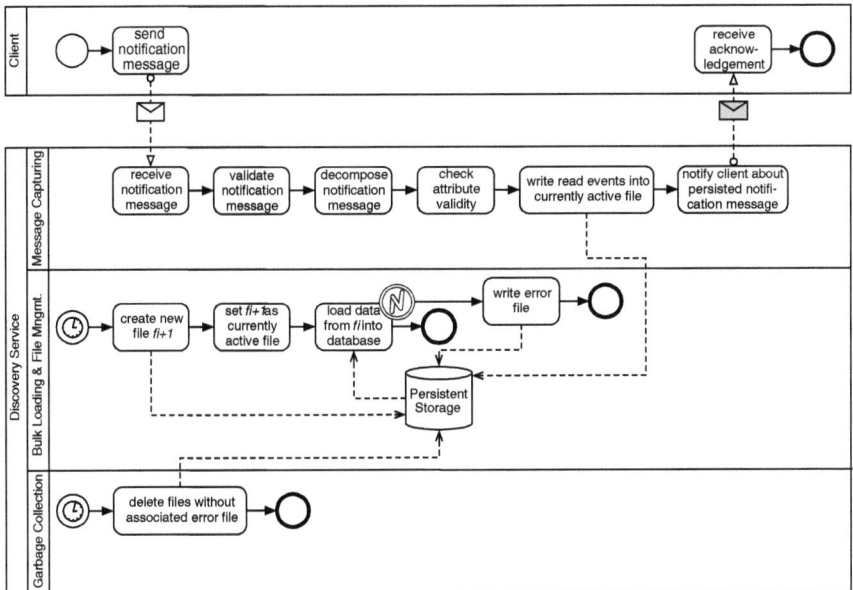

Fig. 6.2 Simplified bulk loading process

base (epc, parent_epc, event_time, action, repository_uri). Then, a validity check on attribute level is conducted. If no error occurs, a row is written to a persistent storage into the currently active file f_i for each read event $re \in RE$. The format could be Comma Separated Values (CSV) or binary. The client is informed that the message is valid and persistently stored.

Every few seconds, a new file f_{i+1} is generated on the persistent storage. The time span that is defined here is an indicator for an upper boundary with regard to notification messages to become visible at the discovery service. Three seconds seems to be a good time span as it fulfills the requirement of near real-time and reduces the load for the discovery service. The new file is set as the currently active file. After that, a command is sent to the database to load the data of the previously active file f_i. In case an error occurs, an error file is written.

Every few hours, all files without associated error file are deleted because they are persistently stored in the database.

With this concept, event records are collected for a short period of time and then inserted via bulk loading. As databases can handle bulk loads efficiently [152], the complexity is reduced to the number of bulk loads, i.e. $\mathcal{O}(1)$. For use in production, I would suggest to add a database management system monitoring component in order to prevent overloading the database in a high-load situation and to make sure that quality goals with regard to query performance are met.

This section answered research question RQ_3 about a reasonable data loading concept: data should be loaded leveraging bulk loading. The disadvantage of read event notifications becoming visible with a few seconds delay is still fulfilling the stated requirements.

6.3 In-Memory Data Management

An engineering-based approach to software development includes estimating factors such as expected data volume and system performance [104]. Thus, this section presents the in-memory data management developed [113, 153] for this discovery service and gives an insight into relevant predictions for the prototypical implementation on data volume in Sect. 6.3.1 and expected query performance in Sect. 6.3.3. Such a discussion can only be conducted with certain target hardware in mind. Therefore, I present the targeted hardware in Sect. 6.3.2. This is followed by a discussion about how to leverage partitioning to increase query performance in Sect. 6.3.4, and finally, considerations about bulk loading performance are presented in Sect. 6.3.5.

6.3.1 Expected Data Volume

A column-orientated database with dictionary compression achieves a good compression rate in most use cases [1, 153, 196]. Dictionary compression belongs to

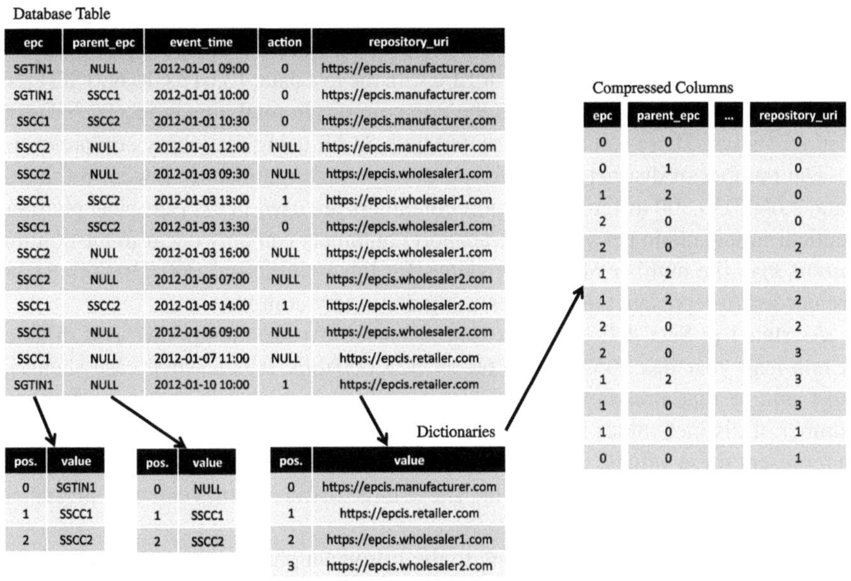

6.3 In-Memory Data Management

Fig. 6.3 Dictionary compression at the discovery service

so called light-weight compression methods [1, 196]. It means that long values are expressed by shorter values [111]. For each distinct value v of a column, a dictionary entry v' is created. Every occurrence of v in the column is replaced by the position of v' in the dictionary [111]. To save space, the position is not explicitly stored. The dictionary is usually sorted to enable searching in $\mathcal{O}(\log(n))$ [153, p. 101]. This dictionary can also be compressed. An example of dictionary compression within the hierarchical-packaging-aware discovery service is given in Fig. 6.3.

This data organization is well-suited for read operations. However, a single write operation can lead to resorting of the complete dictionary. For example, if a tuple with the value $SGTIN0$ for attribute *epc* would be inserted, the dictionary for this column would have to be re-build leading to a dictionary with the following order: $SGTIN0, SGTIN1, SSCC1, SSCC2$. Consequently, all values in the compressed *epc* column would have to be adjusted [153, p. 101.]

In order to avoid frequent costly reorganizations, SAP HANA uses a differential buffer [153, p. 100]. The dictionary of this buffer is unsorted in order to increase insert and update performance [153, p. 39]. Data-changing operations (insert, update, delete) are conducted in the differential buffer [153, p. 100], [102, 103]. From time to time, the differential buffer and the main store are merged [103].

Having given this introduction, I now estimate the data volume for the use case of the European pharmaceutical supply chain. Thus, I estimate the distinct values for each column. All values are based on my supply chain model and the use case of the European pharmaceutical supply chain described in Sect. 1.2. The distinct values are determined for factor 1:100 for 1 year and then extrapolated for factor 1:1 for 1 year.

As 15 billion packages of pharmaceuticals occur in the European pharmaceutical supply chain, the column *epc* will have about 15 billion distinct values plus all transport containers TC that occur as childEPCs. In the test data, 13,613,640,600 SGTINs and 1,989,009,800 SSCCs occur in the *epc* column. In total, this is 15,602,650,400 distinct values. These can be represented with 34 bit using dictionary compression.

The number of distinct values for *parent_epc* are significantly lower. In the test data, 2,060,030,800 different transport containers are used in the European pharmaceutical supply chain per year. As transport containers can only occur in the column *parent_epc*, the number of distinct values for this column is 2,060,030,800. 31 bit are needed to represent these values using dictionary compression.

As stated in Sect. 4.1, the event time consists of year, month, day, and minute. A non-leap year has $365 \times 24 \times 60 = 525{,}600$ min. It is a worst-case scenario but I assume that a read event occurs each and every minute of the year. Thus, the number of distinct values for *event_time* for one year is 525,600. 20 bit are needed to represent these values.

Only three different *action*s occur. These three distinct values can be represented using 2 bits.

About 196,000 companies belong to the European pharmaceutical supply chain. Consequently, about the same number of distinct *repository_uri*s occur. They are encoded using 18 bits.

Table 6.1 gives an overview of the calculations. The first two columns have already been explained. The column 'main store' describes the estimated size of the data in the main store. It is calculated by the number of bits needed to encode the number of distinct values times the total number of event records per year (73.5 bn). The attribute 'parent_epc' is an exception because it is only used for event records belonging to AggregationEvents. Following the test data, about 10 % (= 3.5 billion) of the read events are AggregationEvents. On average, 12 childEPCs are included in one AggregationEvent. Thus, for each AggregationEvent, 12 event records are created on average. The 3.5 billion AggregationEvents result in $3.5\text{bn} \times 12 = 42\text{bn}$ event records.

The calculations for the dictionary assume Universal Character Set Transformation Format – 8-bit (UTF-8) byte character encoding without compression and that all characters in EPCs, actions, and repository URIs only contain US-ASCII characters [26, 202]. Thus, each character can be represented by one byte in the dictionary. For SGTINs, I assume an average length of 44 characters [52]. A SSCCs count up for 34 characters [52]. I assume that a repository URI consists of 40 characters on average. Therefore, the dictionary size is derived from the number of distinct values per column multiplied by the number of characters for the respective values. Further, I assume that the data type *datetime* needs 7 byte to represent the date (4 byte) as well as hour (1 byte), minute (1 byte), and second (1 byte) using 2 packed decimal digits per byte[36]. Even though the second is always set to '00', the space is consumed in the dictionary. Neglecting the compression capabilities of the dictionary, the stated values for the dictionary have to be understood as an upper boundary.

Table 6.1 Data volume by column in the discovery service database (ca. 73.5 bn event records per year)

	Distinct values	Bits needed	Main store size (GB)	Dictionary size	Total size
epc	ca. 15.6 bn	34	ca. 290	ca. 620 GB	ca. 910 GB
parent_epc	ca. 2 bn	31	ca. 220	ca. 60 GB	ca. 280 GB
event_time	ca. 525 k	20	ca. 170	ca. 3 MB	ca. 170 GB
action	3	2	ca. 20	ca. 0 MB	ca. 20 GB
repository_uri	ca. 200 k	18	ca. 150	ca. 10 MB	ca. 150 GB
Total			ca. 850	ca. 680 GB	ca. 1.53 TB

Assuming that all data is stored in the main store, about 1.53 TB of main memory are needed at most to keep all read events for one year in main-memory. The uncompressed data size is about 9.66 TB. Thus, the compression factor is at least 6.3. This section has answered the theoretical part of research question RQ_4: using a column-oriented data store leveraging dictionary encoding, the huge data volume can be reduced to a manageable size.

6.3.2 Target Hardware

The assumption is to store discovery service data of one year in main memory. In enterprise applications, older data can be defined as 'passive' because it is only touched in exceptional situations [153, p. 92]. This also holds true for read events. The database aging strategy is leveraged to store this data persistently on a cheaper storage medium. At the same time, the 'passive' data is still accessible in the exceptional situation that for some reason older data is needed. Data aging is out of the scope of this dissertation. Furthermore, this estimation of hardware is only conducted for the in-memory database. Sizing of application servers, file server etc. is common knowledge and therefore excluded.

Given the fact that 1.53 TB of main memory are needed, I propose to use a common enterprise-class server. It should have 2 TB of main memory. To exploit parallelization [181], I recommend that the system should have eight processors with ten cores each. For each data-modifying access, SAP HANA writes a log file to a persistent storage in order to be able to recover from a system failure [153, p. 137]. This log should be stored on Solid-State Drives (SSD).

The archived data can be stored on SSDs or traditional hard drives. For archiving purposes, SAP HANA's aging mechanism is used [153, p. 92].

If this sizing should become too small, the capacity should be increased by scaling-out the database [162].

6.3.3 Expected Query Performance

The computational complexity of the algorithm is dominated by the search for the respective ObjectEvents and AggregationEvents. Given the presented data structure, the column 'epc' has to be scanned and it has to be determined if 'event_time' is in the range described by the upper and lower boundary. The scan has a complexity of $\mathcal{O}(n)$. When queried, SAP HANA searches for a value in the sorted dictionary in $\mathcal{O}(\log(n))$. After that, it makes a full table scan on the compressed column in $\mathcal{O}(n)$.

By exploiting parallelization, the complexity can be reduced to $\mathcal{O}(\frac{n}{\Phi})$ with Φ being the number of cores available, assuming linear scalability. Using a binary index, the complexity can be reduced to $\mathcal{O}(\log(n))$ [35, p. 286]. Another optimization that is evaluated in the next subsection is partitioning.

6.3.4 Leveraging Partitioning

Two partitioning concepts exist: vertical partitioning [135] and horizontal partitioning [27]. For the present challenge, horizontal partitioning shall be used to split the tuples of the discovery service database table into multiple parts [72]. Partitioning methods frequently used are 'hash', 'round robin', and 'range' [40]. In the search algorithm, only the columns 'epc' and 'event_time' are used as predicates in the SQL query. Thus, these attributes are candidates for partitioning.

Hash Partitioning

Hash partitioning means, that a transformation method f is applied to a value x to transform this value to an integer representation. After that, the modulo operator is applied with the number of partitions Π as the divisor. This results in an index i meaning that the ith partition will be used for this value. Hash partitioning would only make sense for the column 'epc'. A given read event ⊙ with the value ⊙.epc in the epc column would be assigned to a partition as follows:

$$\pi(\odot) = f(\odot.epc) \bmod \Pi$$

Applying hash partitioning on the EPC with $\Pi = \Phi$ number of partitions results in $\frac{n}{\Phi}$ tuples that have to be scanned, resulting in a complexity of $\mathcal{O}(\frac{n}{\Phi})$.

Round Robin Partitioning

Round robin partitioning means that a random starting partition $\pi \in \Pi$ is chosen for the first read event ⊙. The next read event ⊙ will be inserted in partition

6.3 In-Memory Data Management

$$\pi(\odot) = \pi(\bigcirc) + 1 \bmod \Pi$$

and so on. Thus, all tuples are randomly distributed independent of their content. This does not reduce computational complexity because all partitions would have to be scanned in order to retrieve all results for a given item of interest.

Range Partitioning

Range partitioning means that certain value ranges are assigned to a specific partition. It makes sense to use range partitioning for the column 'event_time'. The partition for a event record $\odot$ with $t(\odot)$ describing the 'event_time' of the record would be chosen as follows:

$$\pi(\odot) = \begin{cases} 0 & \text{for } t(\odot) < a \\ 1 & \text{for } a \leq t(\odot) \leq b \\ \ldots & \\ \Pi - 1 & \text{for } t(\odot) > q \end{cases}$$

Usually, the number of partitions would be chosen to be equal to the number of cores available ($\Pi = \Phi$). The number of tuples to be scanned depends on how many partitions are affected by the search query ($= \Omega$). Transport containers and especially returnable transport items are usually used for a long period of time. Thus, pure range partitioning by time is meaningless.

But range partitioning could be used in a setting with multi-dimensional partitioning. First, hash partitioning is applied to the attribute 'epc' of each tuple t to assign it to one of the $\Pi = \Phi$ partitions for the first dimension. In a second step, range partitioning is applied to the attribute 'event_time' of each tuple t. First, a design decision has to be made determining for how many days Θ the events shall be stored in main memory. $\Pi = \Phi$ partitions are created. Each partition stores the data of $\frac{\Theta}{\Phi}$ days. Every $\frac{\Theta}{\Phi}$ days, a new partition is created and the oldest partition is archived. Given the fact that hash partitioning is applied first with $\Pi = \Phi$ partitions, only $\frac{n}{\Phi}$ out of n event records in total have to be considered. As I additionally apply range partitioning, only Ω sub-partitions are affected that can be scanned through using all Φ cores, resulting in a complexity of:

$$\mathcal{O}(\frac{n}{\Phi} \times \frac{\Omega}{\Phi}) = \mathcal{O}(\frac{n \times \Omega}{\Phi^2})$$

In fast moving consumer goods supply chains like the pharmaceutical supply chain, Ω will be very small given the fact that items have a lifespan of weeks or few months from production to consumption. Ω would be high for returnable transport items that are in use for several years but the search algorithm exploits the rather short lifetime of uniquely identified items to reduce the search space with regard to returnable transport items. Thus, I assume that Ω is two on average.

To provide the reader with a better feeling for the computational complexity, I present a back-of-the-envelope calculation based on the European pharmaceutical supply chain scenario. The assumption is that a modern server with eight processors having ten cores each is used ($\Phi = 80$). Furthermore, the discovery service is supposed to store all event records of a rolling horizon comprising one year in memory ($n = 73.5 \times 10^9$; $\Theta = 365$; $\frac{365}{80} = 4.56$ days of data stored per partition).

The runtime is dominated by the number of event records that has to be scanned through, which can be calculated as follows:

$$\frac{n \times \Omega}{\Phi^2} = \frac{73.5 \times 10^9 \times 2}{80^2} = \frac{147 \times 10^9}{6400} = ca.\,23\,\text{million}$$

To get a sense of the time required to do this, I conduct another back-of-the-envelope calculation: 1 core can scan through 1 MB of data in 1 ms [151]. The size of the 23 million event records is equivalent to $23 \times 10^6 \times 34$ bit per event record $= 7.82 \times 10^8$ bit $=$ ca. 93 MB. This sub-partition can be scanned through by one core in ca. 90 ms (omitting the access to the sorted dictionary to identify the integer representation of the unique identifier of the item of interest, which is conducted in $\mathcal{O}(\log(|ER|))$) with $|ER|$ being the number of event records. Theoretically, this could be minimized to $\frac{93}{80} = 1.2$ ms by using all cores for this scan. This has to be conducted for each packaging container that was involved in an item's lifecycle, i.e. three in the simple supply chain example. Thus, I expect that determining all events for an item's lifecycle by scanning through the 'epc' column takes between 3×90 ms $= 270$ ms and 3×1.2 ms $= 3.6$ ms, depending on the parallelization that is exploited. This excludes any additional time to hash the value of the 'epc' column, determine the affected partitions given the range of the 'event_time' of interest, or looking up the unique identifier of the item of interest in the dictionary.

In contrast to this, the approach without partitioning leads to a situation where the whole 'epc' column with its size of 290 GB would have to be scanned through. With the given speed of 1 MB/ms per core, each scan would take between $\frac{290 \times 1024}{1} =$ ca. 5 min for one core and $\frac{290 \times 1024}{1} \times \frac{1}{80} = 3.75$ s leveraging 80 cores.

The approach using an index causes $log_2(|ER|) = log_2(7.35 \times 10^{10}) = 37$ comparison operations. The disadvantage is that the index consumes additional $\mathcal{O}(|ER|)$ space and has to be maintained during insert operations and the merge process [35, p. 484].

Having examined the different approaches, I decide to use the two-dimensional partitioning approach. This inherently answers research question RQ_5 asking how to achieve a desirable query performance.

6.3.5 Expected Bulk Loading Performance

Bulk loading performance is superior to single insert performance [152]. This comes with the disadvantage of more complicated error handling and 'only' near real-time visibility, which is sufficient for the present use case. For the present data schema, single insert performance per instance lies in the order of 8,000 event records per second [152]. In contrast, bulk loading achieves a performance of more than 120,000 tuples per second [152].

In SAP HANA, bulk loading loads the data into the differential buffer [152]. From time to time, the differential buffer has to be merged with the main store [153, p. 103], [103]. However, this is no disadvantage compared to a single insert approach because single inserts also affect the differential buffer and the merge has to be conducted, too.

6.4 Static Structure of the System

The static structure of the Hierarchical-Packaging-aware Discovery Service (HPDS) follows its high-level design overview. The main classes are depicted in Fig. 6.4.

Following the J2EE principles, the client invokes a servlet called *HpdsQueryInterface* to submit a query [123]. This interface accepts client requests, invokes its processing, and sends the response back to the client. To invoke the processing, a reference to the *HierarchicalPackagingSolver* is stored.

The *HierarchicalPackagingSolver* executes the search algorithm as well as the filter algorithm in order to identify all relevant read events. Thus, it holds a reference to an implementation of the *IPersistencyManager* interface. Using an interface instead of a fixed persistency manager allows for replacing one database against another on the fly. This is used for benchmarking different database implementations or versions against each other. In addition, the *HierarchicalPackagingSolver* has a reference to the *EPCISRequestor*.

The *EPCISRequestor*'s duty is to send requests to the identified EPCIS servers in parallel and collect their responses. This implementation is specialized to the EPC Network but technically, any other read event repository with a proper interface could be used as well.

The second servlet is the *CaptureInterface*, which is used by EPCIS servers or alternative systems to send notification messages $n_{RE} \in N_{RE}$ to the discovery service D. Thus, the *CaptureInterface* leverages the *BulkLoadingManager* to insert the read events into the discovery service database.

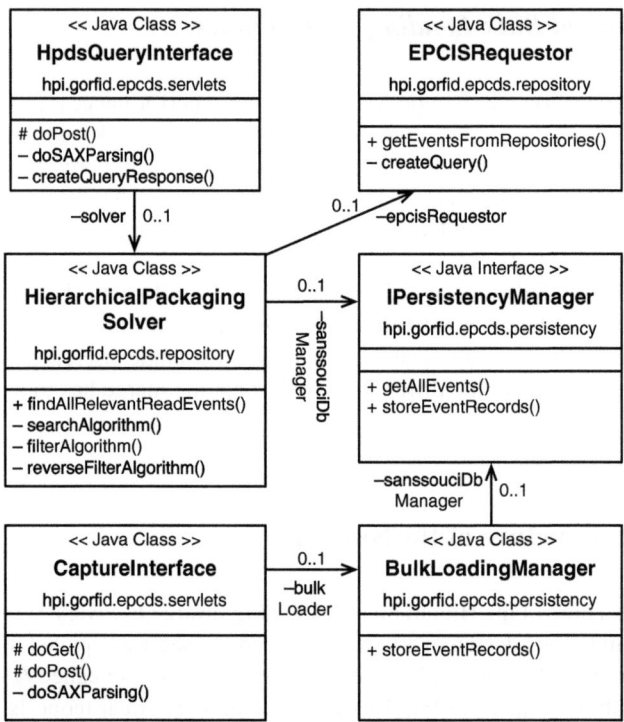

Fig. 6.4 Simplified class diagram of the discovery service

The *BulkLoadingManager*, in turn, holds a reference to an implementation of the *IPersistencyManager*, which is the single point in the discovery service that communicates with the database.

6.5 Dynamic Behavior of the System

In addition to the static structure of the system, its dynamic behavior shall be described in the next subsections. The most interesting use cases are presented. Sect. 6.5.1 shows how notification messages are processed. Lifecycle queries are highlighted in Sect. 6.5.2, last-seen queries in Sect. 6.5.3, and standing queries in Sect. 6.5.4.

6.5.1 Processing Notification Messages

The processing of notification messages N_{RE} is presented in Fig. 6.5 as a UML sequence diagram [139, p. 520]. An *EPCIS Server* or similar component sends the

6.5 Dynamic Behavior of the System 139

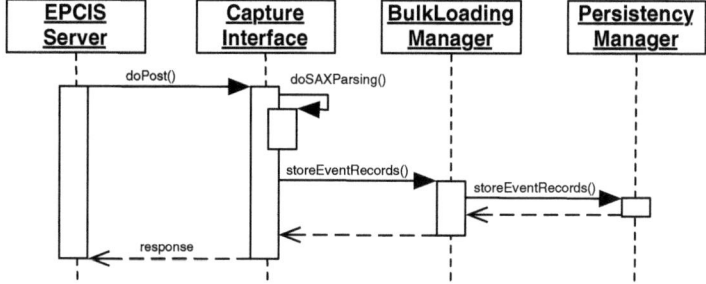

Fig. 6.5 Retrieving and processing notification messages (simplified)

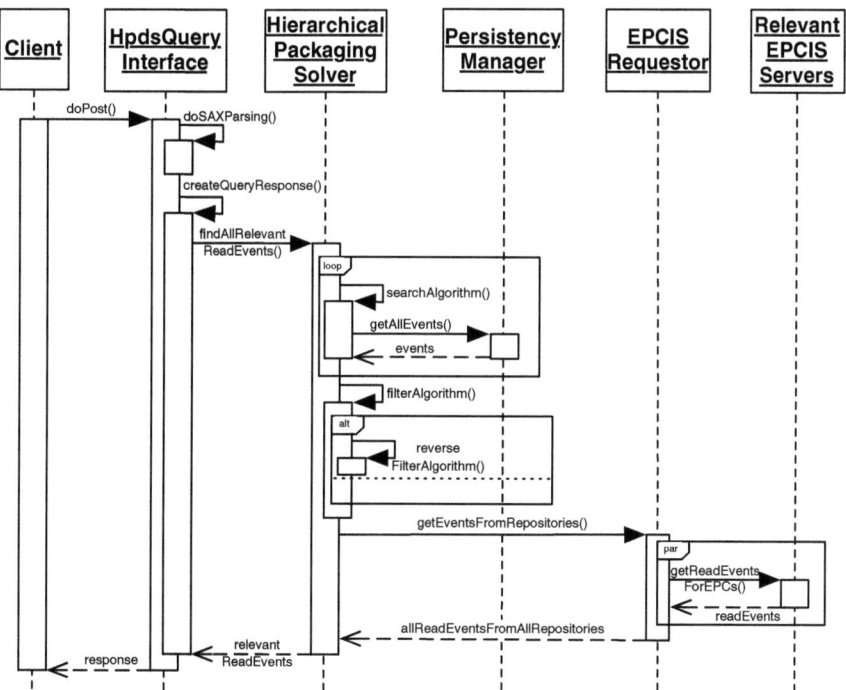

Fig. 6.6 Processing lifecycle queries (simplified)

notification message n_{RE} via a HTTP POST request [63, Sect. 9.5]. The *CaptureInterface* servlet accepts the request. Then, the message is parsed (*doSAXParsing()*) and the read events to be stored are extracted. The *BulkLoadingManager* is invoked in order to store the read events (*storeEventRecords()*). Finally, the *PersistencyManager* receives the event records to be stored and invokes the database to load the event records.

6.5.2 Processing Lifecycle Queries

Lifecycle queries are processed as depicted in Fig. 6.6. A client sends a lifecycle query to the *HierarchicalPackagingAwareDiscoveryServiceQueryInterface (HpdsQueryInterface)* via a HTTP POST request. The message is parsed (*doSAXParsing()*) and the method *createQueryResponse* is called to create the response for the client. While doing so, the *HierarchicalPackagingSolver* is called to find all relevant read events (*findAllRelevantReadEvents*). The *HierarchicalPackagingSolver* invokes the search algorithm (*searchAlgorithm()*), which invokes the message *getAllEvents()* at the *PersistencyManager* in each iteration to submit its SQL query in order to retrieve the event records from the database. After the search algorithm, the filter algorithm (*filterAlgorithm()*) and, if necessary, the reverse filter algorithm (*reverseFilterAlgorithm()*) are called. Next, the *EPCISRequestor* is called to retrieve the read events from the identified EPCIS servers. This is done in parallel for each EPCIS server. The retrieved events are returned to the *HpdsQueryInterface* and the method *createQueryResponse()* includes them in the response to the client.

6.5.3 Processing Last-Seen Queries

Last-seen queries are not implemented in the prototype created throughout this Ph.D. project. Nevertheless, I show how this type of queries would be implemented. For the processing of last-seen queries, two methods are added: In the *HierarchicalPackagingSolver*, a method *findLastRelevantReadEvent()* is created. In the *EPCISRequestor*, the method *getEventFromRepository()* is added. Fig. 6.7 describes the sequence of fulfilling a client's desire to retrieve the last location where an item of interest was observed. Processing last-seen queries happens analog to processing lifecycle queries. The only difference is that the *HierarchicalPackagingSolver* is not called in order to retrieve all relevant read events but only the last read event (*findLastRelevantReadEvent()*). However, since only the last read event is of interest, the search algorithm and filter algorithm(s) have to be invoked as for a lifecycle query. After the algorithms finish, the EPC and EPCIS server of the latest identified event record are used to call the method *getEventFromRepository* at the *EPCISRequestor*, who retrieves a single read event from a single EPCIS server (*getReadEventForEPCs()*). The data about the read events are again returned to the *HpdsQueryInterface* and sent to the client.

6.5.4 Storing and Processing Standing Queries

Processing standing queries is not implemented in the present prototype. However, I show how these kind of queries would be implemented. Standing queries are queries

6.5 Dynamic Behavior of the System

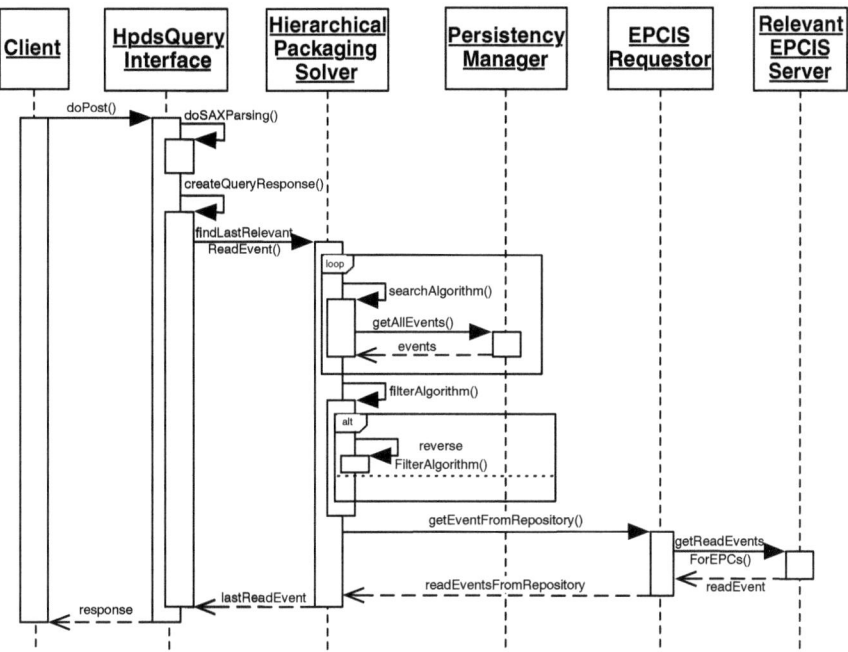

Fig. 6.7 Processing last-seen queries (simplified)

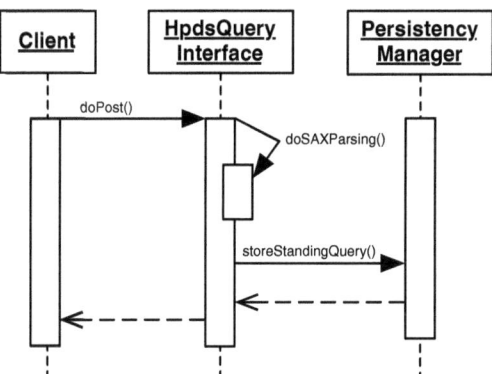

Fig. 6.8 Storing standing queries (simplified)

that are regularly performed. Despite that, they are not different from lifecycle queries or last-seen queries. Thus, the *PersistencyManager* would be extended by a method *storeStandingQuery()* to store standing queries (see Fig. 6.8).

The standing query is executed depending on its defined frequency. To this end, a class *StandingQueryExecutor* is defined, which acts similar to a query interface. It selects a standing query to be executed. Then, all steps are performed to process a lifecycle query or last-seen query, respectively. An example for a lifecycle query is

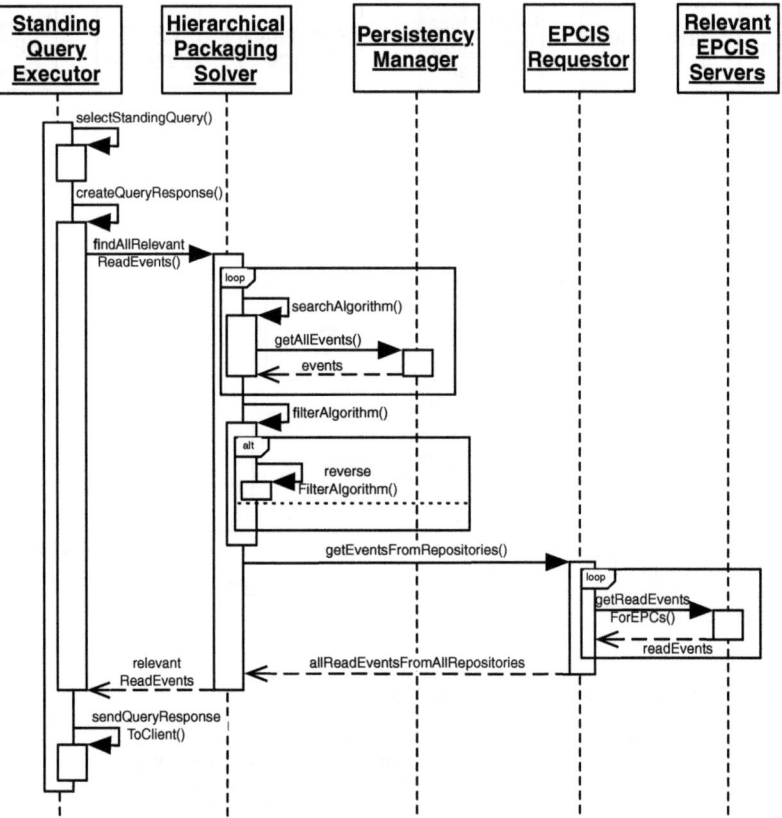

Fig. 6.9 Processing standing queries (simplified)

presented in Fig. 6.9. Finally, the result of the standing query is sent to the callback URI defined in the standing query.

6.6 Summary

This section described how the hierarchical-packaging-aware discovery service was prototypically implemented by describing the high-level design, bulk loading, the in-memory data management, the static structure of the system as well as its dynamic behavior. The next chapter is dedicated to evaluating this prototypical implementation.

Chapter 7
Evaluation

Section 2.3 elicited requirements on a discovery service. Chapters 3, 4, 5 answered all questions except how to ensure performance and scalability for the hierarchical-packaging-aware discovery service. In order to do so, this chapter quantitatively evaluates the prototypical implementation using the realistic test data of the pharmaceutical supply chain.

Performance and scalability of a discovery service can be broken down into the following questions:

1. What is the data volume?
2. What is the notification message performance?
3. What is the query response time and throughput?
4. How would data be distributed when multiple servers are used for a discovery service?

To answer these questions, Sect. 7.1 assesses data volume at the discovery service. Section 7.2 evaluates notification message processing and Sect. 7.3 measures query performance. Section 7.4 describes how the discovery service would scale across multiple servers.

7.1 Data Volume at the Discovery Service

In order to show the feasibility of the hierarchical-packaging-aware discovery service, main memory consumption has to be assessed. Thus, this section evaluates the data volume at the discovery service.

Section 6.3.1 analyzed the upper boundary for main memory consumption of the discovery service. The result was that the discovery service is supposed to consume 1.53 TB at most for all read events in the pharmaceutical supply chain for one year when leveraging columnar storage and dictionary compression. The goal of this assessment is to validate whether the theoretical discussion of main memory consumption is true for a column-oriented in-memory database leveraging dictionary compression.

The hypothesis is that all discovery service data for one year does not consume more than 1.53 TB of main memory when it is loaded into the column-oriented in-memory database that uses dictionary compression, i.e. SAP HANA.

7.1.1 Experiment Setup and Procedure

The server that is used in this experiment is a HP Beta server with eight Intel Nehalem X7560 CPUs with eight cores each running at 2.26 GHz and 2 TB of main memory. SAP HANA as of February 16, 2012 is used.

In this experiment, a subset of the realistic test data described in Sect. 1.2 is loaded into the database. The selected scenarios are:

- Scenario 1:2000, 1 year,
- Scenario 1:1000, 1 year, and
- Scenario 1:100, 1 year.

For this test data, the same calculation as in Sect. 6.3.1 with regard to expected data volume is conducted. This calculated upper boundary is compared to the actual data volume in the database. Having this data at hand, the expected data volume for the pharmaceutical supply chain factor 1:1 for 1 year and factor 1:10 for 1 year is extrapolated. The setup of the experiment is shown in Fig. 7.1.

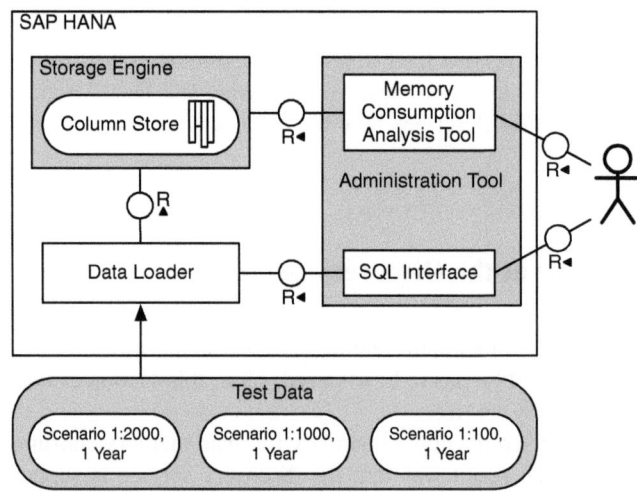

Fig. 7.1 Determining main memory consumption

7.1 Data Volume at the Discovery Service   145

Table 7.1 Data volume by column in the discovery service database, scenario 1:2000, 1 year (32,566,968 event records)

	Distinct values	Bits needed	Main store size (MB)	Dictionary size (MB)	Total size (MB)
epc	ca. 7.5 m	23	ca. 89	ca. 307	ca. 396
parent_epc	ca. 1 m	20	ca. 101	ca. 34	ca. 135
event_time	ca. 525 k	20	ca. 78	ca. 4	ca. 82
action	3	2	ca. 8	ca. 0	ca. 8
repository_uri	97	7	ca. 27	ca. 0	ca. 27
Total			ca. 303	ca. 345	ca. 648

7.1.2 Results

The theoretical calculation of the upper boundary with regard to data volume for scenario 1:2000, 1 year is conducted in Table 7.1. This scenario comprises 32,566,968 event records. The number of distinct values; Bits needed to dictionary encode them; the space this column consumes in the main store; as well as in the dictionary are presented in Table 7.1. In total, this scenario consumes up to 648 MB of main memory. An analogue calculation is conducted for scenario 1:1000, 1 year in Table 7.2. This scenario consumes up to 1.3 GB of main memory.

The calculation for scenario 1:100, 1 year is conducted in Table 7.3. The result is that the upper boundary for main memory consumption is 13.8 GB.

The calculation for scenario 1:10, 1 year is conducted in Table 7.4. The numbers for distinct values and event records are back-of-the-envelope calculations. This upper boundary for this scenario is 149.8 GB.

For readers' convenience, the calculation for scenario 1:1 for 1 year is repeated (see Table 7.5). As described in Sect. 6.3.1, the maximum main memory consumption for the realistic European pharmaceutical supply chain is 1.53 TB.

As indicated in Sect. 6.3.1, additional compression techniques can be used in certain database implementations. Thus, the scenarios 1:2000, 1:1000, and 1:100 for

Table 7.2 Data volume by column in the discovery service database, scenario 1:1000, 1 year (68,108,434 event records)

	Distinct values	Bits needed	Main store size (MB)	Dictionary size (MB)	Total size
epc	ca. 16 m	24	ca. 195	ca. 636	ca. 831 MB
parent_epc	ca. 2 m	21	ca. 170	ca. 79	ca. 249 MB
event_time	ca. 525 k	20	ca. 162	ca. 7	ca. 169 MB
action	3	2	ca. 16	ca. 3	ca. 19 MB
repository_uri	194	8	ca. 65	ca. 0	ca. 65 MB
Total			ca. 608	ca. 725	ca. 1.3 GB

Table 7.3 Data volume by column in the discovery service database, scenario 1:100, 1 year (679,475,785 event records)

	Distinct values	Bits needed	Main store size	Dictionary size	Total size
epc	ca. 156 m	28	ca. 2.2 GB	ca. 6.2 GB	ca. 8.4 GB
parent_epc	ca. 20 m	25	ca. 2 GB	ca. 786 MB	ca. 2.8 GB
event_time	ca. 525 k	20	ca. 1.6 GB	ca. 4 MB	ca. 1.6 GB
action	3	2	ca. 162 MB	ca. 0 MB	ca. 162 MB
repository_uri	ca. 2 k	11	ca. 891 MB	ca. 0 MB	ca. 891 MB
Total			ca. 6.8 GB	ca. 7 GB	ca. 13.8 GB

Table 7.4 Data volume by column in the discovery service database, scenario 1:10, 1 year (ca. 7.2 bn event records)

	Distinct values	Bits needed	Main store size (GB)	Dictionary size Dictionary size	Total size (GB)
epc	ca. 1.6 bn	31	ca. 26	ca. 62 GB	ca. 88
parent_epc	ca. 200 m	28	ca. 23	ca. 7.5 GB	ca. 30.5
event_time	ca. 525 k	20	ca. 17	ca. 4 MB	ca. 17
action	3	2	ca. 1.7	ca. 0 MB	ca. 1.7
repository_uri	ca. 20 k	15	ca. 12.6	ca. 1 MB	ca. 12.6
Total			ca. 80.3	ca. 69.5 GB	ca. 149.8

Table 7.5 Data volume by column in the discovery service database, scenario 1:1, 1 year (ca. 73.5 bn event records)

	Distinct values	Bits needed	Main store size	Dictionary size (GB)	Total size
epc	ca. 15.6 bn	34	ca. 290	ca. 620 GB	ca. 910 GB
parent_epc	ca. 2 bn	31	ca. 220	ca. 60 GB	ca. 280 GB
event_time	ca. 525 k	20	ca. 170	ca. 3 MB	ca. 170 GB
action	3	2	ca. 20	ca. 0 MB	ca. 20 GB
repository_uri	ca. 200 k	18	ca. 150	ca. 10 MB	ca. 150 GB
Total			ca. 850	ca. 680 GB	ca. 1.53 TB

1 year are loaded into an implementation of a column-oriented main memory database with dictionary encoding, i.e. SAP HANA. The scenarios, which are loaded into the database are used to predict larger scenarios 1:10 for 1 year and 1:1 for 1 year. The factor in measured data volume between scenario 1:1000 for 1 year and 1:100 for 1 year is 10.861. This factor is used to extrapolate the data volume in SAP HANA for the scenarios 1:10 and 1:1 for 1 year. For scenario 1:1 for 1 year, this results in a predicted data volume of ca. 602 GB. In comparison with the almost 10 TB of raw data, this is a compression factor of 17. The summarized results of the calculation and the measured data volume is shown in Fig. 7.2. The difference between calculated upper boundary and actual data volume is explained by sophisticated compression techniques that are applied to the main store [1, 111, 159] as well as the dictionary [16]. Compression

7.1 Data Volume at the Discovery Service

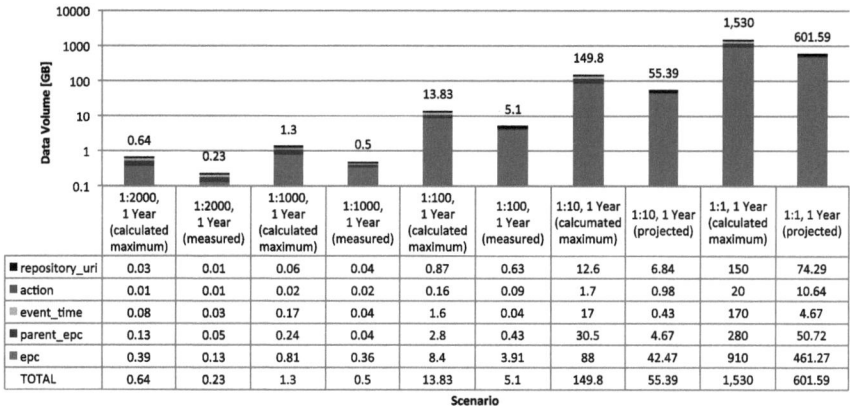

Fig. 7.2 Data volume at the discovery service (summary and extrapolated values)

techniques that can be used are common value suppression [1, 111, 158], run-length encoding [1, 111], cluster coding [111], indirect coding [111], bit compression [160], variable byte coding [171, 187], and patched frame-of-reference [205], among others.

7.1.3 Discussion and Conclusion

Although some parts of this section are based on a back-of-the-envelope calculation, this section answered the practical part of research question RQ_4: using a columnar database leveraging dictionary encoding, the data volume of a large unique identifier network such as the European pharmaceutical supply chain can be reduced to a manageable size.

7.2 Notification Message Processing

The discovery service is required to process up to 8,000 notification messages per second, which result in about 16,800 new event records per second.

The goal of this evaluation is to examine whether the chosen architecture is capable of processing a continuous stream of read events.

The hypothesis is that processing a continuous stream of 8,000 read events per second over a period of two hours of peak time is possible. Thus, the database is supposed to load 16,800 new database tuples per second on average and $16,800 \times 60 \times 60 \times 2 = 120,960,000 = 1.21 \times 10^8$ in total.

7.2.1 Experiment Setup and Procedure

A load process shall take place every three seconds. This results in 2,400 load processes in the 2-h timespan:

$$\frac{2[\text{hours}] \times 60[\frac{\text{seconds}}{\text{minute}}] \times 60[\frac{\text{minutes}}{\text{hour}}]}{3[\frac{\text{seconds}}{\text{loadprocess}}]} = 2,400[\text{load processes}].$$

For each load process, a file with $16,800 \times 3 = 50,400$ event records is prepared for bulk loading in advance. The read events are extracted from the test data set of scenario 1:100, 1 year. These files are stored on a RamDisk to avoid any disturbances caused by hard disk or network [136].

Apache JMeter [130, 182] is used to conduct three operations using the SQL interface of the database:

1. *Bulk Loading*: Every three seconds, bulk loading of the next file is initiated. This instructs a data loader to load the read events, which are stored in a respective file into the discovery service event record table. 32 threads are used to load the data.
2. *Progress Monitoring*: Every three seconds, a query is submitted evaluating how many tuples are currently stored in the database. The timestamp and query result are stored as test results and serve as the basis for the result presentation. Progress monitoring starts two seconds after the initialization of bulk loading.
3. *Merge*: Every 15 min, the merge process is triggered.

The setup of the experiment is shown in Fig. 7.3. The server in this experiment is a HP Beta server with eight Intel Nehalem X7560 CPUs with wight cores each running at 2.26 GHz and 2 TB of main memory. As the database, SAP HANA as of February 16,2012 is used.

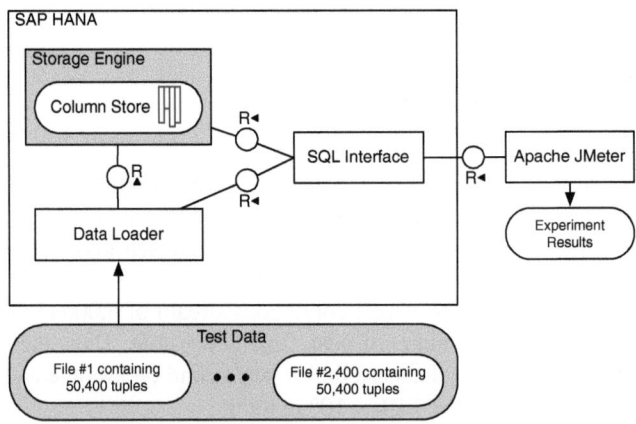

Fig. 7.3 Assessing notification message processing performance

7.2 Notification Message Processing

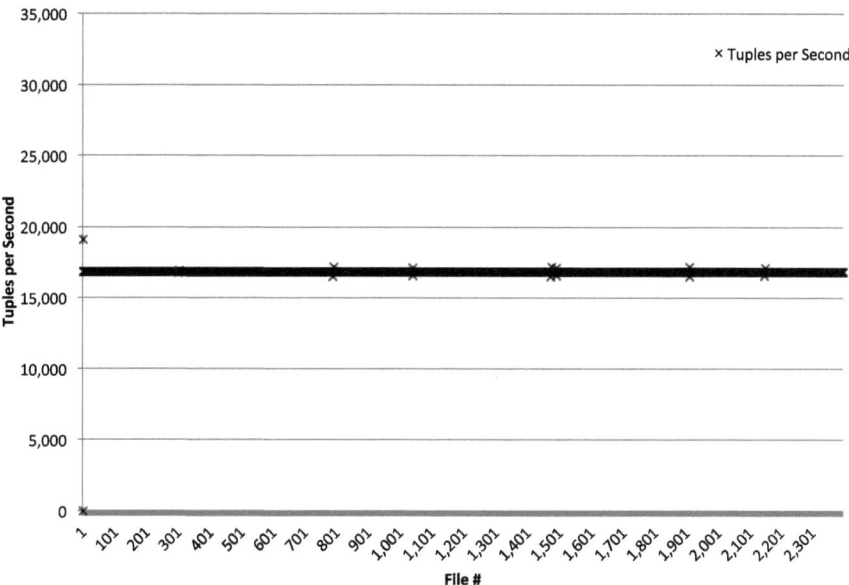

Fig. 7.4 Notification message processing performance

7.2.2 Results

The results are depicted in Fig. 7.4. The axis of the abscissas shows the file number that was processed. This can also be seen as the time elapsed. The axis of ordinates shows number of tuples loaded per second. In the figure, the values for each and every measuring point is shown. For each measurement point, it is calculated how many tuples per second were loaded into the database, i.e. if 50,400 event records were loaded at measurement point i, $\frac{50,400}{3} = 16,800$ is the average throughput for x_i.

The average number of tuples loaded per second is 16,800 with a standard deviation of 22 tuples. The black line at a level of 16,800 consists of many single "x". The loading process could be completed within the 3-s period for 2,393 out of the 2,400 files (99.71 %). In the 0.29 % of the cases where the data could not completely be loaded within the intended time slot, the respective data was loaded in the next time slot, i.e. three seconds later. The average time for a loading process is 474 ms with a standard deviation of 124 ms.

The first two outliers are caused by an initialization effect. The remaining outliers can be justified with the merge process.

7.2.3 Discussion and Conclusion

The experiment was conducted five times. The two best and two worst results are omitted. Quality of the results is judged by standard deviation $\sigma = \sqrt{\frac{1}{N}\sum_{i=1}^{N}(x_i - \mu)^2}$ whereas $\mu = \frac{1}{N}\sum_{i=1}^{N}x_i$ and $N = 2{,}400$. The smaller the standard deviation, the better the result of the experiment.

In a productive setting, the data to be loaded would be stored on a dedicated file server connected to the database server via network technology. This experiment used a RamDisk to avoid disturbances and reduce variance. In the following, it is discussed whether this has an impact on the experiment accuracy. Each of the 2,400 files has a size of about 6 MB. These 6 MB are written to the file server within 3 s and then read within 3 s at most. This leads to a minimum necessary throughput of 2 MB per second, which is no hurdle for today's network technology and performance of persistent storage mediums such as SSDs or traditional hard disks. Throughput of 10 Gigabit network and commercially available SSDs with up to 500 MB/s [85] are sufficient.

The experiment results are as expected: The database is able to load 50,400 database tuples every three seconds on average. As seen in Fig. 7.4, some variance exists, meaning that not all files could be loaded within three seconds. A deeper analysis of the test results showed that the tuples that could not be loaded within the three seconds were always loaded after the next three seconds.

The period of significantly more variance might be caused by internal database re-organization processes like the delta merge [102].

This experiment showed that the necessary discovery service data can be adequately loaded into SAP HANA. This answers the practical part of research question RQ_3 with regard to data loading.

7.3 Query Performance

Query performance is of utmost importance for the desirability of track and trace applications and high throughput is essential from a viability point of view. Thus, this section examines query performance with regard to response time and throughput.

The time from submitting the query to the discovery service to receiving the answer including all relevant read events should be less than one second. This ensures desirability of the service and unrestricted usability, e.g. from mobile devices. Assuming a latency of 20 ms from the client to the discovery service, the slowest read event repository to answer in 460 ms, and a latency of 20 ms back to the client, the discovery service has 500 ms to fulfill a request. This experiment is designed to show whether the HPDS architecture is able to serve clients within this response time while, at the same time, achieving a reasonable throughput.

The hypothesis is that the prototypical implementation of the HPDS has a response time below 500 ms in the 99th percentile, meaning that 99 % of all requests are

7.3 Query Performance

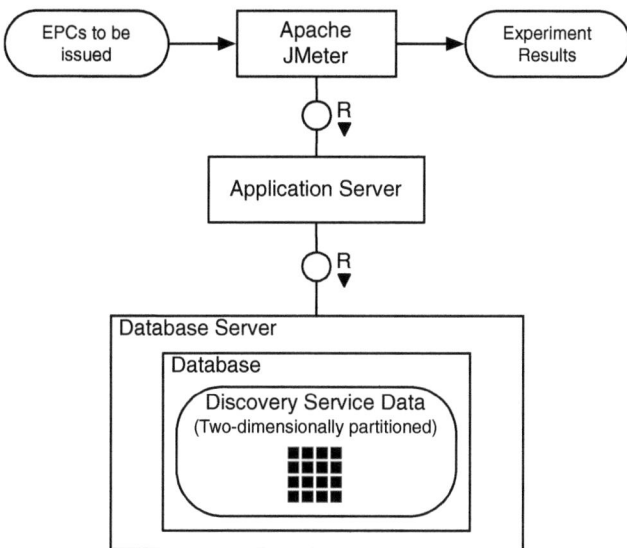

Fig. 7.5 Query performance measurement

processed in less than 500 ms. 1 % of the queries are allowed to violate the 500 ms response time goal.

7.3.1 Experiment Setup and Procedure

For this experiment, the largest test data set is used, scenario 1:100 for 5.5 years. It comprises about 1.9 bn read events and 4 bn event records (see Table 1.1) and consumes approximately 79 GB of main memory when loaded into SAP HANA. The experiment setup is shown in Fig. 7.5. All data is loaded into the discovery service a priori. The EPCs that are included in queries within the loaded scenario are identified and stored in a separate file. During this experiment, these EPCs are issued to the HPDS. Apache JMeter is used to read the EPCs and issue a lifecycle query to the HPDS for each query in the scenario. The HPDS is configured to not query the identified read event repositories. Thus, only the time spent within the HPDS is measured. Furthermore, the HPDS is configured to return the time that was spent for database queries. This time and the total lifecycle query time are stored as experiment results.

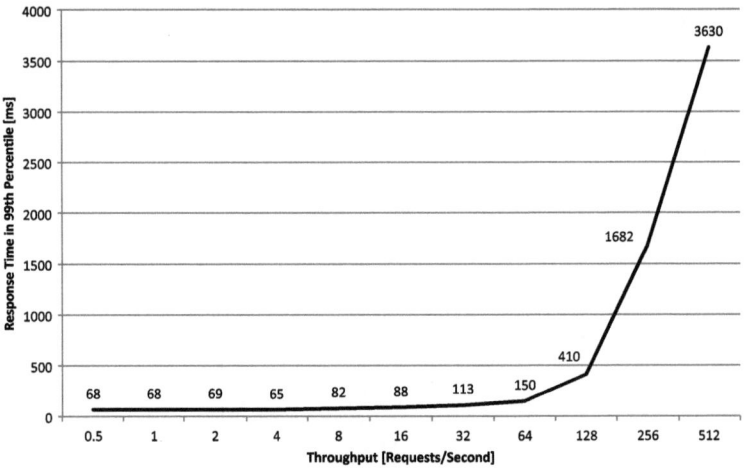

Fig. 7.6 Query performance measurement results

7.3.2 Results

The results are shown in Fig. 7.6. The x-axis shows the throughput, which is gradually increased. The y-axis illustrates the response time in the 99th percentile in ms.

7.3.3 Discussion and Conclusion

The results indicate that a throughput of 128 requests per second can be handled with one database server and one application server. Assuming near-linear scalability and the fact that the current implementation is just a prototype, not more than 20 servers are needed for the complete European pharmaceutical supply chain with 2,000 discovery service queries per second in peak times.

The results of the prototypical implementation show the feasibility with regard to query performance. Thus, this section answered the practical part of research question RQ_5.

The next section evaluates scalability.

7.4 Scalability

Scalability can be achieved by using servers with more resources (scale-up) or using multiple interconnected servers (scale-out) [120].

7.4 Scalability

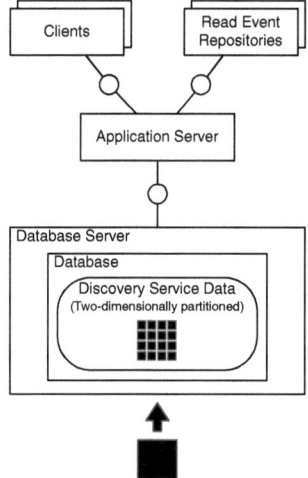

Fig. 7.7 Simplified deployment of a discovery service with one database server and one application server

Figure 7.7 shows a deployment of the discovery service without scale-out.

The data is two-dimensionally partitioned: first, it is hash partitioned by 'epc' and then range partitioned by 'event_time'. Thus, all read events RE are stored in the database server.

Scale-up is handled within a database server, which can store more read events with increasing main memory and increase query processing with an increased number of cores (see Sect. 6.3.4).

Scaling application servers helps handling incoming requests from clients and read event repositories. A load balancer is deployed to distribute the requests across the severs, e.g. by applying a round robin distribution [170]. The discovery service database table is partitioned. The natural choice is to apply the same two-dimensional intra-database partitioning (1. hash partitioned by 'epc', 2. range partitioned by 'event_time') to distribute read events across database servers [17] as presented in Fig. 7.8.

Within a database server, the data is partitioned again using the known partitioning instructions. As a discovery service query only includes 'epc' and 'event_time' in the search condition, a query can be processed by one server without any inter-server communication. Assuming the hash function to evenly distribute 'epc's to database servers, the runtime complexity is reduced from

$$\mathcal{O}\left(\frac{ER \times \Omega}{\Phi^2}\right) \text{ to } \mathcal{O}\left(\frac{\frac{ER}{S} \times \Omega}{\Phi^2}\right)$$

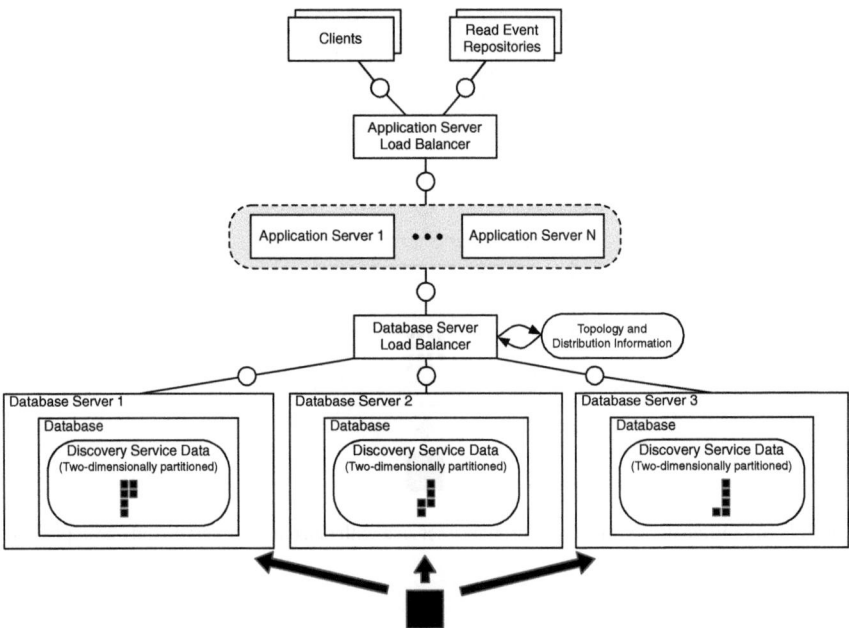

Fig. 7.8 Simplified deployment of a discovery service with multiple database servers and multiple application servers

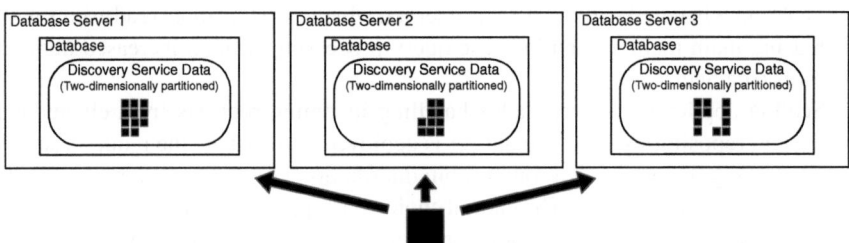

Fig. 7.9 Data replication in a long chain to leverage servers for fail-over and load variations

with $|ER|$ being the number of event records that are stored in the database, S as the number of database servers, Ω representing the number of partitions that are affected by a query, and Φ as the number of available cores.

In order to leverage the different servers for fail-over and load variations, the data can be assigned as follows (see Fig. 7.9, [34]):

1. Server 1 stores all partitions that were previously stored on server 1 and server 2.
2. Server 2 stores all partitions of server 2 and server 3.
3. Server 3 stores all partitions of server 3 and server 1.

7.4 Scalability

That way, a long chain is created, which helps in order to overcome variation of load. This is a modification of the two-flexibility solution to the problem of manufacturing plants that are dedicated to a certain product or product family [91, 173]. Obviously, more main memory is consumed by this data replication. Furthermore, the database load balancer has to be aware of such data replication. A detailed discussion of data placement is a complex topic and out of scope for the present dissertation. Of course the number of servers is not limited to 3. The interested reader is referred to Schaffner et al. [161].

7.5 Summary

This section analyzed the feasibility of the discovery service approach. The result is that the data volume can be significantly reduced by leveraging dictionary compression. Furthermore, unique identifier network data can be loaded fast enough into the discovery service, it can be queried with a sufficient throughput. Finally, the scalability could be confirmed. The next chapter closes this dissertation with a conclusion and directions for future work.

Chapter 8
Conclusion and Future Work

This last chapter gives a conclusion of the present work. I summarize the content of this work in Sect. 8.1 and give an outlook of future work in Sect. 8.2.

8.1 Summary

The thesis started with an introduction, defined key terms, a motivational use case, design science research approach, assumptions, and an outline in Chap. 1.

Chapter 2 presented fundamental technologies as well as related work on discovery services and other approaches.

An overview of the hierarchical-packaging-aware discovery service was given in Chap. 3. In addition, the communication protocol was introduced and exemplified for processing lifecycle queries and last-seen queries.

The search algorithm and its extensions were discussed in Chap. 4. As the search algorithm might return read events that are not belonging to the set of relevant read events, a filter algorithm was introduced in Chap. 5. After these contributions, implementation considerations were presented in Chap. 6.

In Chap. 7, the prototypical implementation was evaluated. The present conclusion closes this thesis. It can be summarized that shortcomings of other discovery service approaches could be overcome by a novel communication protocol, two algorithms to identify relevant read events as well as in-memory data management optimized for this use case.

8.2 Future Work

Future work can be seen in integrating the unique identifier network into established IT infrastructures to profit from the new possibilities.

Furthermore, security is always a huge concern when it comes to sharing data with supply chain partners [94, 163, 165]. This is especially true in "coopetition" situations where companies cooperate with each other but are competitors at the same time [134].

In addition, a benchmark for comparing different implementations of unique identifier network applications such as read event repositories is missing. My contributions [128, 130] could be used as a starting point.

Finally, the concepts described in this work can be applied to further areas of application:

- In the area of supply chain management,
  - recalls could be conducted more effectively and efficiently because with the new discovery service, it can be easily identified where a certain item that is the root cause of the recall was used,
  - participant-spanning supply chain optimization could be realized,
  - supply chain analytics such as supply chain pattern recognition could be run.
- As the presented discovery service approach explicitly integrates changes in hierarchies, this approach could be mapped to Bill Of Material (BOM) problems in the area of asset management. Companies nowadays struggle in keeping track which parts have originally been included in products such as cars, air planes, wind power stations, and so on. Producers of these kind of products must be able to state which parts
  - were planned to be included in the final product (BOM as planned),
  - were actually used in production (BOM as produced),
  - are present in the product right now (BOM as of now),
  - are in the product at any given point in time t (BOM at t).

  The hierarchical-packaging-aware discovery service is suited for these areas of application and could significantly improve bill of material management and open up possibilities in the direction of preventive maintenance applications.
- A more general area of application is the area of complex systems such as aircrafts, electrical generating plants, refineries, and chemical process plants. These systems generate vast amounts of data coming from a variety of sensors and measurements. Currently, small subsets of all the measured data is used for system and process control. As the message capturing component of the discovery service (see Fig. 6.2) is able to process real-time event data, this offers the potential for breakthroughs in control technology.

References

1. D. Abadi, Query execution in column-oriented database systems. Dissertation, MIT, Boston, 2008
2. D. Abadi, P.A. Boncz, S. Harizopoulos, Column oriented database systems. PVLDB **2**, 1664–1665 (2009)
3. Accociation for computing machinery: ACM digital library, http://portal.acm.org. Accessed 1 April 2012
4. Afilias, Afilias discovery services. White paper, 2008
5. Afilias, How Afilias discovery services works. White paper, 2011
6. R. Agrawal, A. Cheung, K. Kailing, Towards traceability across Sovereign, distributed Rfid databases, in *Proceedings of the 10th International Database Engineering and Applications Symposium (IDEAS)*, Dehli, India, pp. 174–184, 2006
7. R. Agrawal, D. Gunopulo, F. Leymann, in *Mining Process Models from Workflow Logs*, ed. by H.-J. Schek, G. Alonso, Saltor, I. Ramos. Advances in Database Technology—EDBT'98 (Springer, Berlin, 1998)
8. R. Agrawal, T. Imielnski, A. Swami, Mining association rules between sets of items in large databases. ACM SIGMOD Rec. **22**(2), 207–216 (1993)
9. J. Al-Kassab, M. Lehtonen, N. Oertel, I. Delchev, Anti-counterfeiting prototypes evaluation report. BRIDGE Project, June, 2009
10. B. Bacheldor, Philip Morris intl. seeks to make serialized bar codes work with EPC network. RFID J. (2007)
11. U. Barchetti, A. Bucciero, M. De Blasi, L. Mainetti, L. Patrono, Implementation and testing of an EPCglobal—aware discovery service for item-level traceability, in *Proceedings of the International Conference on Ultra Modern Telecommunications & Workshops (ICUMT)*, pp. 1–8, 2009
12. S. Beier, T. Grandison, K. Kailing, R. Rantzau, Discovery services—enabling RFID traceability in EPCglobal networks, in *Proceedings of the 13th International Conference on Management of Data (COMAD)*, Dehli, India, 2006
13. W.E. Beller, Y.P. Wang, Bar code dataform scanning and labeling apparatus and method. In US Patent 5,602,377 1997
14. T. Berners-Lee, R.T. Fielding, L. Masinter, Uniform resource identifiers (URI): generic syntax. Internet RFC 2396, August 1998
15. T. Berners-Lee, L. Masinter, M. McCahill, Uniform resource locators (URL) (Network Working Group, The Internet Engineering Task Force, December 1994)
16. C. Binnig, S. Hildenbrand, F. Faerber, Dictionary-based order-preserving string compression for main-memory column stores, in *Proceedings of the 35th SIGMOD International Conference on Management of Data (SIGMOD)*, Providence, Rhode Island, USA, pp. 283–296, June 2009

17. H. Boral, W. Alexander, L. Clay, G. Copeland, S. Danforth, M. Franklin, B. Hart, M. Smith, P. Valduriez, Prototyping Bubba, a highly parallel database system. IEEE Trans. Knowl. Data Eng. **2**(1), 4–24 (1990)
18. C. Bornhövd, T. Lin, S. Haller, J. Schaper, Integrating automatic data acquisition with business processes experiences with SAP's auto-ID infrastructure, in *Proceedings of the 30th International Conference on Very Large Data Bases*, Toronto, Canada, pp. 1182–1188, 2004
19. C. Bowman, P.B. Danzig, D.R. Hardy, U. Manber, M.F. Schwartz, The harvest information discovery and access system. Comput. Netw. ISDN Syst. **28**(1–2), 119–125 (1995)
20. T. Bray, J. Paoli, C. M. Sperberg-McQueen, E. Maler, F. Yergeau, Extensible markup language (XML) 1.0. W3C Recommendation, November 2008
21. D. Brock, The electronic product code (EPC) (White paper, January, 2001)
22. T. Burbridge, M. Harrison, Security considerations in the design and peering of RFID discovery services, in *Proceedings of the IEEE International Conference on RFID*, Orlando, USA, April 2009
23. J. Cantero, M. Guijarro, G. Arrebola, E. Garcia, J. Baos, M. Harrison, T. Kelepouris, Traceability applications based on discovery services, in *Proceedings of the 2008 IEEE International Conference on Emerging Technologies and Factory Automation (ETFA)*, pp. 1332–1337, September 2008
24. J.J. Cantero, M.A. Guijarro, A. Plaza, G. Arrebola, J. Baños, *A Design for Secure Discovery Services in the EPCglobal Architecture*, ed. by D.C.C. Ranasinghe, Q.Z.Z. Shend, S. Zeadally. Unique Radio Innovation for the 21st Century (Springer, Berlin, 2010), pp. 183–201
25. Y. Cao, D. Wang, H. Sheng, PTSP: a lightweight EPCDS platform to deploy traceable services between supply-chain applications, in *Proceedings of the 1st Annual RFID Eurasia Conference*, Istanbul, Turkey, October 2007
26. V. Cerf, ASCII format for network interchange. Internet Engineering Task Force, RFC 20, October 1969
27. S. Ceri, M. Negri, G. Pelagatti, Horizontal data partitioning in database design, in *Proceedings of the 1982 ACM SIGMOD International Conference on Management of Data*, New York, NY, USA, pp. 128–136 (1982)
28. P.P.S. Chen, The entity-relationship model: toward a unified view of data, in *Proceedings of the 1st International Conference on Very Large Data Bases (VLDB)* (ACM, New York, 1975), pp. 173–173
29. E.F. Codd, A relational model of data for large shared data banks. Commun. ACM **13**(6), 377–387 (1970)
30. Commission of the European Communities, *Directive 2001/83/EC of the European Parliament and of the Council on the Community Code Relating to Medicinal Products for Human Use* (Brussels, Belgium, 2001)
31. Commission of the European Communities, *Proposal for a Directive of the European Parliament and of the Council Amending Directive 2001/83/EC as Regards the Prevention of the Entry Into the Legal Supply Chain of Medicinal Products Which Are Falsified in Relation to Their Identity*, History or Source (Brussels, Belgium, 2008)
32. R. Cooley, B. Mobasher, J. Srivastava, Web mining: information and pattern discovery on the world wide web, in *Proceedings of the 9th IEEE International Conference on Tools with Artificial Intelligence (ICTAI)* (IEEE Computer Society, Newport Beach, 1997), pp. 558–567
33. Cooperatives Europe, Co-operative enterprises in the pharmacy sector—opportunities and challenges, Rome, Italy, March 2009
34. G. Copeland, W. Alexander, E. Boughter, T. Keller, Data placement in Bubba, in *Proceedings of the 1988 ACM SIGMOD International Conference on Management of Data (SIGMOD)* (ACM, New York, 1988), pp. 99–108

35. T.H. Cormen, C.E. Leiserson, R.L. Rivest, C. Stein, *Introduction to Algorithms*, 3 edn (The MIT Press, New York, 2009)
36. M. Cowlishaw, Densely packed decimal encoding. IEE Proc. Comput. Digital Tech. **149**(3), 102–104 (2002)
37. F. Curbera, M. Duftler, R. Khalaf, W. Nagy, N. Mukhi, S. Weerawarana, Unraveling the web services web: an introduction to SOAP, WSDL, and UDDI. IEEE Internet Comput **6**(2), 86–93 (2002)
38. B. Cute, M. Young, Finding your way in the internet of things, White paper, September, 2008
39. P. Deitel, *Java: How to Program*, 8 edn. (Pearson Prentice Hall, Upper Saddle River, 2010)
40. D. DeWitt, J. Gray, Parallel database systems: the future of high performance database systems. Commun. ACM **35**, 85–98 (1992)
41. T. Diekmann, A. Melski, M. Schumann, Data-on-Network vs. Data-on-Tag: managing data in complex RFID environments, in *Proceedings of the 40th Annual International Conference on System Sciences (HICSS)*. Big Island, HI, USA, 2007
42. Director Supply Chain Management of a German Sales Company of an International Researching Pharma Company, Interview on the structure of the European pharmaceutical supply chain, 2009
43. D. Engels, *EPC-256: The 256-bit Electronic Product Code Representation* (Auto-ID Center, MIT, Cambridge, 2003)
44. EPCglobal Inc, Discovery Services Standard (in Development). http://www.epcglobalinc.org/standards/discovery,. Accessed on 1 April 2012
45. EPCglobal Inc, EPC Information Services, Version 1.0.1, 2007
46. EPCglobal Inc, Pedigree Ratified Standard Version 1.0, 2007
47. EPCglobal Inc, Application Level Events Version 1.1, 2008
48. EPCglobal Inc, Class 1 Generation 2 UHF Air Interface Protocol Standard Version 1.2.0, 2008
49. EPCglobal Inc, Object Name Service Version 1.0.1, 2008
50. EPCglobal Inc, Architecture Framework Version 1.4, 2010
51. EPCglobal Inc, EPC Radio-Frequency Identity Protocols EPC Class-1 HF RFID Air Interface Protocol for Communications at 13.56 MHz, Version 2.0.3, September 2011
52. EPCglobal Inc, Tag Data Standard Version 1.6, 2011
53. European Commission, Safe innovative and accessible medicines: a renewed vision for the pharmaceutical sector, December 2008
54. European Commission, Directive 2011/62/EU of the European parliament and of the council of 8 June 2011 Amending Directive 2001/83/EC on the community code relating to medicinal products for human use, as regards the prevention of the entry into the legal supply chain of falsified medicinal products, in *Official Journal of the European Union*, pp. 74–87, July 2011
55. European Directorate for the Quality of Medicines; Healthcare, Creation of a live demo of the EDQM track and trace service for medicines, in *Miscellaneous*, 2010
56. European Hospital Healthcare Federation; DEXIA, Hospitals in the 27 member states of the European union. Collection Europe, 2009
57. S. Evdokimov, B. Fabian, S. Kunz, N. Schoenemann, Comparison of discovery service architectures for the internet of things, in *Proceedings of the, IEEE International Conference on Sensor Networks, Ubiquitous, and Trustworthy Computing*. Newport Beach, CA, USA, pp. 237–244, 2010
58. B. Fabian, Secure name services for the internet of things. Dissertation, Humbold-Universität zu Berlin, Berlin, Germany, June 2008
59. B. Fabian, O. Günther, Security challenges of the EPCglobal network. Commun. ACM **52**(7), 121–125 (2009)

60. B. Fabian, O. Günther, S. Spiekermann, Security analysis of the object name service, in *Proceedings of the 1st International Workshop on Security, Privacy and Trust in Pervasive and Ubiquitous Computing (SecPerU)*, (Diavlos Publishing, Santorini Islands, 2005), pp. 71–76, July 2005
61. D.C. Fallside, P. Walmsley, XML Schema Part 0: Primer Second Edition. W3C Recommendation, October 2004
62. U. Fayyad, G. Piatetsky-Shapiro, P. Smyth, From data mining to knowledge discovery in databases. AI Mag. **17**(3), 37–54 (1996)
63. R. Fielding, J. Gettys, J. Mogul, H. Frystyk, L. Masinter, P. Leach, T. Berners-Lee, Hypertext Transfer Protocol—HTTP/1.1, in *RfC (2616)*, 1999
64. R.T. Fielding, Architectural styles and the design of network-based software architectures, Dissertation, University of California, Irvine, California, USA, 2000
65. K. Finkenzeller, *RFID Handbook: Fundamentals and Applications in Contactless Smart Cards, Radio Frequency Identification and Near-Field Communication*, 3rd edn. (Wiley, Chichester, 2010)
66. M.C. Fisk, Toyota Recall Cost to Exceed $2 Billion, Lawyers Say. Bloomberg News, February 9 2010
67. S. Führing, *Interview on the New Legal Requirements Related to the Secure European Pharmaceutical Supply Chain* (Brussels, Belgium, 2009)
68. B. Gilchrist, A. Shenkin, The impact of scanners on employment in supermarkets. Commun. ACM **25**(7), 441–445 (1982)
69. B. Glover, H. Bhatt, *RFID Essentials* (O'Reilly Media Inc, Sebastopol, 2006)
70. E. Grummt, M. Müller, R. Ackermann, Access control: challenges and approaches in the internet of things, in *Proceedings of the IADIS International Conference WWW/Internet 2007*. Vila Real, Portugal, pp. 89–93, October 2007
71. M. Grund, J. Krueger, H. Plattner, A. Zeier, S. Madden, P. Cudre-Mauroux, HYRISE—hybrid main memory storage engine, in *VLDB* 2011
72. M. Grund, J. Krüger, J. Müller, A. Zeier, H. Plattner, Dynamic partitioning for enterprise applications, in *IEEE International Conference on Industrial Engineering and, Engineering Management*, 2011
73. GS1 Australia, Bar Code Technical Details. GS1 Australia, January 2011
74. GS1 US, An Introduction to the Global Trade Item Number. GS1 US, December 2006
75. M.A. Guijarro, G. Arrebola, J.J. Cantero, E. García, F.J. Núñez, J. Baños, M. Harrison, C. Condea, H. Casalprim, Working Prototype of Serial-Level Lookup Service. Public Deliverable of the BRIDGE Project, February 2008
76. S. Haller, S. Karnouskos, C. Schroth, in *The Internet of Things in an Enterprise Context* ed. by D. John, D. Fensel, P. Praverso. Future Internet—FIS 2008 (LNCS 5468, Berlin, 2009), pp. 14–28
77. C.M. Harland, in *Supply Chain Management, Purchasing and Supply Management, Logistics, Vertical Integration, Materials Management and Supply Chain Dynamics* ed. by N. Slack. Blackwell Encyclopedic Dictionary of Operations Management (Blackwell, UK, 1996)
78. M. Harrison, H. Moran, J. Brusey, D. McFarlane, PML server developments, in *White paper*, June 2003
79. S. Helal, N. Desai, V. Verma, L. Choonhwa, Konark-a service discovery and delivery protocol for Ad-Hoc networks, in *Proceedings of the 2003 Wireless Communications and Networking Conference (ECNC)*. IEEE, pp. 2107–2113, March 2003
80. A.R. Hevner, S.T. March, J. Park, S. Ram, Design science in information systems research. MIS Q. **28**(1), 75–105 (2004)
81. L.E. Hicks, *The Universal Product Code* (Amacom, New York, 1975)
82. D. Huang, M. Verma, A. Ramachandran, Z. Zhou, A distributed ePedigree architecture, in *Proceedings of the 11th IEEE International Workshop on Future Trends of Distributed Computing Systems (FTDCS)*. IEEE, Sedona, AZ, USA, pp. 220–230, 2007

References 163

83. A. Iamnitchi, I. Foster, in *On Fully Decentralized Resource Discovery in Grid Environments. Grid Computing—GRID* (Springer, LNCS 2242, Heidelberg, 2001)
84. IEEE computer society, IEEE Portal. http://www.computer.org. Accessed on 1 April 2012
85. Intel, Intel solid-state drive 510 series—product specification. http://www.intel.com/content/www/us/en/solid-state-drives/ssd-510-specification.html, March 2011
86. International Organization for Standardization (ISO), Software Engineering—Product Quality (ISO/IEC 9126-1) 2001
87. International Organization for Standardization (ISO), Data Matrix Bar Code Symbology Specification (ISO/IEC 16022:2006) 2006
88. IP Crime Group, 2008–2009 IP Crime Report 2009
89. IP Crime Group, IP Crime Annual Report 2009–2010 (2010)
90. S.R. Jeffery, M. Garofalakis, M.J. Franklin, Adaptive cleaning for RFID data streams, in *Proceedings of the 32nd International Conference on Very Large Data Bases (VLDB).* VLDB Endowment, Seoul, Korea, pp. 163–174, 2006
91. W.C. Jordan, S.C. Graves, Principles on the benefits of manufacturing process flexibility. Manag. Sci. **41**(4), 577–594 (1995)
92. Y. Kang, H. Jin, Y.H. Lee, A development of traceability services in EPCglobal network environment, in *Proceedings of the 10th Asia Pacific Industrial Engineering and Management Systems Conference (APIEMS).* Kitakyushu, Japan, pp. 1604–1611, December 2009
93. C. Kern, *Anwendung von RFID-Systemen* (Springer, Berlin, 2006)
94. F. Kerschbaum, L. Weiss Ferreira Chaves, Encrypted searchable storage of RFID tracking data, in *Proceedings of the 13th IEEE International Conference on Mobile Data Management (MDM).* Bengaluru, India, July 2012
95. W.R. Killingsworth, K.W. Sullivan, An integrated approach to preventing counterfeits in defense supply chains, in *Diminishing Manufacturing Sources and Material Shortages (DMSMS).* Orlando, FL, USA, September 2009
96. J. Kim, H. Kim, E-Pedigree discovery system and its verification service for consumer's mobile RFID device, in *Proceedings of the 2007 IEEE International Symposium on Consumer Electronics*, pp. 1–4, June 2007
97. KIND InfoService, Directory of pharmaceutical companies in Europe. http://www.pharma-info.com/sites/en/ph_static/ph_en_countries_europe.html,. Accessed on 1 April 2012
98. R.-D. Klein, U. Rohde, Verfahren zur Zweidimensionalen Speicherung von Daten auf einem Bedruckbaren oder Fotografisch Entwickelbaren Medium. Munich, Germany, Patent DE4107020A1, September 1992
99. G. Klyne, C. Newman, Date and Time on the Internet: Timestamps Network Working Group, The Internet Engineering Task Force, July 2002
100. A. Knopfel, B. Grone, P. Tabeling, in *Fundamental Modeling Concepts: Effective Communication of IT Systems* (Wiley, Chichester, 2006)
101. D.E. Knuth, Big Omicron and big Omega and big Theta. SIGACT News **8**(2), 18–24 (1976)
102. J. Krüger, M. Grund, C. Tinnefeld, H. Plattner, A. Zeier, F. Färber, Optimizing write performance for read optimized databases, in *Proceedings of the 15th International Conference on Database Systems for Advanced Applications (DASFAA).* Tsukuba, Japan, 2010, pp. 291–305
103. J. Krüger, M. Grund, J. Wust, A. Zeier, H. Plattner, Merging differential updates in in-memory column store, in *Proceedings of the Third International Conference on Advances in Databases, Knowledge, and Data Applications (DBKDA).* (St. Maarten, The Netherlands Antilles, 2011), pp. 196–201
104. J. Krüger, M. Grund, A. Zeier, H. Plattner, Enterprise application-specific data management, in *Proceedings of the 14th IEEE International Enterprise Distributed Object Computing Conference (EDOC).* Vitória, ES, Brasil, pp. 131–140, October 2010

105. C. Kürschner, C. Condea, O. Kasten, in *Discovery Service Design in the EPCglobal Network*, ed. by C. Flörkemeier, M. Langheinrich, E. Fleisch, F. Mattern, S. Sarma. The Internet of Things, (Springer, Berlin, 2008), LNCS 4952, pp. 19–34
106. S.K. Kwok, S.L. Ting, A.H.S. Tsang, C.F. Cheung, A counterfeit network analyzer based on RFID and EPC. Ind. Manag. Data Syst. **110**(7), 1018–1037 (2010)
107. S. Lahiri, in *RFID Sourcebook* (IBM Press, Upper Saddle River, 2006)
108. D. Laming, *Information Theory of Choice-Reaction Times* (Academic Press, Oxford, 1968)
109. J. L. Le Moulec, J. Madelaine, I. Bedini, Discovery services interconnection, in *Proceedings of the 3rd International Workshop on RFID Technology (IWRT)*. Milan, Italy, pp. 59–68, May 2009
110. G. Lee, J. Shin, D. Park, H. Kwon, Discovery architecture for the tracing of products in the EPCglobal network, in *Proceedings of the IEEE/IFIP International Conference on Embedded and Ubiquitous Computing (EUC)*. IEEE Computer Society, Shanghai, China, pp. 553–558, December 2008
111. C. Lemke, K.-U. Sattler, F. Faerber, Compression techniques for column-oriented BI accelerator solutions, in *Proceedings of the 13. GI-Fachtagung Datenbanksysteme für Business, Technologie und Web (BTW)*. Münster, Germany, pp. 468–497, March 2009
112. B. Liu, W. Hsu, Y. Ma, Integrating classification and association rule mining, in *Proceedings of the 4th International Conference on Knowledge Discovery and Data Mining* (AAAI Press, Menlo Park, 1998), pp. 80–86
113. P. Loos, J. Lechtenbrger, G. Vossen, A. Zeier, J. Krüger, J. Müller, W. Lehner, D. Kossmann, B. Fabian, O. Günther, R. Winter, In-memory Databases in Business Information Systems, in *Business and Information, Systems Engineering*, 6-2011, 2011
114. M. Lorenz, J. Müller, M.-P. Schapranow, A. Zeier, A distributed EPC discovery service based on Peer-to-Peer technology, in *Proceedings of the 7th European Workshop on Smart Objects: Systems, Technologies and Applications (RFID SysTech)*. Dresden, Germany, 2011
115. H. Ma, Distribution design for complex value databases. Dissertation, Massey University, New Zealand, 2007
116. P. Manzanares-Lopez, J.P. Muñoz-Gea, J. Malgosa-Sanahuja, J.C. Sanchez-Aarnoutse, An efficient distributed discovery service for EPCglobal network in nested package scenarios. J. Netw. Comput. Appl. **34**(3), 925–937 (2010)
117. M. Mealling, a uniform resource name namespace for the epcglobal electronic product code (epc) and related standards. The Internet Engineering Task Force: Network Working Group, January 2008
118. A. Melski, J. Müller, A. Zeier, M. Schumann, Assessing the effects of enhanced supply chain visibility through RFID, in *Proceedings of the 14th Americas Conference on Information Systems (AMCIS)*. AIS, Toronto, Canada, pp. 1–12, August 2008
119. A. Melski, J. Müller, A. Zeier, M. Schumann, Improving supply chain visibility through RFID data, in *Proceedings of the 1st IEEE International Workshop on RFID Data Management (RFDM)*. Cancun, Mexico, pp. 102–108, April 2008
120. M. Michael, J.E. Moreira, D. Shiloach, R.W. Wisniewski, Scale-up x Scale-out: a case study using Nutch/Lucene, in *Parallel and Distributed Processing Symposium, International 2007*, p. 441
121. N. Mitra, Y. Lafon, SOAP Version 1.2 Part 0: Primer (Second Edition). W3C Recommendation, April 2007
122. Y. Monden, *Toyota Production System: An Integrated Approach to Just-in-Time*, 3rd edn. (Institute of Industrial Engineers, Norcross, 1998)
123. R. Mordani, *Java Servlet Specification—Version 3.0* (Sun Microsystems, Inc., Santa Clara, 2009)
124. J. Müller, M. Faust, D. Schwalb, M.-P. Schapranow, A. Zeier, H. Plattner, A software as a service RFID middleware for small and medium-sized enterprises, in *Proceedings of the 5th European Workshop on RFID Systems and Technologies (RFID SysTech'09)*, Bremen, Germany, 2009

125. J. Müller, M. Lorenz, F. Geller, M.-P. Schapranow, T. Kowark, A. Zeier, Assessment of communication protocols in the EPC network: replacing textual SOAP and XML with binary google protocol buffers encoding, in *17th IEEE International Conference on Industrial Engineering and Engineering Management (IE &EM)*, Xiamen, China, 2010
126. J. Müller, J. Oberst, S. Wehrmeyer, J. Witt, A. Zeier, H. Plattner, An aggregating discovery service for the EPCglobal network, in *Proceedings of the 43rd Hawaii International Conference on System Sciences (HICSS)*. IEEE Computer Society, Koloa, Kauai, Hawaii, pp. 1–9, January 2010
127. J. Müller, H. Plattner, A Real-Time RFID discovery service for the extended enterprise enabled by in-memory data management (to appear). Int. J. RF Technol 2012
128. J. Müller, C. Pöpke, M. Urbat, A. Zeier, H. Plattner, A simulation of the pharmaceutical supply chain to provide realistic test data, in *Proceedings of the 1st International Conference on Advances in System Simulation (SIMUL)*. IEEE Computer Society, Porto, Portugal, pp. 44–49, September 2009
129. J. Müller, M.-P. Schapranow, M. Helmich, S. Enderlein, A. Zeier, RFID Middleware as a service—enabling small and medium-sized enterprises to participate in the EPC network, in *Proceedings of the 16th International Conference on Industrial Engineering and Engineering Management (IE &EM)*. IEEE Computer Society, Beijing, China, pp. 2040–2043, October 2009
130. J. Müller, M.-P. Schapranow, C. Pöpke, M. Urbat, A. Zeier, H. Plattner, Best practices for rigorous evaluation of RFID software components, in *Proceedings of the 6th European Workshop on Smart Objects: Systems, Technologies and Applications (RFID SysTech)*. VDE Verlag, Cuidad, Spain, pp. 1–10, June 2010
131. J. Müller, R. Tröger, A. Zeier, R. Alt, Gain in transparency versus investment in the EPC network—analysis and results of a discrete event simulation based on a case study in the fashion industry, in *Proceedings of the International Workshop on Service Oriented Computing in Logistics at the 7th International Joint Conference on Service Oriented Computing (ICSOC-ServiceWave)* (Springer, Berlin, 2009), LNCS 6275, Stockholm, Sweden pp. 145–155, 2009
132. J. Müller, M. Uflacker, J. Krüger, M.-P. Schapranow, A. Zeier, noFilis CrossTalk 2.0 as device management solution, experiences while integrating RFID hardware into SAP auto-id infrastructure, in *16th International Conference on Industrial Engineering and Engineering Management (IE &EM)*, Beijing, China, 2009
133. J.P. Muñoz-Gea, J. Malgosa-Sanahuja, P. Manzanares-Lopez, J.C. Sanches-Aarnoutse, Implementation of traceability using a distributed RFID-based mechanism. Comput. Ind. **61**(5), 480–496 (2010)
134. B.J. Nalebuff, A.M. Brandenburger, Co-opetition: competitive and cooperative business strategies for the digital economy. Strategy Leadersh. **25**(6), 28–35 (1997)
135. S. Navathe, S. Ceri, G. Wiederhold, J. Dou, Vertical partitioning algorithms for database design. ACM Trans. Database Syst. (TODS) **9**(4), 680–710 (1984)
136. M. Nielsen, How to use a RAMdisk for Linux. In Linux Gazette (44), August 1999
137. OASIS, Universal Description, Discovery and Integration (UDDI) Version 3.0.2. Organization for the Advancement of Structured Information Standards (OASIS) 2004
138. OASIS, Web Services Dynamic Discovery (WS-Discovery) Version 1.1. Organization for the Advancement of Structured Information Standards (OASIS) 2009
139. Object Management Group, OMG Unified Modeling Language (OMG UML), Superstructure, V2.1.2. November 2007
140. OECD, The Economic Impact of Counterfeiting and Piracy 2008
141. OECD, Magnitude of Counterfeiting and Piracy of Tangible Products 2009
142. D.L. Olson, S. Kesharwani, *Enterprise Information Systems: Contemporary Trends and Issues*. (World Scientific Publishing Company, New Jersey, 2010)
143. Oracle Inc., Java. September 2011
144. Oracle Inc., Stack - java.util.stack, 2011

145. Oversity Ltd., CiteULike. citeulike.org, http://www.citeulike.org/ Accessed on 1 April 2012
146. M.T. Özsu, P. Valduriez, *Principles of Distributed Database Systems*, 2nd edn. (Prentice Hall, Upper Saddle River, 1990)
147. M. Papazoglou, D. Georgakopoulos, Service-oriented computing. Commun. ACM **46**(10), 24–28 (2003)
148. PHOENIX Pharma, PHOENIX Group Annual Report 2003/2004. 2004
149. C. Plain-Jones, Data matrix identification. Sens. Rev. **15**(1), 12–15 (1995)
150. H. Plattner, in *The World is Not Plug and Play: Why Design Will be a Critical Competency for Enterprise Software Providers, Partners, and Customers* ed. by P. Loos, H. Krcmar. Architekturen und Prozesse (Springer, 2007), pp. 3–9
151. H. Plattner, Lecture: complexity of enterprise applications—sequential scanning, in *Trends and Concepts in the Software Industry*, Hasso Platner Institute for IT Systems Engineering, Potsdam, Brandenburg, Germany, July 2010
152. H. Plattner, In-Memory technology, in *6th Annual Symposium on Future Trends in Service-oriented Computing*. Potsdam, Brandenburg, Germany, June 2011.
153. H. Plattner, A. Zeier, *In-Memory Data Management—An Inflection Point for Enterprise Applications* (Springer, Berlin, 2011)
154. E. Polytarchos, S. Eliakis, D. Bochtis, K. Pramatari, in *Evaluating Discovery Services Architectures in the Context of the Internet of Things*, ed. by D.C.C. Ranasinghe, Q.Z.Z. Sheng, S. Zeadally. Unique Radio Innovation for the 21st Century (Springer, Berlin, 2010), pp. 203–227
155. D. Power, Knowledge-driven DSS: what is the "true story" about data mining, beer and diapers? DSS News **3**(23), 1–5 (2002)
156. A. Rezafard, Extensible supply-chain discovery service problem statement. Internet Engineering Task Force, Internet Draft, Work-in-progress, November 2008
157. D. Rosenkranz, M. Dreyer, P. Schmitz, J. Schönborn, P. Sakal, H. Pohl, Comparison of DNSSEC and DNSCurve securing the object name service (ONS) of the EPC architecture framework, in *Proceedings of the 6th European Workshop on Smart Objects: Systems, Technologies and Applications (RFID SysTech)*, VDE Verlag, Cuidad, Spain, pp. 1–6, June 2010
158. M.A. Roth, S.J. Van Horn, Database compression. SIGMOD Rec. **22**(3), 31–39 (1993)
159. D. Salomon, *Data Compression*, 3rd edn. (Springer, New York, 2004)
160. P. Sanders, F. Transier, Intersection in integer inverted indices, in *Proceedings of the Workshop on Algorithm Engineering and Experiments (ALNEX)*. New Orleans, Louisiana, USA, January 2007
161. J. Schaffner, B. Eckart, D. Jacobs, C. Schwarz, H. Plattner, A. Zeier, Predicting in-memory database performance for automating cluster management tasks, in *Proceeding of the 27th International Conference on Data, Engineering (ICDE)*, pp. 1264–1275, April 2011
162. J. Schaffner, D. Jacobs, B. Eckart, J. Brunnert,A. Zeier, Towards enterprise software as a service in the cloud, in Second IEEE Workshop on Information & Software as Services in Conjunction with ICDE 2010, Long Beach, CA, USA, 2010
163. M.-P. Schapranow, Real-time security extensions for EPCglobal networks. Dissertation, Hasso Plattner Institute for IT Systems Engineering, Potsdam, 2012
164. M.-P. Schapranow, J. Müller, S. Enderlein, M. Helmich, A. Zeier, Low-cost mutual rfid authentication model using predefined password lists, in 16th International Conference on Industrial Engineering and Engineering Management (IE&EM). IEEE Computer Society, Beijing, China, pp. 889–893, October 2009
165. M.-P. Schapranow, J. Müller, A. Zeier, H. Plattner, Secure RFID-Enablement in Modern Companies: A Case Study of the Pharmaceutical Industry (to appear). Handbook of Research on Industrial Informatics and Manufacturing, Intelligence 2012

166. M.-P. Schapranow, A. Zeier, F. Leupold, T. Schubotz, Securing EPCglobal object name service—privacy enhancements for anticounterfeiting, in Proceedings of the 2nd International Conference on Intelligent Systems, Modelling and Simulation (ISMS). IEEE Computer Society, Phnom Penh, pp. 332–337, January 2011
167. M.-P. Schapranow, A. Zeier, H. Plattner, A dynamic mutual rfid authentication model preventing unauthorized third party access, in Proceedings of the 4th International Conference on Network and System Security (NSS). IEEE Computer Society, Washington, 2010, pp. 371–176
168. J. Schweim, H. Schweim, Internet pharmacies and counterfeit drugs. Medizinische Klinik **104**(2), 163–169 (2009)
169. A. P. Sheth, J. A. Larson, Federated database systems for managing distributed, heterogeneous, and autonomous databases. ACM Comput. Surv. (CSUR) (Special Issue on Heterogeneous Databases) **22**(3), 183–236 (1990)
170. M. Shreedhar, G. Varghese, Efficient fair queuing using deficit round-robin. IEEE/ACM Trans. Netw. **4**(3), 375–385 (1996)
171. E. Silva de Moura, G. Navarro, N. Ziviani, R. Baeza-Yates, Fast and flexible word searching on compressed text. ACM Trans. Inf. Syst. (TOIS) **18**(2), 113–139 (2000)
172. D. Simchi-Levi, P. Kaminsky, E. Simchi-Levi, *Designing and Managing the Supply Chain: Concepts, Strategies, and Case Studies*, 3rd edn. (McGraw-Hill, Irvine, 2007)
173. D. Simchi-Levi, Y. Wei, Optimality and Supermodularity of the long chain, in *Proceedings of the Manufacturing and Service Operations Management Society Annual Conference* (Ann Arbor, 2011), June 2011
174. A. Smith, F. Offodile, Information management of automatic data capture: an overview of technical developments. Inf. Manag. Comput. Secur **10**(3), 109–118 (2002)
175. K. Solling, L. Masinter, Functional requirements for uniform resource names. IETF, Networking Group, December, 1994
176. Springer, SpringerLink—electronic journals, protocols and books. http://www.springerlink.com, last Accessed 1 April 2012
177. T. Staake, F. Thiesse, E. Fleisch, Extending the EPC network: the potential of RFID in anti-counterfeiting. in *Proceedings of the ACM Symposium on Applied Computing (SAC)*. (ACM, Santa Fe, 2005), pp. 1607–1612
178. State of California, Senate Bill No. 1307: wholesalers and manufacturers of dangerous drugs and devices April 2004
179. H. Stockman, Communication by means of reflected power. Proc. IRE **36**(10), 1196–1204 (1948)
180. J. Sun, H. Zhao, K. Wang, H. Zhang, G. Hu, in *Design and Implementation of an Enterprise Internet of Things* ed. by T. Kim, H.-K. Kim, M. Khan, A. Kiumi, W. Fang, D. Slezak. *Communications in Computer and Information Science: Advances in Software Engineering* (Springer, Berlin, 2010), pp. 254–263
181. H. Sutter, The free lunch is over: a fundamental turn toward concurrency in software. Dr. Dobb's J. **30**(3), 202–210 (2005)
182. The Apache Foundation, Apache JMeter. http://jmeter.apache.org. last Accessed 1 April 2012
183. The Apache Software Foundation, Apache Tomcat. September 2011
184. F. Thiesse, C. Floerkemeier, M. Harrison, F. Michahelles, C. Roduner, Technology, standards, and real-world deployments of the EPC network. IEEE Internet Comput. **13**(2), 36–43 (2009)
185. F. Thompson, Extensible supply-chain discovery service commands, Version 4. Internet Engineering Task Force, Draft, Work-in-progress, 2008
186. F. Thompson, Extensible supply-chain discovery service schema, Version 4. Internet Engineering Task Force, Draft, Work-in-progress, 2008
187. F. Transier, Algorithms and data structures for in-memory text search engines. PhD thesis, University of Karlsruhe, 2010

188. University of Cambridge; AT4 Wireless; BT Research; SAP Research: High level design for discovery services. Public deliverable of the BRIDGE project, August 2007
189. University of Cambridge; AT4 Wireless; BT Research; SAP Research; ETH Zurich; GS1 UK: Requirements document of serial level lookup service for various industries. Public deliverable of the BRIDGE project, August 2007
190. M. Urbat, Designing EPCBench—a benchmark for the EPCglobal network. Master Thesis, Potsdam, Brandenburg, Germany, March, 2011
191. M. Van Alstyne, E. Brynjolfsson, S. Madnick, Why not one big database? ownership principles for database design. Decis. Support Syst. **15**(4), 267–284 (1995)
192. W. Van der Aalst, B. van Dongen, J. Herbst, L. Maruster, G. Schimm, A.J.M.M. Weijters, Workflow mining: a survey of issues and approaches. Data Knowl. Eng. **47**, 237–267 (2003)
193. W. Van der Aalst, T. Weijters, L. Maruster, Workflow mining: discovering process models from event logs. Knowl. Data Eng. **16**(9), 1128–1142 (2004)
194. Z. Wang, D. Chen, M. Du, J. Le, A novel RFID event data integration approach via EPC network, in *Proceedings of the IEEE International Conference on Intelligent Computing and Intelligent Systems (ICIS)*. IEEE, pp. 289–292, 2010
195. J. Webster, R.T. Watson, Analyzing the past to prepare for the future: writing a literature review. Manag. Inf. Syst. Q. **26**(2), 13–23 (2002)
196. T. Westmann, D. Kossmann, S. Helmer, G. Moerkotte, The implementation and performance of compressed databases. SIGMOD Rec. **29**, 55–67 (2000)
197. WHO: European Health for All Database (HFA-DB). World Health Organization Regional Office for Europe, 2007
198. J.R. Williams, A. Sanchez, *EPCIS and Pharmaceutical Supply Chain* (Auto-ID Laboratory, Boston, 2008)
199. J.P. Womack, D.T. Jones, D. Roos, *The Machine That Changed The World: The Story of Lean Production* (Harper Perennial, New York, 1991)
200. J. Worapot, Y. Li, A. Somjit, Design and implement of the EPC discovery services with confidentiality for multiple data owners, in *Proceedings of the 2010 IEEE International Conference on RFID-Technology and Applications (RFID-TA)*. IEEE Computer Society, Guangzhou, China, pp. 19–25, June 2010
201. Q. Yan, R. Deng, Z. Yan, Y. Li, T. Li, Pseudonym-based RFID discovery service to mitigate unauthorized tracking in supply chain management, in *Proceedings of the 2nd International Symposium on Data, Privacy and E-Commerce (ISDPE)*, pp. 21–26, September 2010
202. F. Yergeau, UTF-8. Internet Engineering Task Force, RFC 3629, November 2003
203. M. Young, Extensible Supply-chain Discovery Service Concepts, Version 4. Internet Engineering Task Force, Draft, Work-in-progress, 2008
204. H. Ziekow, O. Günther, Sharing RFID and complex event data among organizations. Inf. Syst. Frontiers **12**(5), 541–549 (2010)
205. M. Zukowski, S. Heman, N. Nes, P. Boncz, Super-scalar RAM-CPU cache compression, in *Proceedings of the 22nd International Conference on Data Engineering (ICDE)*, Atlanta, Georgia, USA, pp. 59–70, April 2006

MIX
Papier aus verantwortungsvollen Quellen
Paper from responsible sources
FSC® C105338

If you have any concerns about our products,
you can contact us on
ProductSafety@springernature.com

In case Publisher is established outside the EU,
the EU authorized representative is:
**Springer Nature Customer Service Center GmbH
Europaplatz 3, 69115 Heidelberg, Germany**

Printed by Libri Plureos GmbH
in Hamburg, Germany